Social Change and Labor Unrest in Brazil Since 1945

Salvador A.M. Sandoval

Routledge
Taylor & Francis Group
LONDON AND NEW YORK

First published 1993 by Westview Press, Inc.

Published 2019 by Routledge
52 Vanderbilt Avenue, New York, NY 10017
2 Park Square, Milton Park, Abingdon, Oxon OX14 4RN

Routledge is an imprint of the Taylor & Francis Group, an informa business

Library of Congress Cataloging-in-Publication Data
Sandoval, Salvador A.M.
Social change and labor unrest in Brad since 1915 / Salvador A.M. Sandoval.
p. cm.
Includes bibliographical references (p.) and index.
1. Strikes and lockouts—Brazil—History—20th century.
2. Irtdustrial relations—Brazil—History—20th century. I. Title
HD5353.526 1993
331.89'2981 '09045—dc20 93-1 6955
CIP

ISBN 13: 978-0-367-28748-1 (hbk)
ISBN 13: 978-0-367-30294-8 (pbk)

To the memory of

Carmen Hernandez Sams, my grandmother, whose vivid recollections of the Mexican Revolution first aroused my interests in popular protest

Contents

Tables and Figures

Tables

Figures

Foreword

Beleaguered Brazil has known many political regimes since 1945, some more democratic than others. In his vigorous vindication of social science's contribution to political understanding, Salvador Sandoval shows us that changes of regime over the 45 years in question strongly affected the character of Brazilian industrial conflict. He uses a variety of sources, including his own meticulous, voluminous compilations from newspaper reports, to document change and variation in strike waves, general strikes, mass strikes, firm-by-firm strikes, and the voicing of different kinds of demands. He demonstrates that in Brazil repressive regimes muted the relationship between economic fluctuations and strike activity, whereas under more permissive regimes fluctuations in such factors as real wages had stronger effects on the rise and fall of industrial conflict. Ironically, a regime's attempt to depoliticize strikes and workers by repressing unions and working-class leaders *increased* the responsiveness of industrial conflict to political conditions.

Another irony: Successive regimes' own promotion of economic expansion recurrently generated changes in the Brazilian labor force and industrial organization that undermined repressive strategies. The encouragement of capital-intensive industry formed whole new groups of workers while authoritarian governments were concentrating their fire at the older, smaller-scale sites of production, which had earlier served as bases for radicals. The creation of large state sectors in manufacturing and services eventually facilitated massive strikes against the state. The liberal dismantling of the old paternalist arrangements under which governmental taxes paid established unions freed union organizers to act on their own against the government.

This last point catches the eye. In a day when the share of North American unions' income from dues is declining while their reliance on government-regulated pension and welfare funds is rising, Sandoval's analysis opens the way to a neglected comparative study (comparable to the "fiscal sociology" that has flourished in studies of the state) of how the source and form of union revenues affect labor militancy. Although he concentrates on the decay of corporatist institutions, Sandoval's treatment opens the path to a much wider set of comparisons.

Although a few scholars have carried on parallel studies of North America and Western Europe, Salvador Sandoval serves comparative analysis well by his rigorous treatment of a great Latin American industrial power. Not only does he give us a lucid chronicle of Brazilian political and economic history since World War II but he also puts his observations of industrial conflict in a form that lends itself readily to comparison in both directions: with national histories that have already been analyzed in the same perspective and with similar studies of other Latin American (or, for that matter, Asian) countries that have yet to be done, that need urgently to be done. Sandoval has shown the way.

Social Change and Labor Unrest in Brazil also raises questions about democracy. "Democracy" is intensively, inevitably, and even desirably a contested term -- nowhere more so than in Latin America today. (Are Brazil, Paraguay, Colombia, Cuba, Peru, El Salvador, Mexico, Argentina, and Chile now democracies? In what senses of the term?) Yet one can draw from the diversity of definitions three widely-recognized elements. A state is democratic *in so far as* it guarantees:

1. a broad, equal definition of citizenship;
2. binding consultation of citizens with respect to state personnel and policies;
3. protection of citizens, especially members of minorities, from arbitrary state action.

Thus a state democratizes if (among other things) it broadens and equalizes the franchise; if elections sweep out old powerholders and policies in favor of new ones; or if it checks the political autonomy of the army, the police, and other armed forces. By these criteria, the regimes Sandoval identifies as more repressive were also less democratic.

By extension, then, Sandoval's study of Brazil illuminates one of the paradoxes and pleasures of democracy: The establishment of democratic rights frees citizens to pursue their own non-political interests by political -- or at least politically protected -- means. The rights to unionize, to strike, to meet, to demonstrate, and to publish complaints or demands all increase the likelihood that workers will respond collectively and vigorously to short-run changes in their wages and working conditions while turning away from direct attempts to seize political power -- not that workers and their leaders who turn to questions of wages and working conditions necessarily lose political awareness and will. On the whole, they remain sensitive to questions of rights, obligations, and justice. But so long as democratic institutions are operating reasonably well, workers can join other interests in seeking to use their collective strength with respect to capitalists and the state on behalf of their own material welfare. *Social Change and Labor Unrest in Brazil* also argues implicitly but effectively that infringements of democracy regularly promote politicization of industrial conflict. The book thereby allows us to observe the struggles of Latin American labor -- and, by extension, of labor throughout the world -- with eyes refreshed.

—Charles Tilly
New School of Social Research

strike, to meet, to denounce, and to publish complaints or demands all [illegible]

Introduction

This study describes the patterns of strike activity in Brazil over a period of forty-five years from the end of the Second World War to 1989. Brazilian strikes have changed substantially over these years in form, frequency, and content. Our task in this book is to explain these changes through an analysis of their quantitative dimensions.

Trends in the characteristics of strike activity can be used to assess interpretations about modifications in the nature of worker protest, even though strikes are not the only indicators of protest in a society. Nonetheless, strikes can be seen as a distinct form of contention involving the collective refusal to work. As such, they represent a situation of overt conflict between workers, employers and the state. Thus, they can be distinguished, to a greater or lesser extent, from other forms of popular protest. The purpose of focusing on the strike is to see how often it is used, under what circumstances it is employed, by which workers, and with what effects.

An analysis of strike patterns in a country like Brazil is of interest for several reasons. Of the "third world" countries, Brazil is among the most industrially developed. In this respect, it is relatively closer in many aspects to the nations of the industrialized West than to most of the nations of Latin America, Asia and Africa. Nevertheless, in spite of its economic strides, as of yet no adequate longitudinal study of strike patterns has yet been done.

Because Brazil occupies a key position among the developing nations, the study of strike patterns has important sociological interest. By examining the transformation of labor conflict over a period of accelerated economic growth and frequent changes in the power relations between workers, capitalists and the state we can contribute with another perspective to the debates over economic development and democratization in the context of political and economic conditions of late-industrialization.

We set out to accomplish three general objectives in this study. First, we present an overview and quantitative description of Brazilian strikes to show more precisely what labor conflict looked like over the years. Secondly, we examine the patterns of work stoppages in order to analyze the characteristics of workers' political participation through strike actions. Third, we explore the importance of political, economic, and organizational processes in the occurrence of strike activity.

The beginning date of 1945 was chosen for a number of reasons. First, 1945 was the start of an era of elected civilian governments after the fall of the *Estado Novo* dictatorship. Second, the labor laws which to a large extent govern labor relations were consolidated in the early forties and have only recently been altered by the 1988 Constitution. Third, the era after the Second World War represents a phase of accelerated economic growth in Brazilian history which clearly distinguishes it from previous periods.

The years since 1945 have been divided into periods characterized by the type of political rule and governmental tolerance toward working-class strike activity. Thus, the forty-five year time span encompasses nine periods: (1) 1945-1946, the years of re-democratization following the end of the *Estado Novo* dictatorship; (2) 1947-1949, the period of repressive populism in the government of Eurico Gaspar Dutra and his Cold War policies; (3) 1950-1955, the times of clientelistic populism under the government of Getúlio Vargas; (4) 1956-1960, the years of liberal populism under the government of Juscelino Kubitschek; (5) 1961-1963, the period of crisis in populist rule covering the presidencies of Jânio Quadros and João Goulart; (6) 1964-1968, the first phase of military rule after the 1964 coup encompassing the governments of General Castelo Branco and General Costa e Silva; (7) 1969-1977, the second phase of military rule characterized by heightened political repression and accelerated industrial growth; (8) 1978-1980, the *Abertura Política* period marked by the beginning of the re-democratization of the political system and the resurgence of overt strike activity and popular discontent; and (9) 1981-1989, which includes the end of the last military government of João Figueiredo and the *Nova República* period, the first civilian government of José Sarney.

The intent of analyzing strike activity for a period of forty-five years required considerable statistical data on workers' strikes. Though Brazil, like other countries, keeps abundant official statistics on various aspects of workers and unions, official strike data have not been available for study prior to 1985. As a result the statistical strike data for this study were obtained from both government and non-governmental sources.

For the years between 1945 to 1980, we compiled an archive of strike actions relying primarily on newspaper reports of work stoppages from the *Folha de São Paulo,* one of the country's major national newspapers. In spite of the drawbacks in using newspaper accounts we found that the data's limitations did not indicate any significant distortion in the analysis of the general tendencies in strike activity for this period.

More recently, for the 1981-1989 period we have worked largely with strike data from two institutional sources. The first, the Nucleo de Estudos de Políticas Publicas/NEPP of the Universidade Estadual de Campinas, has compiled data based primarily on strike reports from the DIEESE, Departamento Intersindical de Estatística e Estudos Socio-Economicos, which began to systematically record strike actions in 1983 from local union reports and complemented by newspaper information. The second source is the Ministry of Labor's Sistema de Greves/SIGREVE which began in 1985 to compile strike statistics from reports of the Delegacias Regionais do Trabalho (regional labor ministry offices).

Though data sources from both institutions were only jointly standardized in their definitions of strike events in 1987, a comparison of both series of strike data does not indicate significant differentials in the overall statistical levels and tendencies for the years in which data are available. Consequently, in our analysis of strike activity for the 1980s we have used both sources of statistics.

The book begins with a brief description of the legal foundations of the corporative labor relations system in Brazil. Chapter 1 reviews the bases through which the state exercises at its discretion considerable control over workers' organizations. As we shall see, this power to interfere in labor relations has varied greatly from one political period to another and, as a result, has had a strong effect on the nature and dimensions of strike activity.

In Chapter 2 we analyze strike activity in Brazil as it increased in frequency and intensity from 1945 to 1963 while undergoing fundamental changes in composition. The first years following the Second World War showed considerable annual fluctuations in the strike curve, but these gradually turned to a more steady increase in the later half of the 1950s and then peaked in 1963. Over the same period strike patterns changed significantly in form and organization as a response to alternations in political rule.

Chapter 3 examines the geographical distribution of strikes and changes in the occupational composition of strikers over the 1945-1980 period. As was to be expected, to a very large extent strikes have been concentrated in the industrially advanced regions of the Center-South. More important have been the changes in the occupational composition of strikes. In this chapter we argue that the shift in the occupational distribution of strikers closely accompanied structural transformations in the economy; yet changes in strike activity were not primarily the result of structural factors, but rather the consequence of political processes.

Chapter 4 analyzes economic and political factors as determinants of strikes for the period 1945-1980. The objective is to assess the effects of the business cycle and government repression on the fluctuation of strike activity. In Chapter 5, we analyze the transformation of industrial strikes, focus on the political environment and changes in worker organization, and argue that political organizational processes play a predominant role in shaping Brazilian strike patterns. At the same time, we find that workers have generally made organizational innovations as a response to periodic repression by the state.

After the military takeover in 1964, strikes declined dramatically as a result of severe repression. By 1969, overt strike activity had all but ceased though workers took their struggles into the interior of the factories in sporadic collective actions on the shop floors. Since we have only spotty reports of worker protests in these years, a quantitative analysis is impossible. Consequently, for this period our analysis in Chapter 6 will be based on narrative information of the few cases of labor unrest which have come to light.

Strikes erupted once again in 1978. These first years of renewed strike activity, 1978-1980, have been analyzed in some detail in Chapter 7 with the purposes of contrasting the new trends in strike actions with patterns uncovered in previous decades and of examining the emerging tendencies of the contemporary labor movement.

In Chapter 8, we examine the decade of the 1980s when the patterns of strike activity reflected a period of political transition from military to civilian rule under conditions of chronic economic instability. In addition to major increases in labor conflict new segments of the working class joined the ranks of other militants in resorting to strike actions as a means of pressuring economic and political elites. In this respect, the decade is significantly marked by the frequency of strike waves and general strikes indicating not only workers' responses to political and economic crises but also the enhanced militancy and organization of the working class.

Finally, in Chapter 8, we look at the Brazilian case in the light of three important approaches to strike analysis: the economic perspective, the industrial relations model, and the political organizational approach. The economic and industrial relations models are found to be the least explanatory of the three. However, the political organizational perspective, which views strikes as forms of struggle for power and economic advantages, provides the most adequate conceptual framework for analyzing industrial conflict in developing countries like Brazil.

Over the ten years that this study has been in preparation many persons deserve credit for their encouragement and support. Though most likely none of them would entirely agree with all the arguments in my analysis of labor unrest, their suggestions have certainly helped in improving the study.

At the New School for Social Research I am particularly grateful to Dr. Charles Tilly whose friendship and patient guidance provided the solid intellectual foundation upon which this study is based and whose encouragement contributed to its conclusion. Though the analysis and interpretations found in this study are of my own responsibility, Dr. Charles Tilly has been an intellectual model as an outstanding scholar devoted to the study of collective action.

Many others have helped to improve this book especially those colleagues and friends of the Working Group on Labor Studies of the Latin American Studies Association. In particular, I would like to acknowledge the comments, collaboration and support of John D. French.

In Brazil, Dr. Roberto Macedo of the Fundação Instituto de Pesquisas Econômicas of the University of São Paulo was gracious enough to provide several series of economic data used in our analyses. I would also like to mention the indirect contribution of the former Minister of Labor Dorothea Werneck who initiated SIGREV, the Ministry's first sector devoted to gathering and providing strike statistics, and who also introduced the uncommon practice of allowing researchers access to these official data. My thanks to Rosane Maia, formally of the SIGREV-Ministry of Labor, who was most helpful in making available the Ministry of

Labor's strike data for the 1980s, as well as, providing other useful information about industrial relations in Brazil.

Several institutions provided the financial aid over the years which made this study possible. In the first place, I would like to acknowledge the continuous assistance and collaboration of my colleagues of the Graduate Studies Program in Social Psychology at the Pontifícia Universidade Católica de São Paulo for granting me time off in 1984 to conclude the doctoral dissertation. I would like to express my gratitude to the Ford Foundation, CAPES/Ministério de Educação e Cultura, and Fundação de Amparo à Pesquisa do Estado de São Paulo-FAPESP which helped finance various aspects of the study. Furthermore I would like to also express my gratitude to the Horace H. Rackham School of Graduate Studies of the University of Michigan which provided financial support during my graduate studies and dissertation work. In 1989, a small research grant from the Fundação de Apoio à Pesquisa of the Universidade Estadual de Campinas allowed me to collect the data on strike activity for the decade of the 1980s while revising the earlier version of the manuscript and incorporating these new data findings.

In the daily work of writing the study, many provided encouragement at critical junctures. In Brazil, I would like to express my appreciation to Dr. Guillermo O'Donnell and Dr. Herbert S. Klein for their unwaiving encouragement to publish the manuscript. Above all, I owe a special debt of thanks to Sonia de Avelar for her companionship, intellectual influence and support throughout the development of this project, and who in many ways contributed to this book.

1

State Influence on Industrial Relations in Brazil

Any analysis of patterns and characteristics of labor conflicts in Brazil must necessarily be viewed within the context of the specific nature of state control over the relations between labor and capital. It would be mistaken to undertake any analysis of industrial conflict without a clear understanding of the legal basis upon which the state assumes a predominant role in resolving and precluding industrial conflict.

The norms which form the industrial relations edifice were set down by laws and presidential decrees between 1930-1945 by Getúlio Vargas and eventually standardized in the later years of the *Estado Novo* dictatorship under a body of labor laws entitled the *Consolidação das Leis do Trabalho* or *CLT* (Consolidation of the Labor Laws).

The CLT created a corporatist structure of conflict regulation between the bourgeoisie and the working class with the explicit objectives of providing the state with the necessary legal dispositions so as to maintain control over organized labor. In this fashion the *Estado Novo* architects aimed at averting the possibility of major class conflicts through early interference by the government. In this respect, Leôncio Martins Rodrigues, in his essay on the historical origins of the Brazilian corporatist labor structure, claims that "the weaknesses of the industrial and commercial classes in the national economy and the need for protection and governmental concessions in order to survive in face of foreign competition favored state interventionism in a general way, and corporatist unionism in particular".[1] Thus the Brazilian state exercised considerable control over industrial relations and internal union affairs until 1988, when the new constitution restricted government intervention.

State Control over Labor Leaders

The state's control over all labor leaders rested on its authority to depose disruptive elements from elected posts and judge the eligibility of candidates for union offices. By determining eligibility criteria for leaders, the state exercised its broad power to intervene in the internal affairs of working-class organizations.

Until the Constitution of 1988, when state power over labor unions was significantly curtailed,[2] the state's most potent weapon against the union movement was intervention. Under the intervention laws the state was empowered to seize union headquarters and funds whenever the minister of labor deemed it necessary for the public good. By intervention the minister of labor substituted elected union officers with government appointees (*interventor*). In addition, the ministry could levy any of the following sanctions: (1) union officers could be dismissed; (2) they could be suspended for a period of 30 days; (3) union officers could be dismissed and their rights to participate in union affairs canceled, while an appointed *interventor* assumed the direction of the union until the labor ministry called for new elections. Over the years the threat of intervention had been an effective weapon in discouraging militant actions by unions. Often, selective and exemplary interventions were sufficient to intimidate and immobilize unions planning collective actions.[3]

In addition to the more direct interventions, the state was also empowered to deny workers access to union posts by judging their eligibility. This allowed governments to prevent more "radical" elements from entering key union offices. In this respect, union leaders who had been dismissed through acts of intervention were often denied future union envolvement by cancelling their rights to participate in union affairs. This cancellation was a surgical mechanism through which the Ministry of Labor expelled from the union movement leaders that it regarded as threatening to the *status quo.*

Apart from the more coercive forms of suppressing undesirable union leaders, the state had several opportunities and mechanisms of leader cooptation, which were the main ones through which more tolerant governments maintained some control over the labor unions. Union leaders did not have significant social mobility as a direct result of union benefits from holding office. By law, salaries and benefits could not exceed those of the officers' full-time jobs, a provision which attempted to eliminate some opportunities to use union positions for significant personal gain.

Outside the union organization, however, the state labor regulatory apparatus provides other extra-union opportunities for individual advancement. On the one hand there is the extensive network of tripartite labor courts in which the unions are represented in these corporate bodies through "class" justices (*vogais*) chosen by the President of the Regional Labor Court from lists submitted by the local union leaderships. These judges are appointed for three-year renewable terms and play an important role in the elaborate judicial structure which adjudicates industrial disputes.

The attractiveness of these positions is the prestige attributed to the judges, the relative political importance attached to the labor courts as legitimizers of state adjudication, and the high salaries. The labor courts are important mechanisms of cooptation, given the relatively large numbers of class judgeships available. This is exemplified in the case of São Paulo, where in 1973 the municipality had available 32 "class" judgeships (32 labor courts) and 80 local unions which compiled the lists of possible candidates. In the same year, the labor judges in São Paulo were earning 13 times the prevailing minimum wage.[4]

There are class judgeships for local, regional, and national levels of the labor court system in which the state-level labor federations recommend candidates for the regional labor courts, and the national labor confederations provide the candidates for the Supreme Labor Court. In this manner, the labor judicial structure parallels the labor union structures providing collateral channels of leader cooptation.

Prior to the Coup of 1964, there were also a large number of public agencies dealing with working class issues and needs, such as the social security institutes and medical care agencies which were directed by tripartite bodies and, like the labor courts, served as effective mechanisms of cooptation. The military governments after the 1964 coup reduced and re-structured these agencies to achieve cheaper functional efficiency and to marginalize the participation of the unions in their administration. In this respect, the opportunities of cooptation were restricted as the military governments chose to deal with the union movement through more authoritarian methods, rather than continue the populist strategies of control through cooptation characteristic of the civilian governments of the fifties and early sixties.[5]

Though the participation of labor leaders in public agencies was reduced and restricted, the Ministry of Labor still provides a variety of union leadership training programs ranging from practical courses in union bookkeeping, labor law, social welfare, the labor courts, and job indemnity rights, to courses on moral and civic education and national reality, and representational activities in national and international conferences.[6] These activities more often than not provide some opportunities for limited indoctrination but are probably much less effective as cooptation mechanisms.

State Control over the Workers' Organization

The Ministry of Labor exercised control over labor organizations basically through three mechanisms: (1) through the power to extend and withdraw recognition of a union as the workers' legal representative; (2) through the collection and distribution of union revenues; and (3) through the supervision of the use of federally collected union funds.

Brazilian unions, in order to legally represent their members, had to be officially recognized by the Ministry of Labor and more recently, according to the 1988 Constitution, by some "competent" body. Under the labor union system in Brazil, any defined geographical unit can have only one union representing a specific occupational category (*unicidade sindical*),[7] and it was the function of the Ministry of Labor to determine which workers' organization would represent the interests of a particular category in any location. This ministerial recognition was the prerequisite for unions to have access to the labor courts, to legalize collective agreements with management, and to receive guaranteed government funds. To qualify as a union, a local association of workers must have one-third of the workers in the a specific occupational category within a given geographical area as its affiliated members, except "under exceptional circumstances" when the minister of labor can recognize a union with fewer members.[8]

In the same manner that the Ministry of Labor extended recognition to a union, it could also cancel its recognition. Cancellation of a union's charter is an extremely serious matter, inasmuch as it implies the extinguishing of a class organization. In practice, the measure has only been used in rare circumstances when there is a complete re-structuring of labor organizations in a geographical jurisdiction and/or when the members of a union have become too politicized. The solutions have been to incorporate one group with another less politicized occupational category or to reduce the geographical jurisdiction of the union by gerrymandering its membership. Given the multiple forms of control over union leaders, usually the removal of a union's leadership or intervention in the union have been sufficient to handle strong opposition, without the government's resorting to the cancellation of the union's legal status.[9]

On the financial side, the state also plays a key role in union funding, which affords yet another source of interference in union matters. The union structure is financed from two main sources: (1) a government trade union tax (*contribuição sindical*) and (2) union membership dues (*contribuição assistencial*).[10]

The union tax is collected from *all workers* in the union's jurisdiction, *whether or not they are affiliated with the union.* The tax is equal to the wage the worker receives for one day's work during the month of March and is deposited by employers in specially designated accounts in the Bank of Brazil. The unions are responsible for seeing that the tax is collected and distributed according to the following proportions:[11]

5% to the national confederation
15% to the state federation
6% to the Bank of Brazil for handling charges
54% to the local union
20% to the Ministry of Labor

Furthermore, union members must pay monthly dues to qualify as members, and union benefits are often conditioned to the payment of union dues. Over the past years some unions have created a special deduction withheld from all workers' wages during the first month after the annual round of salary increases. This deduction is negotiated with management and is usually included in the collective agreements establishing the annual salary increases. Since these fees are part of the labor-management agreements which must be sanctioned by the labor courts, the possibility of this independent source of funding still comes under scrutiny of the labor court apparatus.[12] Among the changes introduced by the 1988 Constitution, the trade union tax became a constitutional norm and, furthermore, allowed for the deduction from the workers' pay of additional assistance contributions while maintaining the role of the Ministry of Labor in the reallocation of union tax funds among the various levels of the official union structure. It is important to note that under the 1988 Constitution independent national labor organizations, called *centrais sindicais,* are not recipients of union tax funds as are the official national and regional trade union confederations.

As a consequence of this highly institutionalized form of guaranteeing union revenues under state auspices, most Brazilian labor unions are, to a large extent, dependent on these official sources of funds. In general, the union tax is the most important source of revenues for many Brazilian labor unions, though there are significant variations from region to region and between occupational categories. In his 1972 study, Kenneth S. Mericle showed that dependence on the union tax was reduced from 71 percent nationally to 59 percent among the large São Paulo labor unions. Mericle's observation about this difference is still pertinent today:

> [I]t is very difficult to reduce this dependence through raising union dues [though at the time of Mericles' study the union discount was not as widespread]. Not only are the low salaries and membership resistance a constraint, but the process of raising dues is very complicated and increases must be approved by the Regional Labor Delegate.[13]

In addition to making labor unions financially dependent on the state, the trade union contribution has also facilitated the emergence of pro-government career union bossism or *peleguismo*. These *pelegos*, as union bosses have been called, have maintained their control over many labor unions through a variety of the mechanisms and with the support from the Ministry of Labor and the labor courts. The trade union tax created a situation in which union leaders can rely more on government favor to support union activities and its leadership instead of relying on rank-and-file mobilization and contributions. Since the union tax is collected from all the workers, regardless of their affiliation status, *pelegos* have sought to maintain only minimal worker participation in order to avoid challenges to their authority.

Furthermore, the low worker participation resulting from the lack of union bosses' concern for mobilization also facilitated high levels of corruption among these entrenched union lackeys. Since stability in union offices often depended on a leader's support for the authoritarian regime, the Ministry of Labor's reward for political loyalty has been to overlook frequent mismanagement of union funds. This situation seems to have become much more common after the 1964 coup, as authoritarian governments successively replaced more committed union leaders with interventors and supported the election of pro-government candidates to union offices. During this period, in contrast to the civilian populist period, union office became a viable channel of personal socio-economic mobility. For these reasons, many serious labor leaders and scholars have come to view the union tax as serving to facilitate the process of cooptation of leaders and a major factor in the demobilization of workers.

As a corollary to the direct effects of government guaranteed funding, the state also has the right to oversee the day-to-day activities of the labor union, that is, to verify whether union tax funds are used in the activities prescribed by the labor legislation. Article 592 of the labor code enumerates the following activities as approved applications for union tax funds: (1) medical, dental and hospital assistance; (2) maternity assistance; (3) legal assistance; (4) professional and vocational training schools; (5) job placement agencies; (6) credit and consumer cooperatives; (7) vacation facilities; (8) libraries; (9) social and sporting activities; 10) funeral expenses; and (11) expenses resulting from the administration of these activities. Other types of assistance activities and programs are permitted, though they must be approved by the Ministry of Labor.[14] In the legislation, it is very clear that union tax funds cannot be used for strike benefits or other forms of militant activities.[15] To insure the correct application of funds, unions are required to keep very detailed accounts of their expenditures as well as to file annual reports demonstrating that funds are used only for authorized activities.

The inspection of and tutelage over union activities obliges the leadership to assume extensive bureaucratic responsibilities in the administration of the organization's activities. Through this extension of the state apparatus periodic reporting necessitates frequent contact with government agencies. This administrative nexus creates another instance in which union leadership can be intimidated and controlled by state officials.

The Constitution of 1988 not only maintained the trade union tax but also assured its use in supporting the corporatist national and state labor organizations. Similarly, the new 1988 Constitution allowed these often complacent organs to obtain a share of the funds collected from the assistance contributions as well.

State Control over Workers

In Brazil the worker's job security has never been well protected. The worker's security depends on his rights under the law and on the judgments of the labor courts rather than on a strong local union and shop level organization which make worker mobilization the power behind job guarantees.

Prior to 1966, the labor law established two types of job security:

1. Workers with one to ten years of service were entitled to indemnity payments from the employer equal to one month's salary per year of effective service in the event of permanent dismissal; any worker with one or more years of service was also entitled to a 30 day advance layoff notice or, in its absence, a full month's salary.
2. Workers with ten or more years of service were considered stable and could not be dismissed without a prior court hearing in which the employer was obliged to prove the worker guilty of serious misconduct which justified the discharge.

Job stability was the most important provision of the pre-1966 labor code because it was either very costly or almost impossible to dismiss a "stable" worker without a proven "just cause". Thus stable workers had considerable security and workers employed for less than ten years had limited but real security based on the financial constraints involved in firing them.

In December 1966, the military government reformed the job security provisions and created the *Fundo de Garantia por Tempo de Serviço* (FGTS),[16] designed to replace these job stability provisions. This new system differed from the previous one in two fundamental aspects: (1) stability status was not recognized in the FGTS system; (2) the employer's costs of discharging a worker were greatly reduced.

The FGTS eliminated in dismissal practices the distinction made between workers based on their seniority. Employers now deposit a monthly 8 percent of the workers' wages in individual accounts in the workers' names. These deposits become a fund which replace the indemnity obligations of the employer under the previous legislation. This procedure removed all major financial restraints on the part of employers in dismissing employees.[17] This "vesting" alternative to job security strengthened the power of management over the workers, since all financial constraints in dismissals are pre-paid. Because the funds are vested, workers can voluntarily quit their jobs without losing the cash rights accumulated, in contrast to the previous legislation where the workers were entitled to indemnity only if fired.

The transitions from the old system of job stability to the FGTS was accomplished by allowing labor *and* capital to choose the system to be applied in each individual case. In this sense the FGTS program was optional; in practice, employers sought to hire workers who opted for the FGTS, since employers had greater freedom to manipulate the labor market. In addition, government also provided financial incentives for workers covered under the old system to opt for the FGTS.

In general, the replacement of the job stability system by the FGTS system has had negative impacts on union organizing and participation. In the past, job stability was important to labor unions because it provided workers with effective job security which allowed them to undertake union activities inside and outside the factory with little threat of dismissal. Since Brazilian unions have not historically had extensive penetration and strength at the shop floor level, union representatives in the plants, the *delegados sindicais,* were very much dependent on employment stability to remain on the job as union activists. With the introduction of the FGTS, this type of union representation was greatly weakened, "hindering the emergence of a strong and militant shop steward system."[18] This situation was significantly altered with the reforms introduced in the 1988 Constitution which have guaranteed workers the right to have an elected workplace representative, though not necessarily a union delegate, who accounts to his fellow workers for his acts.

With a faciliated worker layoff system, management has come to use planned turnover as a mechanism to reduce labor costs, especially in periods of market contraction and prior to salary increases, when employers dismiss workers only to rehire them under new wage agreements at starting wages. This picture of utilizing turnover to lower wages has also been used to attempt to intimidate unionized workers during periods of salary negotiation. While, on the one hand, this intimidation has had some effect, in general workers' reactions to this form of intimidation has led to labor protest against high turnover policies and the legal structure which allow for easy dismissal.

State Control over Workers' Right to Strike

The workers' right to strike was guaranteed by the Constitution of 1946, though specific provisions for striking were to be delineated in subsequent complementary legislation. Eighteen years passed, however, before the regulatory specifications were decreed in 1964, after the military coup. During the civilian governments, strikes were informally regulated by interpretations of the general guidelines set down in 1946. These guidelines required the following for a strike to be considered legal:[19]

1. That the dispute had to be submitted to previous conciliation attempts or to adjudication by the regional labor courts;
2. That the strike could only occur in activities not considered fundamental to the well-being of the nation. The Minister of Labor was empowered to define which activities fell into this category;
3. Federal and state governments reserved the right to declare any strike illegal without any judicial process.

Early in the military government, on June 1, 1964, complementary legislation regulating strikes was issued. This new regulation for strike actions was one of the few changes made in the legislation governing labor relations, a clear illustration of how adequate the labor laws were for the newly installed military regime.

Under the 1964 regulations, strikes had to be called by a general assembly of the union membership, to be presided over by the regional public attorney of the labor judiciary. At least four days prior to the strike deadline, a list of assembly approved demands were to be sent to the employers and to the regional delegate of the Ministry of Labor, who could immediately begin mediating the dispute. Once the strike was called, the public attorney could submit the question of the strike's legality to a decision of the labor court. The ruling of the labor court was binding on the union; if the strike was determined to be illegal, the union was to terminate it at once or prevent it from occurring.[20]

If a strike was declared illegal, the law was very specific about the behavior of both strikers and employers. Persons breaking the norms established by law could be fined and prosecuted for "inciting disrespect for the decisions of the labor courts or attempting to block the execution of such a decision."[21] It was also illegal for anyone outside the union's jurisdiction to incite workers to strike.

The law quite clearly forbade strikes with political, social, religious, or solidarity motives which did not make demands of direct interest to the specific category of workers involved. Furthermore, workers were not permitted to strike during the tenure of a collective contract or labor court decision or to call for strike action over issues which the labor court had dismissed in the previous year. To avert strikes, employers could initiate a court case soliciting court intervention thirty days prior to the expiration of the old contract or court decision.

During legal strikes, employers could not dismiss workers. More importantly, if the union won the strike, or if the labor court granted all or part of the union's demands, the employer was obliged to pay the wages corresponding to the work days lost during the strike.[22]

Although the legislation allowed strikes over wages and working conditions, in fact the government used its regulatory powers to prevent strikes over these issues. The fact that the labor laws provided for various opportunities before a strike erupted in which the intervention of the labor courts could be solicited by employers or government officials meant that the courts were empowered to decide which strikes would be tolerated. In this respect, conflicts over wages and working conditions were generally settled by court decisions before a strike occurred.

Under the post-1964 regulations, strikes were permitted in only two situations, both involving violations by employers of court decisions or labor agreements:

1. Strikes were permitted with the objective of obtaining back wages when employers failed to pay wages;
2. Strikes were authorized when employers were not paying the wages established in collective agreement or court decision.

Since the labor laws restricted legal strike action to a very narrow and highly-regulated range of issues and behaviors that were acceptable to government leaders, strike activity by workers and their organizations, even for specific workplace "bread and butter" issues, ran the risk of challenging the state's control. This tendency of "politicization" of strike activity, that is, the strike as a collective action against state regulations or policies, became more pronounced with the military government's attempts to eliminate the use of strikes in disputes over wages. By assuming responsibility for the determination of the rates for wage increases, the government attempted to reduce the union's role in the bargaining process dealing with this important issue.

The central government's wage control policy was first introduced by Decree # 54.018 on July 4, 1964, for workers in the public sector. On July 13, 1965, Law 4725 extended wage controls in collective contracts and labor court decisions for the private sector. Under this policy, the Ministry of Finance controlled the amount of all salary increases, thus almost eliminating from the negotiation process any wage issues and reducing the role of the labor courts from dispute arbitration to the simple administration of the wage-setting system.[23] All wage increases, whether by negotiated agreement between union and management or by court decision, were to conform to the levels established by the Ministry of Finance. Under this system neither the courts nor the unions had any role in determining official wage rates.

The government's centralization of the indexing of wage increases created a third mechanism directed at eliminating working-class organizations from interfering in the political and economic affairs of the nation. By greatly restricting legal strike actions and by withdrawing the issues of wage increases and working conditions from the arena of collective negotiation, the military government sought to perfect the autocratic labor structure and eliminate class conflict, while the unions retained only the tasks of administering their welfare activities. Government surveillance, the power to intervene, guaranteed funding for trade unions and control over the types of issues to be advocated favored a type of bureaucratic union leadership which placed the aims of social welfare services above active union organizing and more "militant" demand-making.

The constraints of the labor laws placed on union leadership often became issues of criticism and debate among the more militant unionists. Studies have demonstrated that many union leaders preferred to be more independent of the state and to have a less bureaucratized form of unionism. In his 1963 study J.V. Freitas Marcondes found that more than one-half of the union leaders interviewed in the São Paulo area favored abolition of the union tax because of its negative effects on the union.[24] Ten years later, in 1973, Kenneth S. Mericle, in his study of industrial relations in Brazil, found that slightly less than half of the leaders he interviewed favored the abolition of the union tax. The reasons for many union leaders' preferences against the union tax continued to be the demobilizing effects of the tax on unions and their leadership in stunting their liberty and autonomy to act on behalf of workers'interests.[25] In a 1984 study of union leaders' attitudes, Grondin found a similar pattern of opinion among São Paulo unionists. Of those interviewed, 45 percent preferred that the union tax continue, 30 percent would abolish it and 23 percent would have some significant change in its structure.[26] When inquired as to the use of the funds from the union tax, 43.3 percent used the money mainly on social welfare activities, 15 percent used it mainly for union headquarter's expenses, 10 percent on recreational activities and only 1.6 percent used it for union organizing.[27]

Several other studies[28] have shown that the unions' reliance on the tax and emphasis on welfare services has led workers to regard the unions as primarily concerned with social welfare activities. These attitudes have been reinforced by union bossism which has dominated much of union life. Because of the multiple control mechanisms of the government over unions and labor confederations, many unions have come to be run by self-interested careerists, who seek support in the political regime and who have thrived personally under its tutelage.

In spite of the rigidity of government institutions which confront the Brazilian labor movement, in the late 1970s several segments of the working class once again began to oppose the maze of controls and constraints on their collective actions, both through the revival of a new militant unionism and through independent grass-roots organizations acting collectively on their interests.

Under a democratizing impetus of the 1988 Constitution, which was to usher in a new era of democratic rule in Brazil, few but important reforms were introduced in the *getulista* corporatist labor relations structure, which have contributed to significant changes in this largely verticalized edifice. These constitutional reforms can be briefly summarized in the following manner:[29]

1. The end of the Labor Ministry's power to intervene in the internal affairs of the labor unions;
2. The unrestricted right of workers to strike with restrictions for the so-called "essential activities" occupations;
3. The right of civil servants to unionize and strike;
4. The right of workers to elect their workplace representatives in establishments of 200 or more employees.

The state institutions regulating and containing labor conflict are important factors in shaping both class relations and the forms and frequency of working-class contention. As is discussed in this chapter, the institutional arrangements in Brazil are residues of previous authoritarian regimes and reflect the efforts by dominant classes to incorporate the working class into the economy and political arena under systematic controls by the state as a means of restricting labor unrest.

The labor relations system created in the Vargas period not only survived many institutional and political changes since 1945, but also withstood profound social, economic and cultural transformations of Brazilian society. Clearly, this institution capable of maintaining its control functions in the constitutions of 1937, 1946, 1967 and 1988 regardless of the political regime (the *Estado Novo* dictatorship, national populism, the military governments or the recent elected governments) has left profound marks on Brazilian political and social life.

Yet in spite of the elaborate web of official checks and controls, these institutions are themselves dependent on the power structure and political conjuncture in Brazilian society. The varying importance of these institutional controls and their relative obsolescence in relation to changes in society and in the political process are revealed in the following chapters which examine the transformation of strike activity in Brazil since 1945.

Notes

1. Leôncio Martins Rodrigues, "O Sindicalismo Corporativo no Brasil," *Partidos e Sindicatos: Escritos de Sociologia Política* (São Paulo: Editora Atica, 1990), p. 63.

2. For the first time since 1943, the year when the CLT was enacted, the corporatist union model was significantly reformed. Under Article 8, Paragraph 1 of the Constitution of 1988, the Minister of Labor can no longer decree the intervention of union organizations and the unions can organize as determined by their membership without following any model imposed by the Ministry of Labor.

3. Kenneth Scott Mericle, "Conflict Regulation in the Brazilian Industrial Relations System" (Ph.D. Dissertation, The University of Wisconsin, 1974), p. 99.

4. Ibid., p. 108.

5. Still the most informative analysis of the collaboration and cooptation of labor leaders by civilian governments prior to the 1964 military coup is Kenneth P. Erickson, *The Brazilian Corporative State and Working Class Politics* (Berkeley: University of California Press, 1979).

6. Mericle, "Conflict Regulation," p. 110.

7. One of the first detailed discussions on the problems with the single occupation or trade union in a given geographical area (*unicidade sindical*) is the work of Evaristo de Moraes Filho, *O Problema do Sindicato Unico no Brasil* (São Paulo: Editora Alfa-Omega, 2nd edition, 1978).

8. Mericle, "Conflict Regulation," p. 111.

9. Ibid., p. 112.

10. Ibid.

11. Ibid., pp. 112-113.

12. Ibid., p. 113.

13. Ibid., p. 115.

14. Ibid., p. 116.

15. Ibid.

16. An excellent study of the impact of the FGTS system is Vera Lucia B. Ferrante, *FGTS: Ideologia e Repressão* (São Paulo: Editora Atica, 1978); for a brief discussion, see Mericle, "Conflict Regulation," pp. 123-127.

17. Mericle, "Conflict Regulation," pp.120-125, passim.

18. Ibid., p. 127.

19. Ibid., p. 129.

20. Ibid.

21. Ibid.

22. Ibid., p. 130-131.

23. Ibid., p. 221.

24. Ibid., p. 133.

25. Ibid., p. 134.

26. Marcelo Grondin, *Perfil dos Dirigentes Sindicais na Grande São Paulo* (São Paulo: CECODE-Centro de Cooperação do Desenvolvimento, 1985), p. 140.

27. Ibid., p. 140.

28. See Celso Frederico, *Consciência Operária no Brasil* (São Paulo: Editora Atica,1978), p. 60; John Humphrey, *Controle Capitalista e Luta Operária na Industria Automobilistica Brasileira* (Petrópolis: Editora Vozes/CEBRAP, 1982). p. 130; Juarez Rubens Brandão Lopes, *Sociedade Industrial no Brasil* (São Paulo: Difusão Europeia do Livro, 1971), pp. 57-58; Leôncio Martins Rodrigues, *Industrialização e Atitudes Operárias* (São Paulo: Editora Brasiliense, 1970), pp. 101-114; Joseph F. Springer, *A Brazilian Factory Study 1966* (Cuernavaca: CIDOC Cuaderno No. 33,1969, pp. 2121-2125; Luis Flavio Rainha, *Os Peões do Grande ABC* (Petrópolis: Editora Vozes, 1980), p. 281.

29. Leôncio Martins Rodrigues, "O Poder Sindical na Nova Constituição," in *RH-Informação Profissional-Edição Especial: Os Direitos Sociais e Trabalhistas na Constituição de 1988* (São Paulo: Associação Brasileira de Recursos Humanos, October 1988), p. 18.

2

Industrialization and Working-Class Strikes in Brazil: 1945-1980

An analysis of industrial strikes in Brazil from 1945 to 1980 requires some consideration of the general characteristics of the industrialization process during this thirty-five year span. This chapter will (1) describe general trends in the growth of the industrial working class, and (2) compare the patterns of strike actions during this period in terms of both the regional distribution and changing composition of the labor force.

During the thirty years between 1950 and 1980, the industrialization of the country followed a clear path of geographical concentration in the Central-South region comprised of the important states of São Paulo, Rio de Janeiro, and Minas Gerais. This pattern is indicated by the persistently high levels of the industrial labor force in the region, concentrations which accounted for 67.3 percent of the industrial labor force in 1950 and 66.3 percent in 1980. As shown in Table 2.1, the regional distribution of the labor force by decades clearly demonstrates the pattern of regional primacy as a constant feature of the industrialization process, even during the periods of accelerated growth.

The most important industries of the economy and 80 percent of the country's infrastructure[1] are located in the area bounded by São Paulo, Rio de Janeiro and Minas Gerais. Of the three states which comprise this industrial triangle, the state of São Paulo leads the others in economic importance and has steadily increased its share of the industrial labor force as its industries grew. In 1950, 38.6 percent of the workers were employed in São Paulo, over half of the 67.3 percent of the industrial workers in the region. By 1980 the state had increased its share to 48 percent, while the proportion of workers in the state of Rio de Janeiro

Table 2.1 - Distribution of the Industrial Labor Force by Regions and Brazilian States for the Census Years 1950 to 1980 (Totals and Percentages)*

Regions & States	*1950*		*1960*		*1970*		*1980*	
	Nº of Employees	*% of Total*	*Nº of Employees*	*% of Total*	*Nº of Employees*	*% of Total*	*Nº of Employees*	*% of Total*
NORTH	14,719	1.2	19,120	1.3	36,102	1.4	114.143	2.5
N. EAST	211.363	16.8	185,580	12.3	231,157	9.2	463.023	10.0
CENTER-SOUTH	845,545	67.3	1,055,394	70.0	1,797,533	71.6	3.084.762	66.3
Minas Gerais Espirito Santo	117,709	9.4	131,926	8.7	200,698	8.0	400,011	8.6
Rio de Janeiro	242,992	19.3	235,486	15.6	347,619	13.9	453,532	9.8
São Paulo	484,844	38.6	687,982	45.6	1,249,216	49.8	2,231,219	48.0
SOUTH	178,448	14.2	237,739	15.7	411,187	16.4	902,542	19.4
CENTER-WEST	6,673	.5	12,800	.8	27,041	1.0	85,888	1.8
TOTAL	1,256,807	100.0	1,509,713	100.0	2,509,615	100.0	4,650,358	100.0

** Figures of industrial labor force based on data of establishments employing five or more persons.*

Source: Instituto Brasileiro de Geografia e Estatística, *Censo Industrial, 1950, 1960, 1970.*
Instituto Brasileiro de Geografia e Estatística, *Sinopse Preliminar do Censo Industrial 1980.*

decreased from 19.5 percent in 1950 to 9.8 percent in 1980 as it experienced a gradual deindustrialization.

This process of deindustrialization has been, in part, the consequence of the transfer of more dynamic industries to other states, especially São Paulo and Minas Gerais, and also the result of the declining importance of traditional industries located in the old industrial parks of Rio de Janeiro as the economy changed axis and became propelled by modern industries, which to a large extent preferred to locate in other states.

How this regional distribution of the labor force is reflected in strike activity is shown in Table 2.2. Generally speaking, as would be expected, the Center-South represents the area of highest proportion of strike actions over the thirty-five year period. As a region, the percentage of strikes exceeds the proportion of labor in the area, though there are important variations between the states within the region. São Paulo and Rio de Janeiro have had the highest percentages of strikes in the country. While the number of strikes in São Paulo, with a few variations, remained consistently high, in Rio de Janeiro the numbers suggest a more vacillating pattern, especially in the earlier part of the period when the industrial park of Rio de Janeiro was a more dynamic center of industrial growth. In part, the explanation for the fluctuating character of strikes in Rio de Janeiro can be found in the fact that it was the seat of the federal government until the 1960s and consequently was under greater surveillance by the state.

Overall, the regional distribution of strikes indicates a peculiar pattern of oscillation in all the regions, as seen in the total number of strikes for each period, shown in Table 2.2. Although the industrial labor force grew substantially during these thirty-five years between 1945 and 1980, strike figures suggest great fluctuations. Another feature which should be noted is the gradual increase of strike movements of a national character beginning in the early 1950s which seem to have peaked in 1955-1956, when they represented 11 percent of all strikes. In part, the rise of these national strikes indicated growing mobilization capabilities of some segments of the working class and the development of new forms of collective action and organization.

Finally, the gap in the reporting of strikes for the nine-year period between 1969 and 1977 represents a particularly repressive era in the history of the Brazilian working class. Between 1968 and 1977 several significant transformations occurred in the structure of the industrial sector of the economy and the composition and size of the working class

Table 2.2 – Distribution of Strikes by Regions of Brazil as Percentage of Biennial Total Number of Strikes, 1945 to 1980

Regions & States	*1945-1946*	*1947-1948*	*1949-1950*	*1951-1952*	*1953-1954*	*1955-1956*	*1957-1958*	*1959-1960*	*1961-1962*	*1963-1964*	*1965-1966*	*1967-1968*	Total 1945-1968	*1978-1980*
NORTH	-	-	-	-	-	-	-	-	-	-	-	-	-	.3
N. EAST	5.9	3.0	-	10.3	-	-	11.3	4.5	13.0	17.2	-	22.7	10.2	3.0
CENTER-SOUTH	82.7	93.1	100.0	71.9	95.0	83.1	73.0	89.0	82.7	75.2	93.0	72.4	82.7	85.5
São Paulo	62.1	54.3	37.3	58.3	40.0	55.4	46.9	67.2	65.2	43.7	69.8	58.8	56.9	66.6
Rio de Janeiro	19.7	18.0	37.4	6.8	35.0	27.7	21.5	15.1	14.5	24.6	19.9	-	19.4	7.1
Minas Gerais	.9	21.1	25.0	6.8	20.0	-	3.6	6.0	2.0	6.9	3.3	13.6	6.1	11.2
Espírito Santo	-	-	-	-	-	-	-	.7	1.0	-	-	-	.3	.6
SOUTH	9.8	3.0	-	13.6	-	5.5	9.2	2.9	1.0	4.0	6.6	4.5	4.6	8.9
CENTER-WEST	-	-	-	-	-	-	-	-	-	-	-	-	-	1.5
NATION-WIDE	.9	-	-	3.4	5.0	11.1	5.6	3.0	.5	2.3	-	-	2.5	.9
TOTAL	100.0	100.0	100.0	100.0	100.0	100.0	100.0	100.0	100.0	100.0	100.0	100.0	100.0	100.0
TOTAL NO. STRIKES	*101*	*33*	*24*	*29*	*20*	*18*	*53*	*132*	*192*	*215*	*30*	*22*	*868*	*338*

which affected the capacity of political institutions to cope with these changes. The large number of strikes which erupted in the years 1978 to 1980 stand in marked contrast to the conspicuous lack of strikes during the previous years. The gap between 1969 and 1978 represents a watershed in the development of the Brazilian labor movement. In later sections, we shall analyze the specific changes which occurred under the military governments and how these transformations in both industrial society and class relations contributed to the current institutional crisis in Brazil.

Strikes and Changes in the Composition of the Working Class

A few words about the general trends in the rapid industrialization of the Brazilian economy are necessary if one is to understand the evolution of strikes over this thirty-five year period. For this reason, though at the risk of over simplification, we shall examine the major trends in the economy which most influenced the transformation of the strike. In this section in particular we shall focus on the changes in the size and occupational composition of the industrial labor force and how these developments are reflected in the occupational distribution of work stoppages.

One of the more important changes occurring between 1945 and 1980 was the steady rise of the so-called "dynamic" sectors of industry and the relative decline of the traditional ones, a phenomenon which has been observed by many scholars.[2] The classification of industries into traditional, intermediate and modern sectors permits us to follow the changes in sectorial growth and their corresponding levels of strike activity. The classification is based on criteria of levels of capital intensity per worker and rates of technological renovation, which contribute to the sectors' differing rates of growth and position in the economy with regard to employing the industrial labor force. The three sectors can be briefly described as follows:

> **The traditional sector** is composed of those industries which have been less capital intensive per worker and predominated in the earlier phases of industrialization with their more labor intensive production technology. Since 1950 these industries have grown at slower rates than the industries in the other sectors. The

industries classified in the traditional sector are: textiles, leathers, foods, printing, wood manufacturing, clothing and tobacco.

The modern sector is composed of those industries which are more capital intensive and which gained prominence in the post-World War II phase of industrialization through the large amounts of foreign and state investments. Over the thirty years between 1950 and 1980, these industries have registered the highest rates of growth. The modern sector industries are: metallurgy, machines, automobiles, electrical equipment and chemicals.

The intermediate sector is composed of industries which were also important in the earlier phase of industrialization, but unlike those in the traditional sector, registered higher rates of growth between 1950 and 1980, often because of their reinvigorization through the supplying of materials to the modern sector or through new-found markets. The industries in this sector are: ceramics, glass and other non-metallic material, rubber, mining and paper.

The changes in the position of each sector during the period under consideration are indicated by the labor force data shown in Table A-1 of the Appendix. The traditional sector dominated in terms of employment of the largest proportion of the industrial labor force during the 1950s and 1960s, though in terms of production and profits the modern sector industries demonstrated better performance.[3] Gradually over the years, the traditional sector relinquished its lead to the modern sector; the latter increased its share of workers employed from 17.6 percent in 1950 to 40.7 percent in 1980, while the percentage in the traditional sector for these years declined from 66 percent to 43.7 percent, though all sectors grew substantially in absolute terms.

During the first decade of the period, the 1950s, the traditional industries expanded the size of their work force slowly at an annual rate of .88 percent. In spite of this slow growth, the sector's industries still employed twice the number of workers as did the modern sector at that time. On the other hand, the industrial census data (Table A-1) reveal the modern sector growing at an impressive annual rate of 6.6 percent during this decade, due largely to the economic policies of the civilian governments to accelerate industrialization through foreign capital and government investment.[4]

A close look at specific industries in the traditional and modern sectors illustrates these distinct growth trends. In 1950 the textile industry employed the largest number and percentage of workers, 26.7 percent, in comparison to the whole of the modern sector which employed only 17.6 percent (Table A-1 in the Appendix). By 1980, textiles accounted for 8.4 percent of the workers, while some modern sector industries, like metallurgy and machines, each employed above 10 percent. As shown by the data, the decline in predominance of the traditional sector was offset by the rapid growth of the modern sector work force, thus shifting the numerical strength of the unions to this sector.

The two decades between 1960 and 1980 witnessed the greatest growth rates for all the sectors and resulted in the tripling of the industrial labor force from 1.5 million to 4.7 million, if one considers only those establishments employing five or more workers. This extraordinary increase in the industrial working class reflected in large measure the record-setting growth rates achieved under the military regime. While the number of workers in the traditional sector nearly doubled in size, the number of the modern sector workers quadrupled. Consequently, by the time of the 1980 industrial census, both sectors employed about an equal proportion of the industrial labor force (Table A-1).

The changing importance of the traditional and modern sectors was also demonstrated by the sectorial distribution of strikes over the period. As illustrated in Figure 2.1, workers of the modern industries came to assume a greater proportion of strike activities between 1957 and 1964 at the same time that the traditional sector workers reached their peak of strike activities. By 1980, the shift between sectors with respect to strike activity was complete. This process is summarized in the data for the 1950 and 1980 census years presented in Table 2.3. Even though the percentage of workers employed in either sector was about 40 percent (an important change from the 1950 period), the more significant fact was the complete inversion of the proportion of strikes in each sector. Clearly, the shift in the economic importance of each sector was a significant factor in this inversion, but the larger strike rates for the modern sector in 1980 is largely explained by socio-political factors and not economic ones, as we shall see in later chapters. For now, we can observe from the data in Table 2.3 that neither the relative size of the work force in the sector nor the relative levels of sectorial growth in themselves adequately account

Figure 2.1 Strikes by Industrial Sector
1945-1980

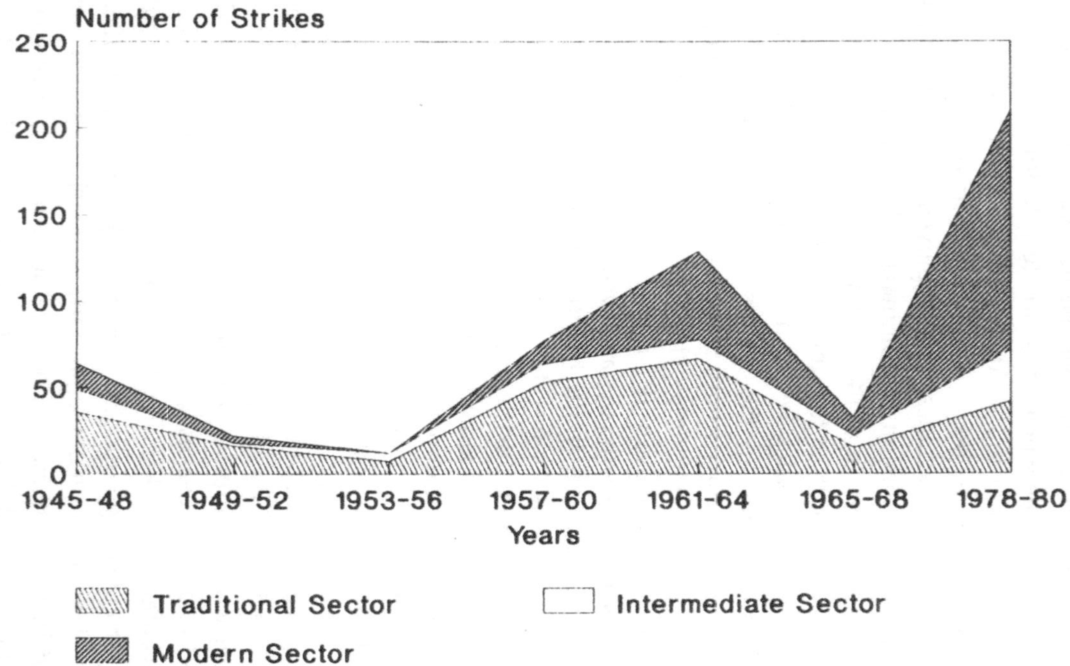

Table 2.3 - Sectorial Changes of the Industrial Labor Force and Changes in Strike Activity, 1950 and 1980

Labor Force Category	*1950*			*1980*		
	% of 1950 Labor Force (a)	*1948-50 % of Strikes*	*1948-50 Strike Rate*	*% of 1980 Labor Force (b)*	*1978-80 % of Strikes*	*1978-80 Strike Rate*
Traditional	66.0	72.0	1.7	43.7	20.0	2.1
Intermediate	14.9	17.0	1.6	13.4	2.9	.9
Modern	17.6	11.0	1.0	40.7	77.1	8.6
Other	1.5	—	—	2.2	—	---
Total	100.0	100.0	1.6	100.0	100.0	4.6

Source: (a) Instituto Brasileiro de Geografia e Estatística, *Censo Industrial - 1950.*
(b) Instituto Brasileiro de Geografia e Estatística, *Sinopse Preliminar do Censo Industrial - 1980,* vol. 3, no. 1.

for either the sectorial distribution of the strikes or contrasting strike rates for the two periods.

A close look at the data on strike activities distributed by industrial sectors and occupations permits us to follow the changes in collective actions for the years 1945-1980, as shown in Table 2.4. In terms of numbers of strikes per period, the workers of the traditional industries demonstrated a substantially higher number of stoppages than workers in the other sectors, at least until the period between 1961-1963. The traditional industries accounted for 64 to 70 percent of the strikes, except for the two years of 1945-1946, when widespread strikes in other sectors reduced the share of the traditional sector strikes to 54 percent.

In the modern sector the number of strike actions was often less than a third of the traditional sector's until 1961-1963, when there occurred an almost equal number of work stoppages in the modern sector as in traditional industries. From this time on, the occurrence of strikes among modern sector workers continued to be numerous until 1969, when governmental repression virtually ended all overt labor conflicts. Yet by 1978-1980, after nine years of harsh repression, the revival of labor strikes was led by workers in the modern sector, in particular, the metalworkers.

When we examine the changes in strike rates, as shown in Table 2.4, the trends are less clear than before. On the whole, the traditional sector tended to be slightly more strike-prone between 1945 and 1960, with considerable variation over the period. During 1961-63, for the first time in fourteen years, the modern sector demonstrated a strike rate higher than that of the traditional sector, and from then on the modern sector workers remained the most inclined to strike.

Still another indicator of the changes in sectorial predominance is the persistence of strike activity over the period. Between 1945 and 1960 certain key traditional industries such as textiles, foods and leather maintained strike rates which were generally higher than the national rates. On the other hand, the industries in the modern sector tended to exhibit greater fluctuations in strike rates, though in general between 1947 and 1960 strike rates among the largest occupational group of the modern sector, the metalworkers, were below the national rates (Table 2.4).

Among the workers of the intermediate sector, miners appear as the most militant occupational group, as demonstrated by their consistently high strike rates. More often than not, miners had strike rates several times higher than the national rates and were often the most strike-prone

Table 2.4 - Distribution of Strikes by Sectors, Branches of Industry and Selected Occupational Groups According to Political Periods, 1945-1980

Category & Branch of Industry	*1945-1946 End of Estado Novo*			*1947-1949 Repressive Populism*			*1950-1955 Clientelistic Populism*			*1956-1960 Liberal Populism*			*1961-1963 Crisis of Populism*			*1964-1968 Military Government*			*1978-1980 Democratic Opening*		
	Nº	*%*	*Rate*[a]	*Nº*	*%*	*Rate*	*Nº*	*%*	*Rate*	*Nº*	*%*	*Rate*	*Nº*	*%*	*Rate*	*Nº*	*%*	*Rate*	*Nº*	*%*	*Rate*
TRADITIONAL INDUSTRIES:	29	54.7	4.4	12	70.6	1.6	16	64.0	1.8	55	68.7	5.6	56	49.6	5.2	26	53.0	2.3	42	20.0	2.1
Textiles	10	18.9	3.8	9	52.9	2.9	7	28.0	2.0	19	24.0	6.3	12	10.6	3.8	7	14.3	2.5	9	4.3	2.3
Leathers	1	1.9	1.5	1	5.9	5.9	1	4.0	1.0	5	6.0	25.0	4	3.5	4.4	2	4.0	1.7	1	.5	2.6
Foods	8	15.0	4.7	1	5.9	.5	5	20.0	2.6	17	21.0	7.7	17	15.0	7.4	3	6.1	1.4	5	2.4	.9
Non-Metal Materials	2	3.8	2.6	1	5.9	.4	3	12.0	2.7	4	5.0	2.9	1	.9	.8	6	12.2	4.6	2	1.0	.5
Printing	2	3.8	7.1	--	--	--	--	--	--	1	1.2	2.2	3	2.7	7.5	1	2.0	1.7	3	1.4	2.1
INTERMEDIATE INDUSTRIES:	11	20.8	6.8	3	17.6	1.7	4	16.0	3.3	11	13.8	12.2	9	7.9	9.0	4	8.2	2.2	7	2.9	.9
Rubber	2	3.8	3.6	--	--	--	--	--	--	1	1.2	7.1	2	1.8	11.1	--	--	--	3	1.4	5.0
Paper	--	--	--	--	--	--	1	4.0	3.4	2	2.5	5.7	4	3.5	10.0	--	--	--	1	.5	1.0
Mining	5	9.4	16.7	3	17.6	9.4	3	12.0	7.9	7	8.8	20.0	1	.9	nd	4	8.2	9.3	2	1.0	2.4
MODERN INDUSTRIES:	10	24.5	8.1	2	11.8	.9	5	20.0	1.8	14	17.5	3.5	48	42.5	7.1	19	38.8	2.4	162	77.1	8.6
Metalworks	11	20.8	11.0	2	11.8	1.4	4	16.0	2.0	5	6.3	1.7	28	24.8	6.7	17	34.8	3.5	147	70.0	9.5
Chemicals	2	3.7	4.3	--	--	--	1	4.0	1.0	9	11.2	10.0	20	17.7	18.0	2	4.0	1.5	12	5.7	3.5
ALL INDUSTRIAL STRIKES	53	100.0	5.5	17	100.0	1.5	25	100.0	1.9	80	100.0	5.4	113	100.0	6.1	49	100.0	2.4	210	100.0	4.6

(a) Strike rates calculated as the number of strikes per 100,000 workers for establishments of five or more employees.

Source: Instituto Brasileiro de Geografia e Estatística, *Censo Industrial, 1940, 1950, 1960, 1980.*

Instituto Brasileiro de Geografia e Estatística, *Produção Industrial, 1966, 1968.*

Instituto Brasileiro de Geografia e Estatística, *Transformação Industrial, 1964.*

of the occupational categories in the industry. Like their counterparts in textiles, foods and leather, miners also demonstrated their combativeness through a persistent series of strike actions over the different political periods, even during the 1947-1949 Cold War repressions when miners and textiles workers accounted for 70 percent of the strikes (Table 2.4). The extensive history of labor organization and collective actions which characterized many of the traditional sector industries was also found among the miners, particularly those in Minas Gerais and Santa Catarina, who were among the most militant.

As indicated by the strike rate, the emergence of the modern sector as a leading force in the labor movement is apparent by 1961-1963. By this time, 42.7 percent of the strikes were among modern sector workers, almost equally distributed between metal and chemical workers, while strikes in the traditional industries had declined to 49.6 percent of the total. In addition, the modern sector exhibited a higher strike rate than the traditional sector, though in this period of serious economic crisis, high inflation and growing class polarization, all sectors registered high strike rates. Nevertheless, compared to previous years, by 1961-1963 the metalworkers definitely had a prominent position in labor conflicts.

After the collapse of the populist government with the Coup of 1964, industrial strikes declined drastically as the new military government of General Castelo Branco proceeded to break the militant labor organizations and to subjugate them to state controls. In spite of these setbacks, workers in both sectors, particularly in those occupational groups which had been more militant, continued to offer resistance to the authoritarian regime. But the growing repression, especially after the decree of the "Fifth Institutional Act" giving the military president dictatorial powers, forced those committed groups of workers away from militant union activities to seek alternative forms of waging their struggle in the workplace.

The years between 1969 and 1977 were punctuated by several censored and, therefore, unreported work stoppages. The few scattered references of industrial conflict in this period suggest that a large number of incidents occurred in industries of the modern sector, in particular among the automobile industry workers. These work stoppages were more often isolated occurrences within factories and rarely involved a large proportion of the employees. Nevertheless, the fact that collective efforts to respond to employers' abuses continued, often even under the threat of severe personal risk, is testimony to a growing swell in labor which was gathering momentum under the seemingly calm of Brazil's "economic miracle".[5]

The years 1978-1980 mark the revival of a combative labor movement. In part as a consequence of the absolute increases in the industrial working class, the re-emergence of class conflict was marked by almost double the number of strikes as in the troubled years of 1961-1963. Yet in this renewal of workers' collective actions, the traditional sector accounted for only 20 percent of the strikes, even though about 43 percent of the work force was still employed in traditional industries. On the other hand, the modern sector, and in particular the metalworkers, emerged as the predominant force in industrial conflict.

The overshadowing of the traditional sector by the militancy of the modern industries' workers is further demonstrated by the differences in the levels of strike propensity. Workers in the modern sector clearly came through the years of repression better prepared to confront their employers and the state as suggested by the 8.6 strike rate for the three-year period 1978-1980. Neither the traditional nor the intermediate sectors produced similar levels of labor conflict, though in the latter sector the rubber industry workers, who maintained strong ties to the more militant automobile workers, registered the second highest strike rate.

The eventual decline of the role of the traditional sector in industrial conflicts is vividly demonstrated by the data on the number of man-days lost in strikes.[6] According to the data in Table 2.5, the traditional and intermediate sectors were by far the more aggressive segments of the working class prior to the late 1950s. During the period between 1956-1960, the modern sector appeared to match the other sectors in man-days lost, though it accounted for a lower proportion of the strikes.

By 1961-1963, the modern sector assumed the largest number of man-days lost while also accounting for 42.5 percent of the strikes in the period. After this, the sector continued to lead in this aspect in both the period following the military coup and in 1978-1980 at the beginning of the re-democratization. This shift in predominance, indicated by the several measures of strike activities, is further confirmed in an examination of the strike behavior of those occupational groups which led the changeover.

The changes in the occupational composition of strikers were not rapid, but rather a long and complex process which first showed signs as early as the end of the 1950s. At this time, as the data in Table 2.6

indicate, the metalworkers undertook few strike movements but were extremely successful in attaining a high number of lost man-days. Within the 1956-1960 period they were the occupational group with the largest number of days lost in strike activity. The data also show that the intensity of strikes among the textile workers was beginning its decline in terms of man-days lost from previous years, though other traditional sector occupations, such as food and leather workers, maintained previous levels.

While the metalworkers continued to rank high in man-days lost compared to other groups, the textile workers never recovered the levels achieved in previous years. Since the calculation of man-days lost is determined by the products of the median strike duration and mean number of strikers, the amount of man-days lost is conditioned by those factors affecting the number of workers willing to strike and resist. Consequently, a low number of man-days lost alone does not necessarily mean a decline of militancy. In the case of the textile workers, the decrease of man-days lost may have represented not so much a weakening of militancy or capacity to mobilize workers as an emphasis on other tactical options, such as other forms of collective actions, demonstrations, and petitions or more intense participation of unions' leaders in elite level organizations and political lobbying. Considering that the textile workers were among the better organized industrial groups at this time and the frequent mention of textile workers activities in mass political organizations, more likely the decline in textile worker strike actions was the result of political calculation.

In the case of the metalworkers, the data indicate low levels of man-days lost from 1945 until the end of the 1950s, which confirms the previous observations. The final years of the 1950s seem to have been the beginning of future combativeness. At this time there was a dramatic leap in the number of days lost in strikes, initiating a trend which was to continue to the present. From 1964-1968, the first years of military rule, many of the traditional sector unions were placed under government intervention (Table 2.7), leaders were arrested and persecuted, employers took advantage of the situation to purge their personnel of union activists. In this atmosphere, a few unions, headed by metalworkers, continued to resist, as is clearly visible in the much higher number of man-days lost between 1964 and 1968 (Table 2.6). It seems that through the repression the metalworkers, at least those in São Paulo and Minas Gerais, were able to undertake some mobilizations which enabled them

Table 2.5 - Man-Days Lost in Industrial Sector Strikes According to Political Period, 1945-1980

Category & Branch of Industry	1945-1946 End of Estado Novo (Dictatorship)	1947-1949 *Repressive Populism*	1950-1955 *Clientelistic Populism*	1956-1960 *Liberal Populism*	1961-1963 *Crisis of Populism*	1964-1968 *Military Dictatorship*	1978-1980 *Democratic Opening*
TRADITIONAL INDUSTRIES:							
% of Total Strikes	54.7 (29)	70.6 (12)	64.0 (16)	68.7 (55)	49.6 (56)	53.0 (26)	20.0 (42)
Man-Days Lost	13,555.5	4,465.6	46,291.2	9.834.0	7,813.5	24,828.5	11,497.5
INTERMEDIATE INDUSTRIES:							
% of Total Strikes	20.8 (11)	17.6 (3)	16.0 (4)	13.8 (11)	7.9 (9)	8.2 (4)	2.9 (6)
Man-Days Lost	12,009.2	6,666.6	13,518.0	9,556.2	6,431.1	2,532.0	9,920.0
MODERN INDUSTRIES:							
% of Total Strikes	24.5 (13)	11.8 (2)	20.0 (5)	17.5 (14)	42.5 (48)	38.8 (19)	77.1 (162)
Man-Days Lost	8,655.2	6,690	3,920	9,348	19,095.2	140,718.0	31,368

Note: Number of strikes in parenthesis.

Table 2.6 - Man-Days Lost in Strikes for Selected Occupational Groups According to Industrial Sectors and By Political Periods, Brazil 1945-1980

Sector & Branch of Industry	*1945-1946* *End of Estado Novo (Dictatorship)*	*1947-1949* *Repressive Populism*	*1950-1955* *Clientelistic Populism*	*1956-1960* *Liberal Populism*	*1961-1963* *Crisis of Populism*	*1964-1968* *Military Dictatorship*	*1978-1980* *Democratic Opening*
TRADITIONAL INDUSTRIES:							
Textiles	19,537	21,344.4	70,169.4	7,169.4	2,114.8	4,926	7,245
Foods	3,000	2,000	5,000	4,000	6,148.2	2,000	4,386
Leathers	3,600	3,600	135,000	75,583.2	5,407.5	69,710	---
INTERMEDIATE INDUSTRIES:							
Ceramics & Non-Metal. Materials	15,300	5,300	43,932	5,250	23,175	13,299.4	4,025
Mining	32,490	6,666	15,357.2	11,396.7	75,192	2,532	6,031.3
MODERN INDUSTRIES:							
Metalworks	6,690	6,690	2,000	252,736	26,207.6	156,246	34,164
Chemicals	19,800	---	5,400	4,800	11.422	1,455.7	3,297.8

Table 2.7
Distribution By Sector and Industry of Unions Identified As Being Under Government Intervention In Early 1965

Sector and Branch of Industry	*Nº of Unions*	*% of Interventions*
TRADITIONAL SECTOR	121	73.7
Textiles & Clothing	40	24.3
Foods	17	10.3
Construction	30	18.2
Leathers & Others	31	18.9
Printing	3	1.8
INTERMEDIATE SECTOR	3	1.8
Glass	2	1.2
Mining	1	.6
MODERN SECTOR	40	24.3
Metalworks	25	15.2
Chemicals	15	9.1
TOTAL	164	100.0

Note: Most of the unions subjected to government intervention had been released by June 1966, two and a half years after the military coup.

Source: United States Department of Labor, *Labor Law and Practice in Brazil* (Washington: U.S. Government Printing Office, BLS Report No. 309, 1967), p. 76.

express their discontent with government policies and defy military rule.

The influence of the rise of the modern sector on the transformation of the Brazilian labor movement has been a largely unexplored question. In this chapter we have focused primarily on the changing occupational and sectorial composition of industrial strikes over the thirty-five years between 1945 and 1980, but certainly other aspects of the complex combination of economic and socio-political factors must be examined in order to better understand the evolution of the working-class movement.

Indeed, the analysis of the shifting importance of the modern and traditional sectors of industry seems to also be true for the service sector. As we can see from the data in Table 2.8, the service workers' strikes also underwent a similar transition from the predominance of the traditional service occupations until 1964 and subsequently declined under military

Table 2.8 - Distribution of Service Sector Strikes for Selected Occupational Categories Grouped According to Traditional and Modern Sectors, 1945-1980

Service Sector & Occupational Category	1945-1948		1949-1952		1953-1956		1957-1960		1961-1964		1965-1968		1978-1980	
	Nº of Strikes	% of Total	Nº of Strikes	% of Total	Nº of Strikes	% of Total	Nº of Strikes	% of Total	Nº of Strikes	% of Total	Nº of Strikes	% of Total	Nº of Strikes	% of Total
TRADITIONAL SERVICE SECTOR:		67		74		54.2		77		58.9		13.4		22.1
Transit Workers	15	22.3	6	22.2	6	25	22	22	49	20.5	1	6.7	16	13.6
Railroad Workers	15	22.3	7	25.9	--	--	15	15	9	3.8	--	--	--	--
Port/Dock Workers	9	13.4	5	18.5	2	8.3	18	18	36	15.0	1	6.7	2	1.7
Maritime Workers	--	--	--	--	4	16.7	14	14	18	7.5	--	--	--	--
Civil Service	6	9.0	2	7.4	1	4.2	8	8	29	12.1	--	--	8	6.8
MODERN SERVICE SECTOR:		16.5		22.2		16.7		18		30		53.5		59.3
Bus Drivers	--	--	--	--	--	--	4	4	5	2	--	--	--	--
Truckers	1	1.5	1	3.7	--	--	4	4	10	4.2	1	6.7	13	11
Airline Workers	1	1.5	1	3.7	4	16.7	5	5	1	.4	1	6.7	2	1.7
Bank Workers	5	7.5	3	11.1	--	--	--	--	30	12.6	4	26.7	4	3.4
Health Workers [a]	--	--	1	3.7	--	--	3		6	2.5	1	6.7	16	13.6
School Teachers	1	1.5	--	--	--	--	3	3	8	3.3	1	6.7	31	26.3
Radio/TV Workers	--	--	--	--	--	--	--	--	5	2.1	--	--	3	2.5
Telephone Workers	3	4.5	--	--	--	--	2	2	7	2.9	--	--	1	.8
Total Service Strikes	67		27		24		100		239		15		118	
Total Strikes	134		53		38		190		451		54		338	

[a] *Include hospital workers and hospital doctors, residents, nurses and dentists.*

Percentages do not add up to 100% because of the exclusion from the table of some occupations which were not classified in any sector and had an insignificant incidence of strikes.

repression. Modern service occupation workers, on the other hand, struck less frequently until 1961. Then between 1961 and 1964 the percentage of strikes by modern service workers increased to 30 percent; finally, after 1965, this sector accounted for over 50 percent of the strikes.

This similarity in the sectorial pattern of service strikes was also the result of the changing structure of the Brazilian economy, though the connection between economic development and labor militancy is more complex. As we argue throughout this book, political factors are a prism-like synapse between economic growth and working-class participation.

One example of this is the fact that for both industrial and service workers, the rupture in the political process represented by the military coup of 1964 marked a watershed in working-class politics. How much longer traditional sector workers would have led in strike activities is a question left unanswered due to the massive interventions by the military governments. As Table 2.7 clearly shows, the brunt of the regime's purges was directed at the more combative and better organized leaders[7] largely found in the traditional sector unions. Of the interventions in labor unions between 1964 and 1970, 80% occurred in the first two years of military rule. Of these, about half were interventions in industrial unions.[8] Of the industrial unions that were still under military intervention two years after the coup, 73.7 percent were unions from the traditional sector, compared to 24.3 percent from the modern sector. This suggests that some modern sector workers, in particular the metalworkers, were better able to recover lost ground and to form new leadership, while most of the traditional sector unions were severely handicapped as a consequence of the imposition of conservative, pro-government union bosses and a closer surveillance of worker discontent.[9]

The Working Class Under Military Rule

The Coup of 1964 inaugurated a regime intent on controlling inflation and resolving the economic imbalances which had resulted from the development policies of the civilian governments. The economic stabilization policies sanctioned by the International Monetary Fund (IMF) included several features, the most important of which was the deliberate lowering of wages, so that by 1968 wages had fallen 57 percent from their 1959 levels as shown by the real wage curve in Figure 2.2. A second policy objective was the lowering of real prices for manufactured goods by the reduction of protectionist measures and official credit subsidies, a course which caused many small, less efficient enterprises to go out of business. Third, a direct assault on the balance-of-payment problem was conducted through measures aimed at encouraging foreign investment, as for example the repealing of the restrictive profit remittance law of 1962.[10] Needless to say, many of the economic policies were extremely unpopular, especially among the working class, and as a consequence could only be implemented through an authoritarian and repressive administration, which some believed to be an essential prerequisite for a new cycle of dependent capitalist growth.[11]

Because the new economic policies required the depression of real wages and the lowering of living standards, the regime executed a systematic campaign to weaken labor's political power by edging it out of the decision-making process. Beginning with the government of Castelo Branco (1964-1966), the government's intention of crushing the power of organized labor was obvious. Virtually all leftist union leaders were deposed and replaced. In the years between 1964 and 1970 over 483 unions, forty-nine labor federations and four confederations were placed under military government intervention; many of their leaders were jailed and/or exiled, usually without formal judicial proceedings, or they simply disappeared.[12] As Figure 2.3 shows, the main thrust of the interventions, used to stifle labor protest, occurred in the first two years of military rule, 1964-1965. But the continued strike activities between 1966 to 1968 resulted in a second wave of interventions which swept the labor movement between 1967 and 1970. After this second round of repression, state interference in unions continued through the 1970s, but at a much lower rate.[13]

As real wages declined, worker resistance erupted, especially among the workers of the modern sector who suffered fewer demobilization effects from the massive state repression. But, in general, the repression was effective; strike activity fell dramatically over the 1964-1968 period (Figure 2.2) and continued until 1969 when a hard line posture was taken toward any type of contention. At this time strike activity ceased and was replaced by sporadic shop floor disputes which have yet to be fully documented because of the stringent censorship placed on the media during the years of military rule.

In addition to the many interventions against the workers' organizations, the military also sought to eliminate industrial strife by

Figure 2.2 Industrial Strikes and Real Minimum Wages, 1959-1974 (Real Minimum Wage Index, July 1940=100)

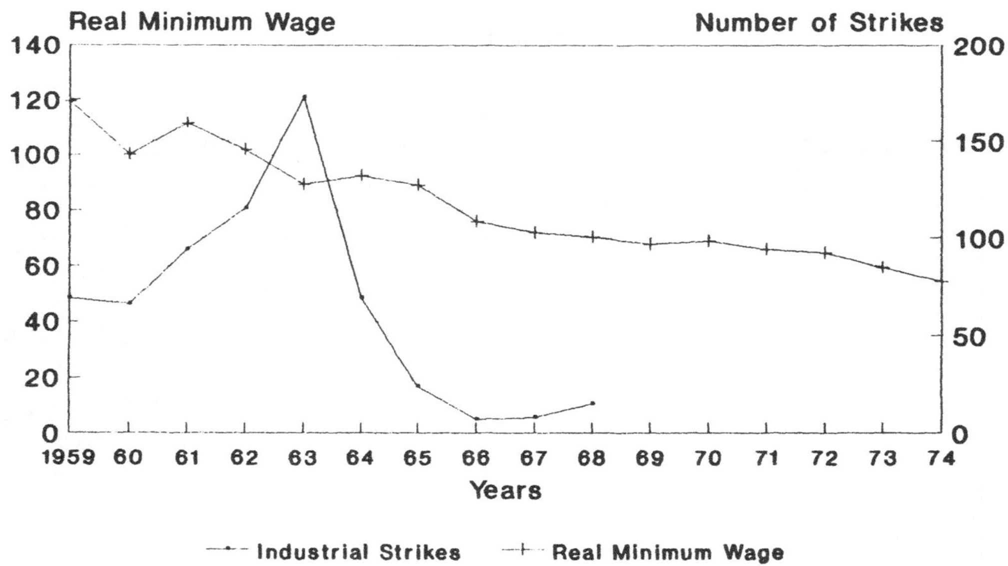

Source: Wage data: DIEESE, *Cinquenta Anos de Salario Minimo,* (Sao Paulo: DIEESE, July 1990), Table 4, p. 4.

Figure 2.3 Government Interventions in Labor Unions, Brazil 1964-1977

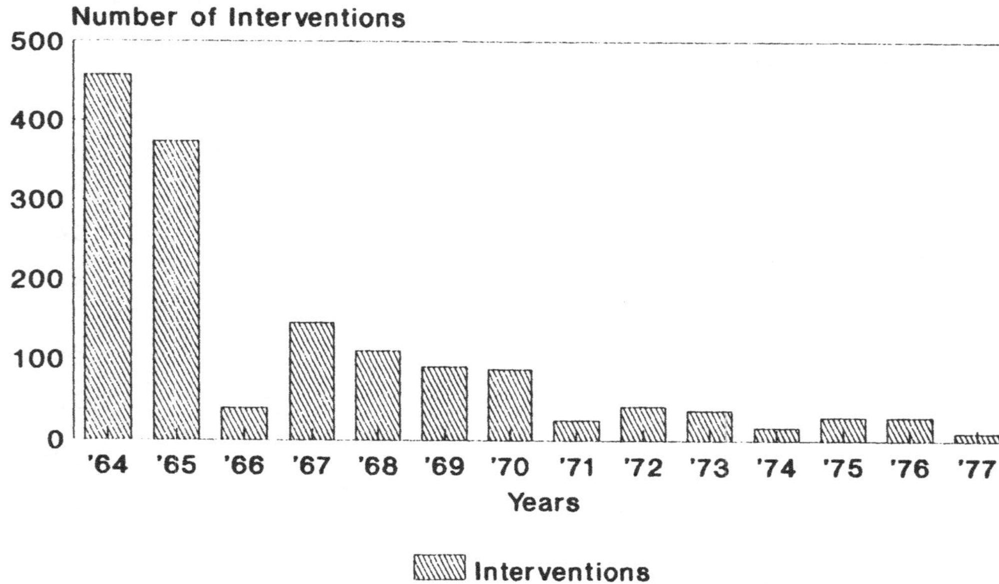

Source: M.H. Moreira Alves, *Estado e Oposicao no Brasil*. (Petropolis: Vozes, 1984), data from Table 8.3, p. 244.

introducing three important reforms to the corporate labor structure. First, the government regulated the conditions under which workers could legally strike, restricting work stoppages to cases of failure by employers to abide by the yearly agreements sanctioned by the labor courts or to failure of employers to pay back-wages owed to the workers. All other reasons for striking became illegal. Second, the system of job security was replaced by one which made the firing of workers for any reason financially insignificant; thus strikers were more vulnerable to employer reprisals. Third, the government took the issue of wage increases out of the domain of negotiation by workers, employers and the labor courts by subjecting salary increases to ceiling levels decreed by the finance minister. As a result, employers conceded to increases equivalent to the ministerial indices, regardless of any correspondence to the cost of living, and the unions and labor courts were legally powerless to obtain higher salary increases. These three measures were the only substantial changes introduced in the labor laws, which illustrates the high degree of compatibility between the corporate industrial relations system and the new dictatorship.

Also hindering the mobilization of workers was the impact of the recession caused by the government's economic policies between 1964 and 1967, when economic growth fell to the lowest levels since 1930. The recession, with its falling wages and increased unemployment, compounded the crisis of organized labor.

After 1968, fueled by the recession of the previous four years and with political opposition largely silenced, the economy entered another period of very rapid expansion. To illustrate this upsurge in economic activity, Brazilian export earnings rose from $1.881 billion dollars in 1968 to $7.951 billion dollars in 1974, representing approximately 9 percent of the exports of the non-oil-producing, less developed countries (LDCs). The importance of Brazil's economic advance within the LDCs is further illustrated by the amount of reserves held by the country prior to the world oil crisis. In the beginning of the 1970s Brazil held 8.7 percent of the LDCs' reserves, and by 1973 it had reached 22 percent of the total reserves of the less developed countries.[14]

During the period of the "economic miracle" (1968-1974), Brazil became a record setter in growth rates. During this period industry experienced growth rates averaging 12.2 percent annually, but this scarcely conveys the magnitude of the transformation during the "miracle". Werner Baer best illustrated the significance of this period by citing:

> ...a few numbers of actual output in both basic industries and consumer goods industries: steel output grew from 2.8 million tons in 1964 to 8.3 million in 1975; installed electric power capacity expanded from 6,840,000 megawatts to 19,500,500 in the same period; cement from 5.6 to 17.9 million tons; motor vehicles from 184,000 to 930,000 and passenger cars from 98,000 to 524,000; television set production had reached 831,000 and production of refrigerators 658,000. The average yearly growth rate of road construction increased from 12 percent in 1968-1972 to 25 percent... and the rate of growth of paving from six percent to 33 percent.[15]

Within the manufacturing sector the highest growth rates were in the modern sector industries largely dominated by multinational and state owned corporations. The traditional manufacturing industries remained to a large extent the reserve of private national capital and grew at more modest rates. During this period, 1968-1973, there was also a slight shift in the pattern of industrial ownership. The division of the industrial sector remained about the same, with multinationals dominating in the production of consumer goods, the state monopolizing the basic input sector, and private national enterprises retaining control over the smaller scale, more traditional areas of the economy.[16]

The balance of power in industry shifted slightly over the 1970s. Both local and foreign private capital decreased their holds over the largest firms as the state productive sector became the fastest expanding segment of Brazilian industry.[17] The expansion of the economy and the increased role of the state in the productive sector also raised the foreign debt of the country. Yet the economic "boom" was not long lasting. Because of the world oil crisis and recession in the international market, the unfavorable terms of trade obliged the government to resort to foreign loans to cover the increasing deficits in the balance of payments.[18]

A concomitant effect of Brazil's economic expansion was the rapid growth of the urban working class. During the past two decades the economically active population in the primary sector decreased from 54 percent of the work force in 1960 to 29.9 percent in 1980. Conversely, the industrial work force increased substantially during the same period. In

1950 Brazilians employed in the secondary sector numbered approximately 2,427,364, rising to 2,940,242 in 1960. A more dramatic increase occurred in the decades between 1960 and 1980. From 1960-1970 the economically active population in the secondary sector almost doubled in size, reaching a total of 5,295,417. By 1980 the working class employed in industry showed extraordinary growth, doubling its size once again in the ten year period to approximately 10,674,977.[19] These significant increases in the size of the urban working class in the decades of authoritarian government and accelerated industrialization inevitably had a fundamental effect on the class relations that evolved, particularly on the capacity of political institutions to handle the demands of this enlarged and modern labor force.

The tertiary sector also demonstrated high rates of growth during this period. Between 1960 and 1980 this segment of the Brazilian working class increased its numbers from 7,532,878 to 20,012,371. Though in absolute terms the tertiary sector was larger than the industrial work force, the latter experienced a more accelerated rate of growth. Be that as it may, the fact remains that the population went from being predominantly rural in 1960 to predominantly urban in 1980.

The quantitative expansion of the industrial proletariat over these decades was rooted in important sectorial changes occurring in the economy. As mentioned above, in 1952 the so-called traditional sectors of the economy predominated as the major employers of the industrial work force. Yet by 1970 there evolved a significant shift as the modern sector industries came to engage a larger proportion of the work force. This shift presents several important points which directly influenced later working-class political behavior.

First, the shift from the traditional to the modern sector is important when one considers that, by and large, the latter is predominantly controlled either by foreign capital (as in the cases of the machine industries, electrical and communication products industries, vehicles and transportation industries, and rubber and tire industries), or by state owned enterprises such as steel and metallurgical industries, chemicals and petro-chemicals. These same sectors continued growing steadily even during the difficult years of the early 1960s (1960-1964), recording positive growth rates while the traditional sectors registered little or no growth. Similarly, during the austerity program of the 1960s imposed by the military governments in Brazil, the modern sector continued to grow at much higher rates than did the traditional sector. This is illustrated in the cases of the textile and metallurgical industries. The labor force in textiles grew by 29 percent between 1960 and 1980, while the metal works industry expanded its labor force by 477 percent.[20]

The shift in each sector's relative importance meant that the modern sector was more dynamic in creating employment and, consequently, contributed more to the growth of the industrial working class. At the same time, the economy became markedly stratified between the foreign and state dominated sectors on the one hand, and the traditional ones controlled by the local private bourgeoisie on the other. The interests of these two groups have often coincided in times of economic boom, but also diverged during economic difficulties and labor unrest, often as a result of their unequal capacity to cope with economic constraints and labor's demands.

The transition to an industrial society has also meant a rapid rate of urbanization. While in 1950 only 21.5 percent of the population lived in cities of 20,000 or more inhabitants, by 1980 this percentage had risen to 45.7 percent.[21] The process of rapid urbanization was characterized by the concentration of seventy percent of the urban population in the cities of the southern regions of the country. By 1980 the country had thirty major urban agglomerations (urban areas of more than 250,000 inhabitants), of which nine had over one million people. Of all the Brazilians living in urban centers, 76.6 percent resided in these major agglomerations, which indicates the very high level of urban concentration and the primacy of a few urban centers.[22] In fact, these thirty agglomerations represented 35 percent of the total population in 1980. Furthermore, the center-south and southern regions actually accounted for 75.9 percent of the inhabitants of these metropolitan areas with the state of São Paulo leading the regions in the number of agglomerations,[23] five of which had over a million inhabitants. The two largest metropolitan areas are São Paulo and Rio de Janeiro. Because of the weight of the Rio-São Paulo axis in terms of urban and economic concentration, working-class politics of the region have the greatest impact on national affairs.

In spite of the advances in economic development, under the military governments, the conditions of the Brazilian working class deteriorated. The tendency in income distribution since 1960 was to concentrate income in a few hands during periods of rapid economic growth. Within the wealthiest 10 percent of the population, 5 percent holds 37.9 percent of the national family income. Since 1960 the top 5 percent has increased its share of the national income from 28.3 percent in 1960 to 37.9 percent in 1976. Conversely, the bottom segments of the population have steadily lost their share. During the period of greatest economic growth, the lower half of the economically active population had their income reduced from 17.4 percent in 1960 to 13.5 percent by 1976.[24]

In her analysis of Brazilian income distribution, economist Sylvia A. Hewlett observed:

> Despite the high growth rates that characterized much of this period, and at least some absolute gain by each decile, the majority of the Brazilian population lost out in relative terms in the years 1960-1975, while the richest 10 percent increased its share of national income from 39.6% in 1960 to 50.4% in 1976. In other words, of the total gain in the Brazilian GNP during this period (and we must remember that the global product more than doubled) the richest strata of the population appropriated three-quarters, and the poorest, 50 percent less than one-tenth. A striking example of the degree of concentration of income in contemporary Brazil is the fact that in 1976 the top 1 percent of the population received a larger slice of the national income than the bottom 50 percent of all Brazilians![25]

While income distribution tables reveal an overall picture of the actual allocation of the socially produced benefits of Brazilian society, other types of evidence help compose a more detailed picture of what the skewed income patterns meant in terms of the lives of the industrial working class. Nothing is more indicative of the fate of the working class during this period than the tendencies in industrial wages. In a detailed study of industrial wages conducted by the *Departamento Intersindical de Estatística e Estudos Sócio-Econômicos* (*DIEESE*) for the period of 1964 and 1969, the first general conclusion is that real wages decreased significantly over the period. Wages seem to have had their greatest decline between 1964 and 1969, when the military government implemented its austerity policies to combat inflation and encourage investment. Then, wages apparently rose slightly during the "economic miracle" around 1970, only to fall once again by 1974. Even though there was a slight increase during 1970-1971, at no time did the working class recover their pre-1960 wage levels.[26]

It is very clear that industrial growth was in part accomplished by the lowering of the working class' wages through strict control of wage increase rates and, more importantly, by a systematic repression of labor discontent through direct intervention in union affairs and other coercive measures.

The decade of the seventies showed a similar pattern of declining wages. In terms of real wages, between 1970 and 1978 the Brazilian worker lost approximately 30 percent. Generally, this decline seems to have been across the board for the working class. As is readily noticeable from Table A-3 of the Appendix, there is not a single occupational group that did not experience a "tightening of the belt", both in the states of São Paulo and Rio de Janeiro. This is so not only for those workers employed in the modern sector, but also for those in the more traditional sector and white collar occupations such as bank clerks and sales clerks. In this respect, it is important to mention that the pushing down of the workers' income, the *arrocho salarial,* was independent of the growth dynamics of the various economic sectors, even though it remains clear that wage differences between sectors still prevailed with some sectors paying higher wages than others.

In the day-to-day lives of the workers, this lowering of wage levels is best understood in terms of the decline in worker's purchasing power. As Table A-4 in the Appendix shows, the work time needed to purchase the monthly minimum ration of essential foodstuffs, the *cesta básica,*[27] for a family of four increased by 69 percent over the 1965-1981 period. That is to say, for the worker in the São Paulo area to purchase the minimum monthly ration in 1965, he had to work approximately 88 hours and 16 minutes. By 1970, the amount of work time necessary to purchase the same quantity of food stuffs rose to 105 hours and 13 minutes, an increase of 19.2 percent. By 1981 the Brazilian worker in São Paulo had to work 148 hours and 40 minutes to acquire his family's essential food stuffs, marking an overall rise of 69.6 percent in the labor power required of the family head to provide for his family.[28]

If one considers that in addition to food stuffs the average family also has other expenses such as housing, medical bills, transportation, and schooling, it is quite clear that the worker had to increase both his income through supplementary jobs, overtime or the like, and also to increase family income through other members of the family entering the labor force. A study entitled *São Paulo 1975: Crescimento e Pobreza* demonstrated that among working-class families the earnings of the head of the household decreased by 38 percent between 1958 and 1969 (see Table A-4, Appendix). To counter this reduction in family income, a second member entered the job market. Yet as the study also showed, even with two family members working, real family income fell over the same period; in fact, together both salaries by 1969 were only slightly higher than the income level of a single worker in 1958.[29] The decline in working-class family income provoked by the contraction of real wages over the 1964-1980 period reflects the social consequences of Brazil's "economic miracle" and manifests one aspect of the objective conditions underlying labor's unrest at the end of the 1970s.

Another factor which contributed to the declining wages of the Brazilian working class was the very high job turnover. The average number of months of worker employment was generally less than a twelve month period. This reflects a generalized situation in which job security was almost non-existent among the work force; employers were given free hands to manage their employees with impunity as the state stifled union initiatives to correct the problem.

The turnover problem was most serious for those workers in the lower salary brackets who were most affected by management policies of gearing employment to seasonal demands, of dismissing employees prior to salary increases in order to rehire them at lower wages, and of reducing business costs through other forms of wage reduction. As Table A-5 shows, industry and the public service sectors generally have a higher average number of months of employment for employees above the three minimum wage levels, which suggests somewhat greater job security among these workers than in other sectors of the economy. Clearly, the higher paid employees have greater job security, as the average number of months of employment approximates the twelve month period; more likely than not, the turnover among these better paid workers, often the most skilled in the sector, is due to transfers to new jobs rather than to a management policy of lowering wages. This seems to have been the case in studies conducted among metallurgical workers in São Paulo[30] and São José dos Campos,[31] where the tendency was for skilled workers to change jobs as a consequence of greater competition among companies to hire the more scarce craftsmen.

Regardless of the peculiarities of the situation among the more skilled workers, the fact remains that for the working class as a whole, the very high rates of job turnover have been another factor contributing to the systematic lowering of wages. Management's use of dismissal practices to accommodate economic cycles and to defend profit margins by firing workers prior to wage increase settlements in order to rehire them at lower salaries resulted in the decline of annual income from lost wages during layoff periods. For this reason, one of labor's main demands has been for greater job security and for the establishment of minimum base salaries for workers within specific sectors of the economy to prevent management from resorting to abusive turnover policies.

In this chapter we have examined the impact of industrial growth on the regional and occupational distribution of strike activity. In general, the major transformation of the Brazilian economy altered only slightly the regional concentration of industry in the center-south region. In fact, the largest proportion of industrial and strike activities is centered in a region which is substantially larger than France or Germany. The main foci of national industrial activity is located in an triangular area bounded by the three largest metropolitan areas: São Paulo, Rio de Janeiro and Belo Horizonte. As would be expected, the bulk of strike activity has taken place within this subregion, though the São Paulo working class has been more active than workers in either of the other states.

Between 1945 and 1980, this pattern altered only slightly. Within the Center-South, Rio de Janeiro has declined proportionately in industrial conflict, while there was an increase in the state of Minas Gerais due to the relative deindustrialization of the former and the more recent industrialization of the latter. Similarly, the growth of industry in the South has also meant an increase in strikes, though the primacy of the Center-South remains uncontested.

Even though accelerated industrial growth did not produce a greater regional diffusion, the more noteworthy consequence was the occupational transformation of the economy and of the working-class population from which strikes arise. Over the years there has been a steady shift in the importance of the old and new industries. The traditional industries of the earlier phases of industrialization gradually gave way in prominence to the modern industries as new markets for durable consumer goods developed.

The shift in sectorial importance is also reflected in a similar change in characteristics of strike activity, though over the long run, the increase in strikes among modern sector workers was not solely the direct effect of the growth of these industries. Instead, the transition from traditional to modern sectorial predominance in strike activity was the result of the complex interaction of political and economic factors affecting the political mobilization process of the working class. As we have seen, a number of traditional sector occupations remained the organizational backbone of working-class mobilization prior to the coup of 1964, and the decline in strike activity after this time was due to the government's suppression of the more militant traditional sector unions, and not to the sector's economic performance.

In the years following the military takeover, economic growth rates reached record heights, especially during the years of greatest repression. Accelerated economic expansion masked a significant worsening of the standard of living among the working population whose attempts at protest were systematically suppressed. Resistance to the abuses under the autocratic regime occurred primarily among modern sector workers in the form of sporadic workplace unrest.

These years proved to be a watershed for the working-class movement because of two complementary mechanisms which contributed to the transformation of strike activity. First, the economic boom accelerated the concentration of workers in large plants (especially within the modern sector) and in several large municipalities and metropolitan areas, particularly in the Center-South. Second, the regime's marginalization of unions and its constant repression of workers' protest led to innovations in working-class organizations more resistant to governmental pressures, such as the development of stronger grass-roots networks at the workplace and alternative forms of organization in proletarian neighborhoods. These changes, which will be examined in later chapters, were of fundamental importance to the resurgence of working-class conflict and the rise of the "new unionism".

Notes

1. John P. Dickenson, *Brazil* (Boulder, Colorado: Westview Press, 1978), p. 153.

2. Two good studies which focus specifically on the differential growth patterns of the dynamic (modern) and traditional sectors of industry are Carlos Lessa, "Fifteen Years of Economic Policy in Brazil," *Economic Bulletin for Latin America*, 9 (November 1964); Ministério de Planejamento e Coordenação Geral-Programa Estratégico de Desenvolvimento 1968-1980, *A Industrialização Brasileira: Diagnóstico e*

Perspectivas (Rio de Janeiro: Ministério de Planejamento e Coordenação Geral, January 1969), pp. 118-166.

3. Carlos Lessa, "Fifteen Years of Economic Policy," pp. 162-172 passim.

4. Ibid., pp. 172-184 passim.

5. The "Economic Miracle" (Milagre Econômico) is the term frequently used to refer to the period between 1968 and 1973 when the Brazilian economy experienced record growth rates, generally the highest of the so-called developing countries.

6. The number of man-days lost in strike activity is calculated by multiplying the number of strikers by the number of days duration of the strike.

7. Leôncio Martins Rodrigues claims that by 1963-1964 practically all the old *pelego* leadership had been replaced in union posts by a new leadership of communists, nationalists, unionists and independents. See Leôncio Martins Rodrigues, *Conflito Industrial e Sindicalismo no Brasil* (São Paulo: Difusão Europeia do Livro, 1966), p. 190.

8. Argelina Cheibub Figueiredo, "Intervenções Sindicais e o Novo Sindicalismo," *Dados*, 17 (1978): 137-146 passim.

9. According to José Albertino Rodrigues, the *pelegos* were the main beneficiaries of the 1964 interventions inasmuch as the military government returned them to leadership positions in the unions, see José Albertino Rodrigues, *Sindicato e Desenvolvimento no Brasil* (São Paulo: Difusão Europeia do Livro, 1966), pp. 153-154, 164.

10. Sylvia Ann Hewlett, *The Cruel Dilemmas of Development: Twentieth-Century Brazil* (New York: Basic Books, Inc., 1980), p. 45.

11. Ibid.

12. Timothy Fox Harding, "The Political History of Organized Labor in Brazil" (Ph.D. Dissertation, Stanford University, 1973), p. 602.

13. Table 2.9 is based on data from Maria Helena Moreira Alves, *Estado e Oposição no Brasil* (1964-1984) (Petrópolis: Editora Vozes, 1984), Table 8.3, p. 244.

14. William R. Cline, "Brazil's Emerging International Economic Role," in *Brazil in the Seventies*, Riordan Roett (ed.) (Washington, D.C.: American Enterprise Institute for Public Policy Research, 1976), pp. 78-79.

15. Werner Baer, "The Brazilian Growth and Development Experience: 1964-1975," in Riordan Roett, (ed.) *Brazil in the Seventies* (Washington, D.C.: American Enterprise Institute for Public Policy Research, 1976), p. 47.

16. Sylvia Ann Hewlett, *The Cruel Dilemmas*, p. 46.

17. Ibid.

18. Ibid., pp. 51-56.

19. Vilmar Faria, "Desenvolvimento, Urbanização e Mudanças na Estrutura do Emprego: A Experiência Brasileira dos Últimos Trinta Anos," in Maria Herminia Tavares de Almeida and Bernardo Sorj (eds), *Sociedade e Política no Brasil Pós-64*, (São Paulo: Editora Brasiliense, 1983), pp. 118-154.

20. See Table 2.1.

21. Vilmar Faria, "Desenvolvimento, Urbanização...," p. 120.

22. Ibid., p. 132.

23. Vilmar Faria, "Desenvolvimento, Urbanização...," Table 2.7, p. 133.

24. See Table 2.2.13 in Sylvia Ann Hewlett, *The Cruel Dilemmas*, p. 231.

25. Ibid., pp. 166-167.

26. DIEESE Departamento Intersindical de Estatística e Estudos Sócio-Econômicos, "10 Anos de Política Salarial," in *Estudos Sócio-Econômicos*, 3 (August 1975), p. 64.

27. The Cesta Básica or the Minimum Essential Monthly Ration is an official measure of 13 basic food stuffs and their specified quantities for the consumption by a family of four members. This ration was defined by the law Decreto-Lei No. 399 in 1938 and used to determine the first minimum wage decrees. See "Instruções," Brasil, IBGE-Fundação Instituto Brasileiro de Estatística e Geografia, *Anuário Estatístico do Brasil*.

28. Fernando Lopes de Almeida, *Política Salarial, Emprego e Sindicalismo 1964/1981* (Petrópolis: Editora Vozes, 1982), pp. 48-49.

29. Cândido Procópio Ferreira de Camargo et al, *São Paulo: Crescimento e Pobreza 1975* (São Paulo: Edições Loyola, 1981.

30. John Humphrey, *Controle Capitalista e Luta Operária na Industria Automobilística Brasileira* (Petrópolis: Editora Vozes - CEBRAP, 1982), pp. 94-99.

31. Salvador A.M. Sandoval and Sonia Maria de Avelar, "Conciencia Obrera y Negociación Colectiva en Brasil," *Revista Mexicana de Sociologia*, 3 (July-September 1983): 1027-1047.

3

Strikes, Economic Fluctuations, and the Power of the State

In the previous chapter we examined the effects of structural changes in the Brazilian economy on the occupational composition of industrial strikes. The capacity of workers to strike depended both on economic factors, such as current wages, prices and production, and political factors. In general, we argue that economic circumstances mediated by conjunctural political factors influence short-term fluctuations in strike activity, while long-term fluctuations depend more on changes in the power alignments within the polity.

The first part of this chapter focuses on the year-to-year variation of median real wages and real industrial production as compared to the fluctuations in strike activity. The purpose is to show that the general relationships between economic activity and industrial conflict are ambiguous unless viewed through the lens of the political dynamic. As a result, we find that the combination of economic factors as they fit together in specific conjunctures pervades the politics of workers challenging employers and the state.

The second part examines strike activity in different political periods in which the levels of government tolerance toward industrial conflict varied considerably. Our analysis focuses on how political factors combine with economic circumstances during the various political periods to significantly influence the fluctuations of strike activity. To this end we examine the impact of police repression on strike actions during each political period in order to illustrate the responses of the different presidential administrations to the challenges of labor protest.

Strikes and Economic Fluctuations

Let us begin by examining the relationship between changes in annual strike activity and the fluctuations of real wages and real industrial product for the years 1946 to 1968. In Table 3.1 the correlations between these economic factors and the number of strikes per year show relationships which are symptomatic of the interaction between political and economic factors. Generally speaking, economic factors such as real industrial product and real wages seem to show a moderate relationship to the number of strikes per year for the entire period, as indicated by the correlations in the first column of Table 3.1.

However, when the twenty-two year period is broken down into the three major subperiods of strike patterns, 1946-1955, 1956-1963, and 1964-1968, the correlation coefficients, presented in Table 3.1, reveal a more complex set of relationships. The three subperiods are characterized by distinct patterns of strike activity. The first period between 1946 and 1955 is one of very noticeable oscillation in strike rates, while the second period between 1956 and 1963 is characterized by a strong and continuous increase in strike activity.[1] The third period, 1964-1968, is marked by a rapid decline in strike activity under the military governments.

Between 1946 and 1955 there was a weak relationship between strikes and the economic variables except for the negative coefficient for the variable food price/wage ratio (-.5001) indicating a inverse relation: as prices/wages rose, strike activity decreased. These correlations reflect the consequences of the influence of authoritarian governments of the period: the repressive civilian administration of Dutra and the clientelistic one of Getúlio Vargas. Both governments, using different control mechanisms, were able to depress the frequency of industrial conflict while the cost of living rose and the economy grew. Thus we find that the strike provoking effects of such economic factors as lowering wages, the rising cost of living or increased industrial output were offset by political controls over organized labor.

On the other hand, the 1956 to 1963 period showed a change in the relationship between strikes and the economic variables. The high coefficient of .9645 between real industrial product and industrial strikes reflects a rise in labor militancy relatively unhindered by the government in this period of economic expansion. The very low correlation coefficient

Table 3.1 - Correlation Coefficients of Strikes Per Year and Selected Economic Variables, 1946-1968

Variable	*Overall Period*	*Sub-Periods*		
	1946-68	*1946-55*	*1956-63*	*1964-68*
Real Industrial Product	.4565	-.2749	.9645	-.6421
Real Wages	.5862	.2415	.2678	.9051
Ratio of Food Price to Money Wage	-.3320	-.5001	.1032	(a)

(a) Data not available for the sub-period 1964-1968.
Source: Time-series data for 1946-1963 for the economic variables, see Raouf Kahil, *Inflation and Economic Development in Brazil 1946-1963*, (Oxford: Clarendon Press, 1973) Table 11.13, pp. 65-66; Time-series data for 1964-1968 for the economic variables, see DIEESE, *Dez Anos de Política Salarial*, pp. 35, 64.

between real wages and strikes (.2415) reflects the success of the government's labor policies of allowing strikes while maintaining relatively stable wages. Thus, with greater governmental tolerance, this period is one of heightened strike activity over the broader issues of economic development as well.

Finally, in the period between 1964 and 1968, the coefficients once again reflect the primacy of the political factors under military rule. The strong correlation between strikes and real wages indicates the simultaneous decline of real wages and strike activity as the new government implemented its stern economic austerity program. Similarly, the strong negative correlation with real industrial product reflects the continued growth of industry and the decline of labor contention (Table 3.1).

The changes in the correlations from one period to another are indicative of the varying importance of economic factors in short-term fluctuations of strike activity. At the same time, political factors are systematically more important in influencing long-run strike fluctuations, because they restrict the contested terrain, and their conjunctural effects may counterbalance the impact of economic factors in determining strike activity.

The complex relationship between political and economic factors is best illustrated in a more detailed example of this dynamic as seen in the periods of civilian rule (1945-1963), when the variability in influence of these factors was more apparent. Beginning with the first period between 1945 and 1955, the marked decline of strike activities from 1946 to 1947 immediately attracts attention (Figure 3.1). Though data are not readily available on levels of industrial growth for that period, all accounts indicate that the years immediately following the Second World War were not economically troubled. On the contrary, the Brazilian economy came out of the war years with the largest foreign reserve up until that time.[2] Thus, the sharp drop in strike actions was not due in any measure to factors related to economic performance. Similarly, the real median wage was not influential in explaining the falling strike rate, since real wages also fell at this time. One would expect that under conditions of economic stability and falling wages that unions would have been more aggressive in defending workers' wages. Instead, the dramatic decline in strikes is the result of the growing intolerance of the Dutra government as it proceeded to implement its Cold War labor policy of reducing the influence of the Communist Party in the labor movement through

Figure 3.1 Real Wages, Real Industrial Product and Strike Activity, 1945-1963 (Wages 1946=100; Ind. Product 1949=100)

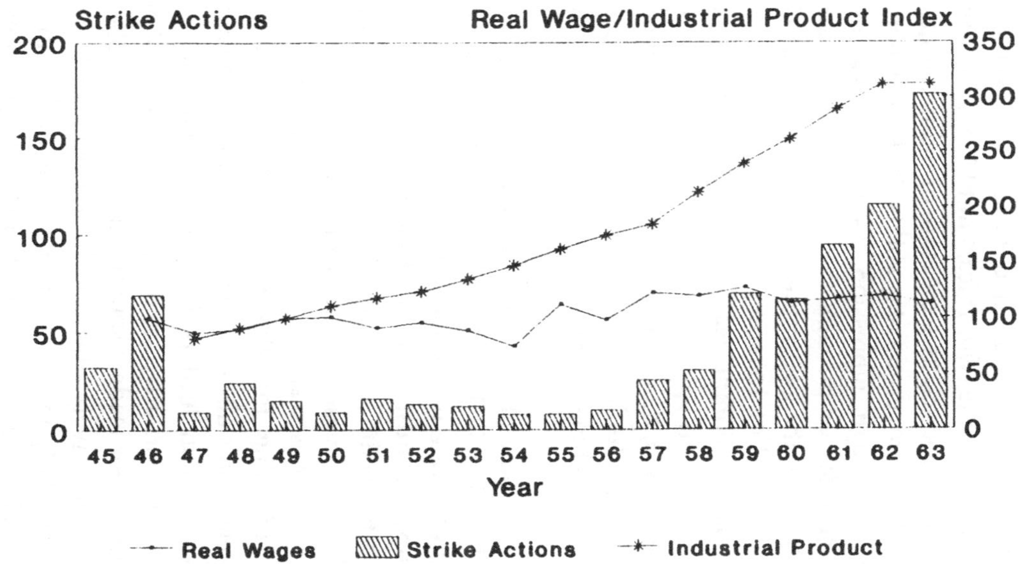

Source: Wage and product data, R. Kahil, *Inflation and Economic Development in Brazil*, (1973), pp. 65-66, 337.

increased ministerial interventions into the labor unions, as illustrated in Figure 3.2.

From this time on, the threat of state repression hung over the labor movement. Examining closely the steadily increasing real industrial product curve and its relation to the strike rate curve, there appears to be no direct relationship between the two. In fact, what stands out most is the dissimilarity between the two, at least until 1956. The continuous rise of the real industrial product, as a measure of industrial growth, was in part the result of the government's ability to keep labor unrest at a minimum, either through repression, as in the case of the Dutra government (1946-1950) or through the cooptation of labor leaders, as frequently practiced by the government of Getúlio Vargas (1951-1954).

After 1949, the level of government intervention in the unions was reduced once many militant leaders had been replaced by more conservative unionists. In spite of this, workers continued to react to falling wages (Figure 3.1), though in a rather irregular fashion depending on the risks and opportunities to act. For this reason we find a slight relationship between falling wages and number of strikes in 1948, 1951, 1952 and 1953.

The Vargas government was quite successful in maintaining wages below their 1950 level while keeping labor discontent under control. This had its effects on the rate of economic growth, especially after 1952, as shown by the upward turn of the real industrial product index while wages continued to decline until 1954. In this scenario, industrial strike activity tended to decrease at the same time that the number of government interventions reached its lowest level in the entire civilian period. Instead of using this direct form of repression, the Vargas administration relied on skillful combinations of nationalist rhetoric and clientelistic ties to union leaders in securing industrial peace. As a consequence of the authoritarianism of the state and Vargas' populist and nationalist posture, labor leaders sought other forms of collective action which could more effectively pressure the government to act on behalf of the workers, especially in increasing the level of the minimum wage through presidential decree. To this end, unions began as early as 1951 to make use of the multiple-category strike, the mass strike, as a mobilization tactic in order to pressure policy makers and to avoid the necessity of individual unions challenging the Vargas government.

The period of 1951 to 1953 was punctuated by several of these mass strikes, though judging from the falling wage levels they seem to have had little effect in securing wage increases and stability; by 1954, wages dropped to the lowest level in the entire nineteen-year period between 1945 and 1963, while real industrial product turned slightly upward (Figure 3.1). The Vargas government decreed a significant minimum wage increase in 1954, months after the great worker agitation of 1953.[3] This increase in the wage level was only in part a response to labor unrest. It was largely the result of Getúlio Vargas' need to bolster support for his government as the armed forces and foreign and national capitalists heightened their opposition to his nationalist and populist policies. The wage increase of 100 percent in 1954 seems to have been the incident which led to the military's threatened coup and Vargas' subsequent suicide.[4]

The second phase in this analysis begins in 1956 with the Kubitschek government, which assumed the presidency after months of uncertainty as to whether the armed forces would respect the election of the new liberal president. The crisis which marked the suicide of Getúlio Vargas continued into 1955 and the election of Juscelino Kubitschek as President. The armed forces opposed Kubitschek's ties to the PDS party of *getulista* origins and appeared to be prepared to block the new administration. General Henrique Lott, in two successive military coups, guaranteed the transfer of the presidency to the duly elected Kubitschek. This event served to illustrate the difficulties of electoral democracy at the hands of the ruling elites.[5] For the labor movement, the Kubitschek years initiated a period between 1956 and 1963 when labor would rise to become a major contender within the polity. This is illustrated by the dramatic increase in strike rates from 1957 until the 1964 military coup (Figure 3.1) and by the relatively small number of ministerial interventions over the eight year period (Figure 3.2).

The Kubitschek years also were characterized by significant acceleration in the rate of industrial growth, as shown in Figure 3.1, which maintained its steady rise until the critical years of 1962 and 1963. Reflected in this increased pace of industrial expansion were the effects of the government's developmentalist policies, which in general came to benefit the dynamic industries of the modern sector of the economy.[6]

It was during this time of economic "boom" that wages rose gradually; between 1956 and 1959 they reached their highest level for the entire period. Since then, as depicted in Figure 3.1, the real median wage drifted downward in spite of the annual increases in the minimum wage decreed by the federal government. As is clear from the diverging curves of real median wage and real industrial product, the gains from accelerated expansion of the economy were not reflected in a similar increase in workers' wages; instead, as wages declined, the gap increased.

At the same time, there was a corresponding but more substantial increase in the level of collective action. It was after 1959 that the gap began to widen, and from that year the strike rate began its marked upward trend. Many of labor's demands were directed at remedying the deteriorating purchasing power of the working class as evidenced by the successive readjustments in the minimum wage. Nevertheless, the substantial increase in the strike rate was not exclusively the consequence of accelerated growth and falling wages. Working-class agitation from the end of the 1950s until 1964 had also at its roots a combination of economic and political factors which pushed the objectives of the workers' struggle beyond the simple goals of wage increases. Many workers' mobilizations were directed at pressuring government not only to correct the declining income, but also to voice organized labor's demands for nationalist reforms as a solution to worsening economic conditions.[7]

The years 1959 and 1960 were marked by efforts to avoid impending economic crisis, as President Kubitschek knew when he broke off negotiations with the International Monetary Fund in 1959. By then economic growth, propelled by injections of foreign capital and large government expenditures, gradually provoked serious balance of payments and inflationary problems which obliged the authorities to turn to the IMF. But the IMF stabilization plan of economic austerity, lowering of working-class incomes, and denationalization of the economy would mean sparing the bourgeoisie and advancing the interests of foreign corporations. In light of this, the Kubitschek government postponed the decision about adopting austerity measures, leaving to his successor, Jânio Quadros, the task of mobilizing popular support for unpopular economic policies.[8]

The significant rise in strike activity in 1961 reflects the country's political predicament. The main factions within the labor movement believed that working-class interests could be advanced through the mobilization of a broad nationalist-reformist front against the conservative forces opposed to nationalist solutions to the economic crisis.[9] The defense of the civilian government to which many militant labor leaders were committed and the support for a multi-class alliance as the political base for nationalist economic reforms were the principle motivating factors behind the dramatic increase in working-class mobilization. As we shall see in subsequent discussion, these factors were also reflected in the concurrent decline in importance of the single-occupational category strike now overshadowed by the mass strike.

The crumbling of the multi-class alliance, the political base of the populist state, obstructed the formulation of solutions for the economic crisis. As the working-class movement showed signs of escaping the controls of government politicians, the dominant classes became more determined in their refusal to widen the political process to allow the new contenders access to the polity.[10] The growing polarization in 1963 was aggravated by a then-record inflation rate of 87 percent per year, which forced wages downward and caused a levelling off of real industrial production (Figure 3.1). By this time, economic and political factors had become inseparable features of the dynamics of class conflict in Brazilian society. The working class increased its agitation in protest to the worsening economic situation and in support of the civilian government of João Goulart which was now threatened by conversative economic, political and military elites. These, in turn, responded with indirect pressures such as restraint in economic activities, thus causing a levelling-off of the index of industrial production.[11] Furthermore, to counterbalance the workers' agitations, conservative groups not only sponsored their own mass political demonstrations in major cities of the country, but also conspired to give a military solution to the political and economic crisis. On March 31, 1964 the armed forces overthrew the civilian government.

Strikes and the Power of the State

In the above analysis we have seen that economic factors generally have played a secondary role in influencing overall strike activity. The case of Brazil[12] demonstrates that working-class strikes are necessarily dealt with in the political arena, since the state assumes the principal role of directly mediating the interests of employers and workers. Leôncio Martins Rodrigues has summarized the causes of the politicization of labor conflicts in the following way:

> The presence of the State politicizes working-class actions and imposes on all groups of workers, independently of the type of

> establishment, a common point of reference. Concretely no union tendency can ignore the government's actions. The difficulty in resisting the interference of the State (with all its repressive power), through forms of struggle outside the plant, stimulates the union leadership to actions of a political nature through the formation of alliances with other forces.[13]

Because of this, the impact of economic factors on strike activity is only understood in the context of the political environment of a particular period which combine to create the conditions determining the varying patterns of industrial conflict.

Looking back over the thirty-five years between 1945 and 1980, there appears a recurring pattern of working class/state relations which indicates the nature of class relations in Brazil and points to a major cause of periodic institutional crises in modern Brazil. The pattern which occurred in the late 1940s, early 1960s, and more recently in the late 1970s is vividly depicted in Figure 3.2. As we can see, the sequence begins with a heightening of labor strikes, as in the years 1945-1946, 1961-1963 and 1978-1979. This is then followed by a period of governmental repression in the form of a substantial increase in the number of ministerial interventions. Finally, there is a relatively long period of decreased strike activity. As we shall see in the concluding chapters, the decade of the 1980s during the critical years of the re-democratization of Brazilian society in the midst of chronic economic and social crises suggests a departure from this model. These changes from the pattern of power relations prevalent prior to 1981 are indicative of current tendencies in the modernization of Brazilian class relations.

Underlying the pattern of recurring repression of strikes is the continuous resistance of the ruling classes in accepting the trade unions as members of the polity, in spite of the major transformations of Brazil's social and economic structures in the emergence of an urban industrial society. In 1950, 19.9 percent of the population lived in cities. By 1980, over 50 percent were urban residents. Similarly, in the years after the Second World War, about 59.9 percent of the economically active population worked in agriculture, but by 1980 this proportion had fallen to 29.93 percent.[14] The persistent appeal by the ruling classes to authoritarian solutions in the face of the rising force of the modern urban working classes has resulted in the periodic waves of repression and political institutional instability.

Figure 3.2 Government Interventions and Strike Activity, 1945-1970

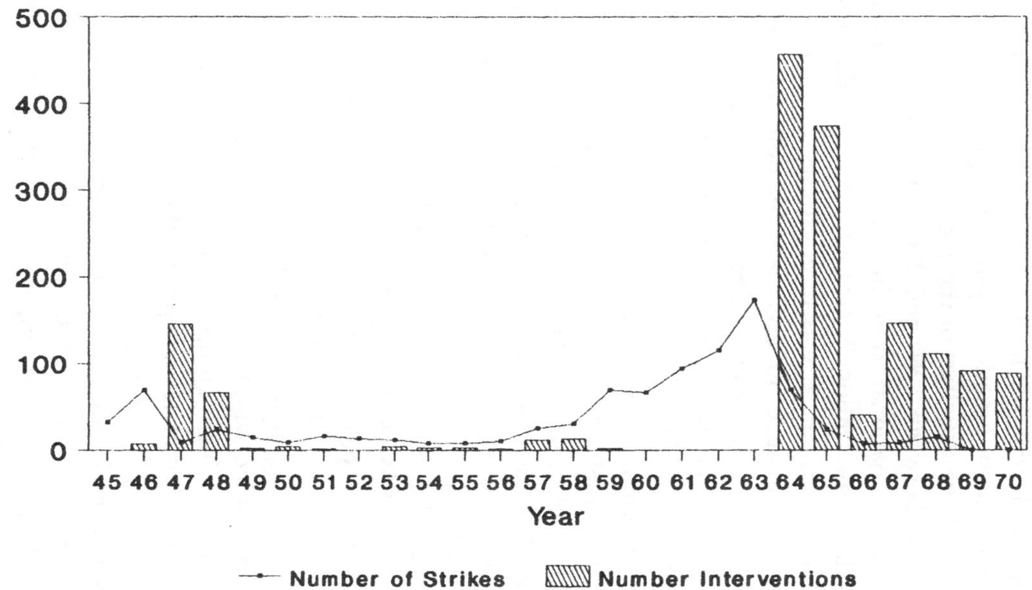

Source: Intervention data: K.P. Erickson *The Brazilian Corporate State*, p. 44-45; Moreira Alves, *Estado e Oposicao*, p. 244.

On the other hand, the workers have grown in numerical strength while developing their capabilities to mobilize resources and to press their claims, even within the shadow of the archaic corporatist institutions. This is evident in the increasingly stronger revivals of contention, as in 1960-1964, when workers attained unprecedented strike levels, and in 1978-1980, when industrial conflict became one of the principal expressions of broader popular discontent, and more recently in the increased strike activities of the 1980s.

In the period between 1960 and 1964, labor achieved a politically significant level of national coordination of their collective actions through "parallel organizations"[15] created outside of the confines of the corporatist union structure. It was through these organizations that the labor movement managed to articulate its political actions and the massive mobilizations of the early 1960s.

The conservative elites' opposition to the challenge of working-class contenders required higher levels of repression in order to turn back the tide of labor militancy. As Figure 3.2 shows, in the decade of the 1960s the number of ministerial interventions far surpassed any previous period. The years of severe military rule that followed further supports the proposition that the ruling elites were unable to bring themselves to modernizing the country's political structures, particularly in the realm of industrial relations. Quite to the contrary, as far as industrial relations were concerned, the reforms of the old labor laws by the military governments after 1964 were designed to reinforce institutional rigidity.

On the whole, the peaks of ministerial interventions followed major upsurges of strike activity, which in turn resulted in part from a broadening of the struggle for power that threatened the interests of the bourgeoisie. Confronted with these new challengers and with heightened strike activity, the dominant groups formed alliances with politicians and the military to use the state to repress labor unrest. This sequence of events is illustrated in Figure 3.3, synthesizing a pattern of class relations which recurred several times during the years of civilian rule until the eventual military takeover in 1964. In essence, the periodic appeals for authoritarian solutions by the ruling classes whenever their interests were challenged highlight the prominence of political factors in the determination of strike activity.

To this point, our analysis has focused on state suppression of militant labor organizations through the timing of ministerial interventions, but equally important are the patterns in the use of

Figure 3.3 Model of Class Relations in Brazil, 1945-1968

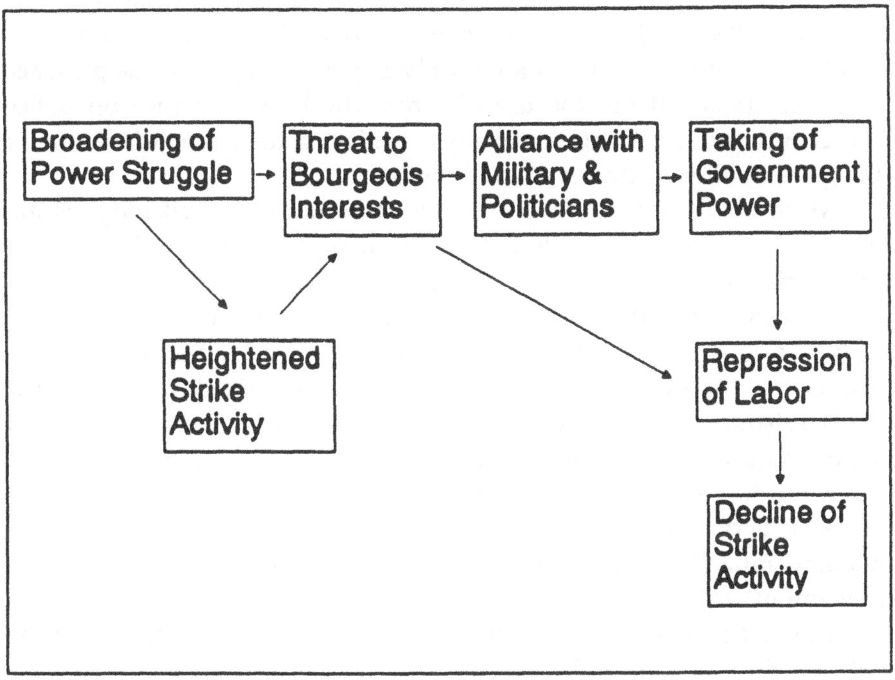

governmental repression of collective actions as another form of state control over the working class and as an expression of the levels of tolerance toward worker agitation among national and local government powerholders.

The newspaper reporting of police repression of strikes is frequently incomplete due to a variety of factors, ranging from technical considerations to problems of external and internal self censorship. Nevertheless, in spite of this drawback, an analysis of strikes in which police activities were reported reveals patterns of police suppression reaffirming the arguments raised in this chapter.

Table 3.2 presents the distribution of strikes over the various political periods according to the type of police involvement: (1) the presence of police units at the sites of the strike actions, or (2) the direct interference of the police with the strikers. The data demonstrate a significant difference between the authoritarian periods and the more liberal ones. As would be expected, the authoritarian periods in which there were strikes (1947-1949, 1964-1968, 1978-1980) were very similar in their much higher percentages of the use of police force to suppress strikers. Of the cases in which police actions were reported, 73 to 80 percent were conflicts involving the use of force; only 20 percent reported the presence of police units but not the use of force. The heavy reliance on police coercion is not surprising, especially considering the autocratic nature of the governments in power at each period.

More interesting is the continued importance of strike repression during the years of more tolerant presidencies, even though the levels of ministerial interventions against unions decreased. Under the more liberal governments the patterns in the use of police coercion are very similar in the various periods; 1945-1946, 1950-1955, 1956-1960 and 1961-1963. Contrary to the autocratic years, these were characterized by a somewhat lesser reliance on police coercion and an increased use of the show of force. As the data show, both categories of police action were about equal in proportion among the reported cases, the only exception being the period between 1945-1946, when the political climate of re-democratization was also reflected in the very low levels of police coercion of strikers (Table 3.2).

The noticeably lower levels of direct police involvement against strikers do not diminish the fact that even during more tolerant governments about 50 percent of the cases reported police suppression. It appears that the liberal governments preferred to respond to labor agitation, at least in 45 percent of the cases, by intimidating workers through the simple show of force, while restraining the use of more violent measures. This variation in the manner in which worker collective actions were handled reflects the underlying authoritarian nature of populist rule; suppression continued to be a significant form of dealing with working-class protest even in the liberal years.

The continued resistance of the dominant economic and political elites is also evidenced by the generally high proportions of the use of coercion against multiple category collective actions (the mass strikes). Since these strikes represented an important advance in the workers' capacity to broadly articulate their interests and to coordinate collective actions, this form of protest became increasingly important over the

Table 3.2 - Distribution of Strikes According to Type of Police Action and Political Period, 1945-1980

Strike Action	1945-1946 End of Estado Novo Dictatorship			1947-1949 Repressive Populism			1950-1955 Clientelistic Populism			1956-1960 Liberal Populism			1961-1963 Crisis of Populism			1964-1968 Military Dictatorship			1978-1980 Democratic Opening		
	N°	T%*	R%	N°	T%*	R%	N°	T%*	R%	N°	T%*	R%	N°	T%*	R%	N°	T%*	R%	N°	T%*	R%
Single- Category Strikes																					
No Mention	43	61	---	12	70	---	17	68	---	60	75	---	84	74	---	35	72	---	170	81	---
Police Presence	8	15	80	1	6	20	4	16	50	9	11	45	13	12	45	3	6	21	11	5	27
Police Involvement	2	4	20	4	24	80	4	16	50	11	14	55	16	14	55	11	22	79	29	14	72
TOTAL	53	100	100	17	100	100	25	100	100	80	100	100	113	100	100	49	100	100	210	100	100
Mass Strikes																					
No Mention	1			0			1			3			14			4			—		
Police Presence	0			1			1			2			3			1			—		
Police Involvement	2			1			2			2			8			0			—		
TOTAL	3			2			4			7			25			5			0		

** T% = percent of total strikes; R% = percent of total strikes in which police action was reported.*

years, especially in the period between 1961-1963, when the mass strike became the major form of pressuring for basic reforms and of displaying support for civilian rule.

The response of the state to these mass mobilizations appears to have been consistent over the various political periods. To a large extent, these strikes were repressed in much greater proportion then were the single-occupational category strikes, particularly during the liberal governments, when over two-thirds of the mass strikes provoked police involvement. Since the claims advocated by the broad mobilizations were largely concerned with political issues, the state tended to react vigorously against this form of political participation.

On the whole, given the relatively high levels of police coercion in all the periods, it is understandable that forms of action involving tens of thousands of workers would develop as an alternative means of struggle for access to the circles of political rule. This is clearly demonstrated by the continuous increase over the 1950s in the use of the mass strike tactic, which peaked in the years 1961-1963 at the end of the populist era (Table 3.2).

Though it is often claimed that political unionism is a constant "problem" in Latin American societies, in this chapter we have attempted to demonstrate that the political nature of the labor movement is evident in the case of Brazil because of the corporatism of the industrial relations system and of the benefits which the political handling of the working-class movement has brought to the dominant economic elites.[16] The analysis shows that the governments' economic policies of depressing wages and repressing working-class protest over the past years have been central elements of programs of accelerated economic development and capital accumulation. Supporting this model of economic growth is a ruling class resistant to democratizing power relations. Its obstruction of working-class access to participation in the polity has largely contributed to the cycles of authoritarianism in Brazilian politics.[17] As we shall see in the next chapter, strike activity patterns have generally responded to the political atmosphere reflecting the various periods in which class relations ranged from semi-democratic to autocratic forms.

Notes

1. Raouf Kahil in his authoritative study identifies three phases in the relationship between wages and profits in his analysis of the period 1947 to 1963. From 1947 to 1954, the industrial wage share and the share of the industrial sector rose together, although before the new minimum wage went into effect in 1954, real wages apparently declined. From 1954 to 1960 the wage share dropped, while the share of industry rose only slightly while real wages rose. From 1960 to 1963 both the share of industrial wages and the share of industry rose, and the behavior of real wages is unclear, see Raouf Kahil, *Inflation and Economic Development in Brazil 1946-1963* (Oxford: Clarendon Press, 1973); for similar findings see John Wells, "Industrial Accumulation and Living-Standards in the Long Run: The São Paulo Industrial Working Class, 1930-1975 (Part I)," *The Journal of Development Studies*, 19:2 (1983): 145-169; John Wells, "Industrial Accumulation and Living-Standards in the Long Run: The São Paulo Industrial Working Class, 1930-1975 (Part II)," *The Journal of Development Studies*, 19:3 (1983): 297-328.

2. Michael Wallerstein, "The Collapse of Democracy in Brazil: Its Economic Determinants," *Latin American Research Review*, 15:3 (1980): 28.

3. For one of the few detailed studies of this mass strike action see José Álvaro Moisés, *Greve de Massa e Crise Política (Estudo da Greve dos 300 Mil em São Paulo-1953-54)* (São Paulo: Editora Polis Ltda., 1978).

4. Thomas E. Skidmore, *Politics in Brazil: 1930-1964: An Experiment in Democracy* (New York: Oxford University Press, 1967), pp. 127-142; John W.F. Dulles, *Unrest in Brazil: Political-Military Crises 1955-1964* (Austin: University of Texas Press, 1970), pp. 4-7.

5. See Thomas E. Skidmore, *Politics in Brazil, 1930-1964*, pp. 149-158; Peter Flynn, *Brazil: A Political Analysis* (Boulder: Westview Press, 1978), pp. 172-182.

6. Raouf Kahil, *Inflation and Economic Development in Brazil*, pp. 306-315.

7. Leôncio Martins Rodrigues, *Conflito Industrial*, p. 193.

8. Michael Wallenstein, "The Collapse of Democracy," pp. 30-31.

9. Leôncio Martins Rodrigues, "Tendências Futuras do Sindicalismo," *Revista da Administração de Empresas da Fundação de Getúlio Vargas*, 19:4 (October-December 1979): 49.

10. Peter Flynn, *Brazil*, pp. 516-517, 520.

11. For an analogous situation, the Mexican sociologist Pablo Gonzalez Casanova has convincingly argued that in the case of Mexico, levels and fluctuation of investment by the private sector often are used by the capitalist class to pressure the federal government. See Pablo Gonzalez Casanova, *La Democracia en México* (México: Ediciones Era, 1965), pp. 16-19.

12. It is worthwhile noting that Mexico also demonstrates broadly similar processes of politicization of the labor movement because of the extensive presence of the Mexican state in industrial relations. Likewise, the tendencies in the labor movement in Mexico are that the most combative are also those unions in the modern sector and segments of workers in the government owned enterprises. See F. Aguilar, "El Sindicalismo del Sector Automotriz," *Cuadernos Políticos*, 16 (1978); Javier Aguilar García, *La Política Sindical en México: Industria del Automovil* (Mexico: ERA, 1982); Ilan Bizberg, *La Acción Obrera en Las Truchas* (México: El Colegio de México, 1982); Ilan Bizberg and L. Banaza, "La Acción Obrera en las Truchas," *Revista Mexicana de Sociología*, 42:4 (1980); E. Contreras and G. Silva, "Los Recientes Movimentos Obreros Mexicanos Pro Independencia Sindical y el Reformismo Obrero," *Revista Mexicana de Sociología*, 34:3-4 (July-December 1972); K. Middlebrook, "International Implications of Labor Change: The Automobile Industry," in J. Dominguez (ed.), *Mexico's Political Economy* (Beverly Hills: Sage Publications, 1982); J. Quiroz, "Proceso de Trabajo en la Industria Automotriz," *Cuadernos Políticos*, 26 (1980); José Luis Reyna, "El Movimento Obrero en una Situación de Crisis: México 1976-1978," *Foro Internacional*, 19:3 (1979); Ian Roxborough and Ilan Bizberg, "Union Locals in Mexico: The 'New Unionism' in Steel and Automobiles," *Journal of Latin American Studies*, 1:15 (May 1983); E. Stevens, *Protest and Response in Mexico* (London: MIT Press, 1974); M. Thompson and Ian Roxborough, "Union Elections and Democracy in Mexico," *British Journal of Industrial Relations*, 20:2 (1982).

13. Leôncio Martins Rodrigues, "Tendências Futuras....," p. 51.

14. Vilmar Faria, "Desenvolvimento, Urbanização e Mudanças na Estrutura do Emprego: A Experiência Brasileira dos Últimos Trinta Anos," in Bernard Sorj and Maria Herminia Tavares de Almeida, (eds.), *Sociedade e Política no Brazil Pós-1964* (São Paulo: Editora Brasiliense, 1983), p. 125.

15. By "parallel organizations" (*organizações paralelas*) is meant those organizations of union leaders created independently of the official union structures for the purpose of coordinating political activities. The first reported parallel organizations appeared around 1946 with the *Congresso Sindical dos Trabalhadores do Brasil*. The parallel organizations became the principal form of political articulation, given the stringent controls imposed on the unions' activities by the labor legislation. See José Albertino Rodrigues, *Sindicato e Desenvolvimento no Brasil* (São Paulo: Difusão Europeia do Livro, 1968), pp. 162-165.

16. The treatment of industrial conflict as a form of struggle for power is an important, if not the dominant, approach to the study of working-class collective actions in an historical perspective. See Reinhard Bendix, *Nation-Building and Citizenship* (Berkeley: University of California Press, 1977 ed.), chap. 3; Edward Shorter and Charles Tilly, *Strikes in France 1930-1968* (London: Cambridge University Press, 1978); Charles Tilly, Louise Tilly and Richard Tilly, *The Rebellious Century 1830-1930* (London: J.M. Dent and Sons Ltd, 1975); John M. Merriman, *The Red City, Limoges and the French Nineteenth Century* (New York: Oxford University Press, 1985); Michelle Perrot, *Les Ouvriers en Greve, France 1871-1890* (Paris: Mouton, 1974); Douglas A. Hibbs, Jr. "Industrial Conflict in Advanced Industrial Societies," *American Political Science Review*, 68 (1976): 1033-1058; Douglas A. Hibbs, Jr., "On the Political Economy of Long-Run Trends in Strike Activity," *British Journal of Political Science*, 8 (April 1978): 153-175; Walter Korpi, "Conflict, Power and Relative Deprivation," *American Political Science Review*, 68 (1974): 1569-1578; Walter Korpi and Michael Shaler, "Strikes, Industrial Relations and Class Conflict in Capitalist Societies," *British Journal of Sociology*, 30:2 (June 1979): 164-187.

17. Peter Flynn also makes a similar argument in Peter Flynn, *Brazil*, pp. 516-522.

4

The Transformation of Strikes and Working-Class Organization in the Era of Populism

Since 1945 there have been profound changes in Brazilian society and the characteristics of the social structure. Yet the authoritarian nature of the relationship between the state, the economic elites and the working class remained almost unaltered until the period of the re-democratization in the later part of the 1980s. In this chapter we will show how the national patterns of strike activity have changed at different periods of political rule between 1945 and 1963, and how these changes reflect the evolution of workers' organization and elite intransigence with respect to working-class protest.

To compare patterns of industrial conflict over the various political periods, we have chosen to combine the three principal measures of strike activity into a three dimensional diagram which will facilitate analysis by producing a visual representation of the relative strength of strike activity at different points in time. Together, the three dimensions form rectangular shapes which represent the strength and volume of labor contention for each period.[1] The rectangle is composed of the horizontal side which shows the median duration of strikes for the specific period; the vertical side which shows the average number of strikers per strike; and the lateral side which shows the strike rate for that period, calculated as the number of strikes per 100,000 workers in the industrial work force,[2] as illustrated in Figure 4.1.

The previous analysis of the correlations between strike rates, economic growth, wage levels and state interventions into labor unions served to demarcate eight different periods, between 1945 and 1980, based on the level of government authoritarianism toward workers'

Figure 4.1 Model of Strike Action

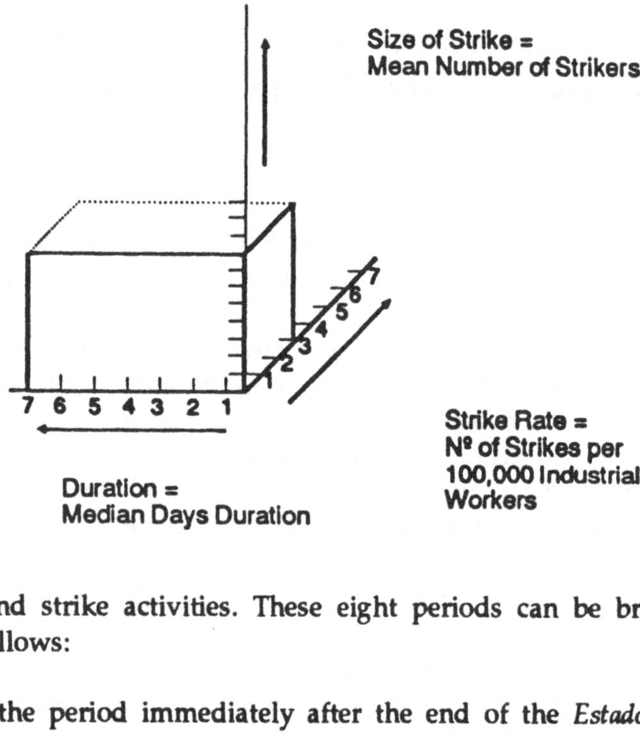

organization and strike activities. These eight periods can be briefly described as follows:

> **1945-1946**: the period immediately after the end of the *Estado Novo* dictatorship and a return to democratic rule, characterized by an upsurge of strike activity, few ministerial interventions into labor unions, and a low level of police repression of strikers;
>
> **1947-1949**: the period of repressive populism, characterized by the extensive use of ministerial interventions, the high level of use of police force against strikers, and a drastic decline in the number of strikes;
>
> **1950-1955**: the period of clientelistic populism, characterized by governmental cooptation of union leaders, few ministerial

interventions, moderate levels of strike activity and moderate use of police coercion;

1956-1960: the period of liberal populism, characterized by few ministerial interventions, rising strike activities and a moderate use of police force;

1961-1963: the period of crisis in populist civilian government, characterized by few ministerial interventions, a marked increase in strike actions, and moderate use of police force.

1964-1968: the period of the first phase of military rule, characterized by a record number of interventions in labor unions, imprisonment and exile of union leaders, substantial use of police force to suppress strikes, and a drastic decline of strike activities;

1969-1977: the period of extensive repression of the labor movement under the military regime characterized by widespread censorship of information on popular unrest, high levels of the use of police coercion and no strike activity except for a few limited workplace manifestions of discontent.

1978-1980: the period referred to as the "democratic opening" characterized by a gradual move to ending military rule and a return to civilian rule, even though the presidency continued to be occupied by military men during these years. The period is marked by an outburst of strike activities, a high degree of police repression and use of ministerial interventions. The period represents the deterioration of military rule, especially after nine years of harsh and severe repression.

Changes in the Shape of Strikes in the Populist Era

The diagrams depicted in Figure 4.2 allow one to visualize the transformation of strike "physiognomy" over the thirty-five years since the Second World War. The shape of each rectangle illustrates the general features of strike activity, while the volume is subdivided to denote the

Figure 4.2 National Strike Shapes 1945-1980

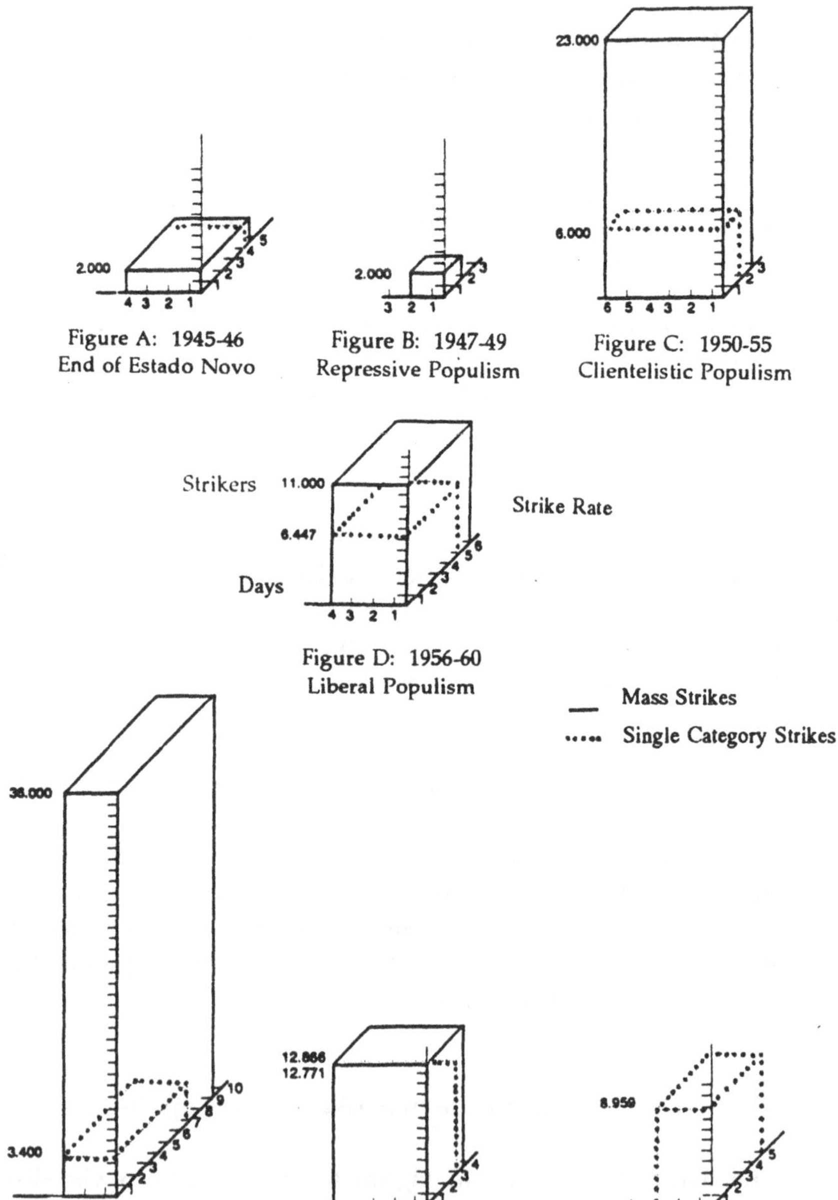

Figure A: 1945-46
End of Estado Novo

Figure B: 1947-49
Repressive Populism

Figure C: 1950-55
Clientelistic Populism

Figure D: 1956-60
Liberal Populism

Figure E: 1961-63
Crisis of Populism

Figure F: 1964-68
Military Dictatorship

Figure G: 1978-80
Democratic Opening

difference between the proportion which corresponds to the dimensions of single-occupation category strikes and to those of multiple-category actions or mass strikes.

The brief upsurge of strikes during the transition years from the *Estado Novo* dictatorship to the elected government of Eurico Dutra (1945-1946) was characterized by strike actions which on the average had a duration of four days similar to strikes of the liberal Kubitschek period, but the size of the strikes was substantially dissimilar, as a consequence of the limitations imposed on workers' capacity to mobilize during the *Estado Novo* years and the smaller size of the industrial labor force in the 1940s. It should be remembered that the take-off of rapid industrial growth did not occur until the early 1950s. Thus, the years 1945-1946 were still a time of smaller establishments, which contributed to the relatively lower average size of strikes during those years. The similarity between 1945-1946 and 1956-1960 with respect to duration and frequency is noteworthy because both periods were years of relative political stability and greater tolerance toward labor unrest on the part of government. The large differences in average size of the strikes seem to have been more the result of growth of the working class and the increase in the size of establishments than of mobilization capacity, considering the high strike rates in both periods.

Another important difference between these two liberal periods is the increased importance of the mass strike in the later period. Comparing Figure 4.2-A for 1945-1946 to Figure 4.2-D for 1956-1960, the proportion of the shape accounted for by mass collective actions is very small in the first period (Figure 4.2-A) because of the workers' lack of broad based organizations. The first inter-occupational organizations, appearing in 1946, were called parallel organizations because they existed outside the official union structure which had no provisions for multiple category organizations. Ten years later, as illustrated in the various figures, the role of the mass strike had gained significant proportions, even though the years 1956 to 1960 were not as important as other periods in the use of mass strike tactics.

The period of repressive populism (1947-1949) saw the dramatic decrease in strike activity. This is vividly illustrated in the contraction of the strike shape (Figure 4.2-B). Strike actions were drastically curtailed because of increased interventions and heightened police suppression of strikes; the shortened duration reflects this harsh reality. The average size of strikes remained about the same as in the previous period because most of the strikes during this time were large single factory stoppages, especially among textile workers.

The repressive tone of the last years of the Dutra government was in keeping with the Cold War tide led by the United States. The aim of the government's actions was to break the communists' influence in the labor unions, outlaw the Communist Party, and weaken what appeared to be a strong challenge from the labor movement.[3] This attack against the labor unions also showed its effects in the disappearance of mass strikes.

The small volume of the strike shape, even in comparison to other autocratic periods, is impressive and was probably the result of two converging factors: on the one hand, the repressive policy of the government and, on the other, restraint by many labor leaders, especially the Communists, in encouraging strike actions as a strategy to secure the return to legality of the Communist Party by avoiding clashes between labor and the government. Consequently, the decline of strike activities seems also to have been due to union leaders' tactical containment of labor unrest in order to better negotiate with other political forces.[4]

The years following the Dutra government, during the Getúlio Vargas presidency of 1950 to 1954, were a time of clientelistic ties between the unions and the government. The specific brand of *getulista* populism molded significantly the strike pattern for this period. Strikes on the average not only increased in their duration to a median of five days, but leaped to an impressive average size of 23,000 strikers, even though the frequency of strike activity remained surprisingly similar to that of the previous period and well below the strike rate for 1945-1946 (Figure 4.2-C). The contrasts in the strike shape for the Vargas years, compared to previous ones especially with respect to the significant increase in duration and size, can only be understood in terms of the peculiar historical phenomenon which was the second Getúlio Vargas presidency.

This period was best noted for the government's support of the unions and the extensive cooptation of labor leaders. At the same time, under a banner of nationalist populism Vargas mobilized support for his government from among the urban masses, particularly in those moments of confrontation with powerful conservative military and economic interests which generally were opposed to both Vargas' manner of relating to the urban working class and to his policy against unrestrained penetration of foreign capital interests in the economy.

Consequently, strike activities followed a pattern similar to the shape depicted in Figure 4.2-C. The large difference between the single-occupational category strikes and the mass strikes reflects the politics of the period. The effects of clientelistic bonds between union leaders and government politicians were reflected in the low strike rate, especially with respect to the lower rate of single-occupational category strikes, depicted by the small rectangle. The few single-occupational category strikes tended to average about 4,000 strikers involving a few establishments. Since labor leaders were closely tied to the Vargas government, particularly through the Vargas created Brazilian Labor Party (PTB), they were less inclined to advocate single-occupational category strikes on their own initiative without tacit support from political leaders.

In addition, opposition to Vargas' labor policies and to his policies toward foreign investment made industrialists more resistant to labor's demands. This is shown in Figure 4.2-C by the large increase in median duration of the strike from the period before and by a slight increase from the 1945-1946 period. Likewise, employers became more intransigent in ceding to labor demands during industrial conflicts, since they could not expect unconditional support from governmental authorities.

For labor leaders, the *quid pro quo* for facilitated access to the government and a lessening of repression was to hold down the level of worker collective actions. Thus, the frequency with which workers struck remained almost the same as under the Dutra government, even though there was less suppression. The major expressions of the labor movement's discontent, in light of the unions' commitments to the government, were the few strategically planned mass strikes designed to pressure the government for economic benefits such as increases in the minimum wage, bonuses, and paid holidays. These mass actions determined the extraordinarily large size of the strike pattern (Figure 4.2-C). By comparing the average size of the single-occupational category strike to the overall average size for the period, the importance of the mass strikes is readily seen. The single category strike averaged 4,351 strikers in contrast to the overall average of 23,337 participants, which illustrates the importance that the mass strikes had on the overall strike pattern.

In terms of man-days lost, the largest proportion was accounted for by the mass strike which overshadowed any other type of work stoppage. The development of the mass strike as an important form of working-class collective action was indicative of the evolution of worker organization; the parallel organizations united labor leaders of several occupational groups in political networks aimed at side-stepping the rigidity of the occupational compartmentalization of the corporatist labor structure. These extra-legal organizations permitted an alternative form of organization free from the government-controlled regional and national occupational based structures and facilitated both the formation of policy consensus among militant labor leaders and the coordination of joint political activities among various occupational categories to press their demands. The unofficial organizations succeeded in bringing about several mass strikes involving hundreds of thousands of workers. These successes, however, often obscured a basic flaw. The parallel organizations were effective in articulating the participation of the union leadership, but, like the labor unions, they lacked a solid grass-roots base, since the unions themselves had very limited penetration into the workplace and few alternative forms of mobilizing the industrial workers.

The labor leaders' preference for the mass strike is evidenced by the fact that 41 percent of the single occupation strikes, for which an organization was reported, were led by some form of grass-roots entity and not by the union (Table 4.1). These rank-and-file groups mobilized fewer workers on the average than did the union-led strikes, and the duration of their strikes was shorter (Table 4.2 and Table 4.3). Yet their large proportion in comparison to other tolerant periods exemplifies the divergence within the working class; the union leadership preferred the mass tactics, while the organized rank-and-file also continued participating in local strikes.[5]

This contradiction, viewed in the light of the government's clientelistic relationship to organized labor, explains why there was such a seemingly weak correlation between economic factors and class militancy. The particular relationship established with the Vargas government, the types of strategies formulated as a result of these political ties, and the ever present threat of military intervention moderated the actions of labor leaders. As the economist Raouf Kahil observed, the working class remained for many months, often as long as a year and a half, without any increase in real wages, while enduring an annual inflation rate which at one time reached 20 percent.[6]

Changes in the strike pattern occurred again under the Kubitschek government which, in contrast to the previous years of crisis, confrontations and repression, stood out sharply as a period of progress,

Table 4.1 – Distribution of Strikes According to Form of Organization in Each Political Period 1945-1980

Form of Organization	1945-1946 *End of Estado Novo (Dictatorship)*	1947-1949 *Repressive Populism*	1950-1955 *Clientelistic Populism*	1956-1960 *Liberal Populism*	1961-1963 *Crisis of Populism*	1964-1968 *Military Dictatorship*	1978-1980 *Democratic Opening*
Single Occupations Strikes							
Unofficial Worker Organizations	14% (8)	47% (9)	24% (7)	9% (21)	15% (21)	7% (4)	24% (50)
Unions: Official Organizations	21% (12)	--- ---	34% (10)	47% (41)	33% (46)	22% (12)	13% (27)
No Mention	65% (36)	53% (10)	42% (12)	44% (33)	52% (71)	71% (38)	63% (133)
TOTALS	100% (56)	100% (19)	100% (29)	100% (87)	100% (138)	100% (54)	100% (210)
Mass Strikes							
Various Occupational Categories	3	2	2	5	17	5	0
General Strikes	---	---	2	2	8	---	---
TOTAL ALL INDUSTRIAL STRIKES:	59	21	33	94	163	59	210

national confidence and political compromise. Kubitschek's association with Vargas politicians and conservative military attempts to prevent him from assuming office after his election facilitated the new president's relations with organized labor. Through the five years of the Kubitschek presidency, the government skillfully balanced the contending interests of the bourgeoisie, the middle classes and the working classes. Rapid industrial growth and national developmentalist ideology diffused popular opposition at least until the final years of the administration, when economic and inflationary pressures began to provoke social unrest.

The strike pattern of these years, 1956-1960, presented an entirely different trend from the more agitated Vargas years. As the total number of strikers increased considerably from 676,760 to 952,130, the shape of the strikes was significantly altered. The strike rate almost tripled from the previous period, seemingly more comparable to the liberal years of 1945-1946. Strike duration shortened slightly because of: (1) the more favorable climate for political compromise espoused by the government, (2) a lessening of employers' resistance under more vigorous government mediation, and (3) the greater economic flexibility resulting from the industrial boom.

On the other hand, the importance of the mass strike declined, as seen in its proportion of the total volume of the strike shape (Figure 4.2-D). This was the result of a number of factors. First, rapid industrial expansion permitted the government to raise real wages for industrial workers, especially those among the modern sector. This atmosphere of growth favored the occurrence of single-ocupational category strikes over "bread and butter" issues, instead of mass mobilizations which only re-emerged in the last two years of the period, when the economy began to exhibit signs of impending difficulties.

Second, the type of mass strike was reduced to strikes involving a few occupational categories, generally in a single locality, instead of broad regional mobilizations. General strikes, stronger in the Vargas years and afterward in 1961-1963, only re-emerged in 1959 as inflation and balance of payment problems began to worsen class relations. The government's tolerance of strike actions and support of negotiations between employers and workers on the one hand, and economic prosperity on the other, made mass strikes to pressure government less necessary, at least until 1959.

Third, the government bent employers' rigidity through compensations with government policies of economic incentives. Thus, the economic factors which had provoked general strikes in the Vargas period were attenuated by the pace of economic growth and a more generous wage policy.

These factors facilitating worker mobilization are evidenced by the tripling of the number of single-occupational category strikes from thirty-three in 1950-1955 to ninety-four strikes in 1957-1960. Furthermore, this type of strike doubled in average size from the previous period, as more workers turned their efforts from national issues to the immediate economic questions of the occupational group.

Also indicative of this shift from the mass strike are the organizational basis of workers' actions. Unlike the earlier years of grass-roots organizing, the unions for the first time since 1945 assumed a predominant role in initiating single category strikes. As the data in Table 4.1 show, 47 percent of the strikes were union-led, while only 9 percent had grass-roots origins. Thus, as the unions assumed the leadership of the single-occupational category strikes, there was a concomitant decline in grass-roots led stoppages.

At least four factors explain the change in the strike shape under the Kubitschek government. In the first place, the effects of industrial growth served to mitigate the wage problem, as wages rose to their highest level for the whole thirty-five year period between 1945 and 1980. Second, the rise of the new occupational groups of the modern sector, which were more concerned with economic benefits than political issues, contributed to the shift in strike form to a single category strike. Third, industrial employers were less reluctant to concede to labor's economic demands during these years of prosperity, thus labor resorted less to the mass strike as a means of exerting pressure. Finally, the government sought to reduce conflict by assuming the role of mediator in industrial disputes.

In contrast to the exuberant years under Juscelino Kubitschek, 1961 to 1963 was a tumultuous period in Brazilian history. The heightening of class conflict was demonstrated by the quadrupling of the number of service and industrial workers' strikes. In the previous governments, about 1,501,300 workers struck in all sectors of the economy, while in 1961-1963 alone the number reached 5,652,600. Several changes stand out with regard to the industrial strikes. The number of strikes increased by 42 percent over the previous period, even though the total number of industrial workers involved remained almost the same. More important is the fact that during 1961-1963 the service sector represented the overwhelming proportion of strikers as workers in the public sector and state owned enterprises became more militant.[7]

The shape of industrial strikes underwent a profound transformation from the previous periods, as depicted in Figure 4.2-E. As mentioned, the strike rate increased dramatically, reaching the highest level until then in Brazil's history. The median duration of the strike decreased to three days, the lowest duration for any period under a tolerant government. More important was the extraordinary rise in the average size of the strike; it increased threefold, from about 11,000, an average of 10,944 strikers per action, in 1956-1960 to approximaterly 36,000 (35,969) in 1961-1963.

The jump in the average size of the strike and its shorter duration were the result of a resurgence of the use of the mass strike. As shown in Figure 4.2-E, the share of the rectangular volume accounted for by the single category strike and by the mass strike illustrates the relative importance of the latter form of working-class collective action. The single category strikes decreased substantially in proportion in comparison to other periods in the 1950s (Figure 4.2-E and Table 4.2), even though this type of strike increased in number.

The mass strikes, on the other hand, had a clear ascendancy as a form of industrial conflict at this time in terms of average size. Because of their large number, the effect on the strike shape was to push the average size to an unprecedented height, while the single category strikes decreased in size (Figure 4.2-E). The importance of the mass strike was also indicated by its more frequent use by the union organizations than at any other period in Brazilian history. The number of mass strikes which occurred in this period was 56 percent greater than the total number of mass actions since 1945 (Table 4.1).

A close look at the mass strikes reveals impressive changes in size. Those strikes which were not explicitly called as general strikes but involving several occupational groups increased in size eight times from the period of the Kubitschek government to a size about as large as that during the Getúlio Vargas period. Similarly, the general strikes doubled in their average size from the two previous periods as well as increasing substantially in frequency. In spite of these mass collective actions' gains in size, their median duration remained about the same as in the 1956-1960 years and shorter than the duration of the single category strikes (Table 4.3).

Table 4.2 – Average Number of Workers per Strike According to Form of Organization and Political Periods 1945-1980

Form of Organization	1945-1946 *End of Estado Novo (Dictatorship)*	1947-1949 *Repressive Populism*	1950-1955 *Clientelistic Populism*	1956-1960 *Liberal Populism*	1961-1963 *Crisis of Populism*	1964-1968 *Military Dictatorship*	1978-1980 *Democratic Opening*
Single Occupations Strikes							
Unofficial Worker Organizations	2,438.1	2,255.8	1,725	1,810.6	2,493.7	19,237	5,163.4
Unions: Official Organizations	1,579.8	---	7,265	15,055.3	10,141.8	15,635.4	21,818.0
No Mention	2,461.2	2,832.2	3,500.4	1,301.4	2,659.0	7,533.8	3,103.4
All Strikes	2,367.5	2,598.7	4,351.6	9,129.4	3,174.0	9,894.9	5,176.4
Mass Strikes							
Various Occupational Groups	1,500	1,500	40,000	4,535	33,500	23,000	---
General Strikes	---	---	225,000	225,000	500,000	---	---

Table 4.3 – Median Duration of Industrial Strikes According to Form of Organization in Each Political Period 1945-1980

Form of Organization	1945-1946 End of Estado Novo (Dictatorship)	1947-1949 Repressive Populism	1950-1955 Clientelistic Populism	1956-1960 Liberal Populism	1961-1963 Crisis of Populism	1964-1968 Military Dictatorship	1978-1980 Democratic Opening
Single Occupations Strikes							
Unofficial Worker Organizations	4 days	3 days	3 days	3 days	4 days	5 days	6 days
Unions: Official Organizations	6 days	---	6 days	5 days	4 days	6 days	5 days
No Mention	4 days	3 days	3 days	4 days	3 days	4 days	3 days
Mass Strikes							
Various Occupational Groups	4 days	2 days	2 days	3 days	3 days	3 days	---
General Strikes	---	---	14 days	1 day	2 days	---	---

The reemergence of this type of strike action was also reflected in the 33 percent decline in the average size of the union-led single category strikes (Table 4.2). In addition, the number of grass-roots based strikes increased in proportion to the period before, though not reaching as high levels as in the Vargas years (Table 4.1). As in previous years, labor leaders' reliance on the mass strike to pressure their demands nationally meant a de-emphasis of local, single category stoppages. As the data show, at this same time workers began to fill the void left by the unions' turning to national strategies.

Organized labor's use of the mass strikes as its major means of exerting pressure in the national political arena was the consequence of the rapidly evolving political crisis of the populist regime and of the growing counterpressures from the military establishment and middle and upper class interest groups. In turn labor stepped up campaigns for economic reforms and exerted their growing influence on the civilian governments, especially during the presidency of João Goulart (1962-1964).[8] Yet the increased use of the mass strike again served to obscure the unions' basic weakness at the grass-roots level. In fact, it seems that labor leaders themselves were unaware of the extent of their real political strength and tended to overestimate the impact of the tactic. Their experiences with the mass strike was restricted to a few, very short demonstrations which had never encountered the full repressive power of the state. The continuous threats of general strikes and solidarity strikes seemed to have been counterproductive as the political situation polarized by the end of 1963[9] and the high commands in the armed forces began plotting the overthrow of the government.

While labor leaders had succeeded over the years in creating strong inter-union leadership networks such as the *Comando Geral de Greve* (General Strike Command), *Pacto de Unidade e Ação* (Unity and Action Pact), *Comissão Permanente de Organizações Sindicais* (Permanent Commission of Union Organizations), *Pacto de Ação Conjunta* (Pact for Joint Action), *Forum Sindical de Debates de Santos* (Union Forum of Debate of Santos),[10] these working-class organizations rested on weak grass-roots structures.[11] The individual unions generally had little penetration in the factories; even among the more militant unions the degree of rank-and-file organization was rudimentary. The consequences of this shortcoming does not appear to have been given much attention, either by steps being taken to remedy the fault or by demands being made for the serious reformulation of the union structure to include its legal extension into the factories with the exception of demanding the legal recognition of the already existent *delegado sindical*. In fact, during the intense mobilizations of these years, organized labor never made any attempt at ending the state's tutelage and subordination of the unions.[12] Subsequently, the coup of March 31, 1964, dispelled the myth of the union's political strength.

The regime inaugurated by the military overthrow of civilian rule was, by all measures, the most repressive in the country's history. In terms of the analysis of strike activities, three broad subperiods are readily identifiable: (1) 1964-1968 was the first phase of military rule; (2) 1969-1977 was the period of severe and harsh repression; and (3) 1978-1980 was the period of the weakening of control of the dictatorship and the beginning of the transition to civilian government.

The overall strike pattern for the first phase of the military dictatorship changed dramatically from the civilian years. As Figure 4.2-F illustrates, the shape of the strike pattern contracted under the weight of repression. There was a substantial decline in both the frequency and the average size of the strikes. On the other hand, there was an increase in median duration, indicating that workers striking at this time were committed to resisting both the force of the state and the pressure of the employers.

The mass strikes which had played such an important role in working-class politics greatly diminished, primarily because of the systematic dismantling of the unofficial parallel organizations and the purging of militant union leaders through the hundreds of interventions decreed by the new government. As a result, the single category strike became the only significant form of strike activity, as illustrated in the very small proportion of the strike shape (Figure 4.2-E) accounted for by the multiple category strike.

In spite of the major setback for the workers, strikes in this first period were still largely led by the unions. The continued, but curtailed, vitality of some unions was reflected in the increase of the average size of union led strikes from 10,141 workers in 1961-1963 to 15,635 in 1964-1968 (Table 4.2). In addition, the resistance of the workers was also evidenced in the substantial increase in the average size of strikes led by some form of grass-roots organization from an average of 2,493 workers in 1961-1963 to 19,237 workers in 1964-1968. Both the grass-roots and union-led strikes lengthened in median duration from the previous periods, which punctuates the commitment of the workers to withstand harsh response by the new regime.

In fact, the strike pattern varied noticeably within this first phase of military rule, as can be seen from an analysis of the two governments that comprised this period. The broad strike shape for 1964-1968 shown in Figure 4.2-F was divided according to military governments in this period, as depicted in Figures 4.3-A and 4.3-B, in order to present a more detailed view of the decline of strike activity as the repressive regime consolidated its control over the working class.

Under the first military government headed by General Castelo Branco (1964-1966), strike activity suffered its first major decline in comparison to the preceding eight years. The strike rate fell by two-thirds with relation to 1961-1963 and was half the rate of the Kubitschek years. At this time, there were two distinct trends within the strike pattern. The average size of strikes greatly decreased from previous periods for both single category and mass strikes to an average of 15,500 strikers in comparison to 36,000 of the 1961-1963 period. Yet the duration of single category and mass strikes clearly diverged. The mass strike fell significantly in relation to the past, but its median duration was characteristically short, as it had always been. These short actions reduced the overall median of strike duration to three days, though as Figure 4.3-A illustrates, single category strikes increased their median duration. The contrast in the durations of both types of strikes is indicative of the weakening of the mass strike tactic in the face of overwhelming military response, and the concentration of the workers' resources to resist in the local single category strikes. In addition, the majority of the mass strikes occurred shortly after the coup. This left the remainder of the period to the single category strike. The diminished effectiveness of the mass strike was clearly demonstrated by the fact that during this first military government, an estimated 657,760 workers struck in 1964 and 1965. By the last year of the Castelo Branco administration, 1966, the total number of strikers had been forced down to 14,610, averaging about 1,421 workers per strike.

The measures enforced to curb labor unrest brought about sharp changes in the strike pattern during the second military government (1967-1968). By this time strike activity had been further reduced, as indicated by the fall in the strike rate (Figure 4.3-B). The average size of the strike also contracted to a level comparable to the late 1940s and early 1950s. Despite the repression, however, the endurance of the workers

Figure 4.3 National Strike Shapes, 1964-1968

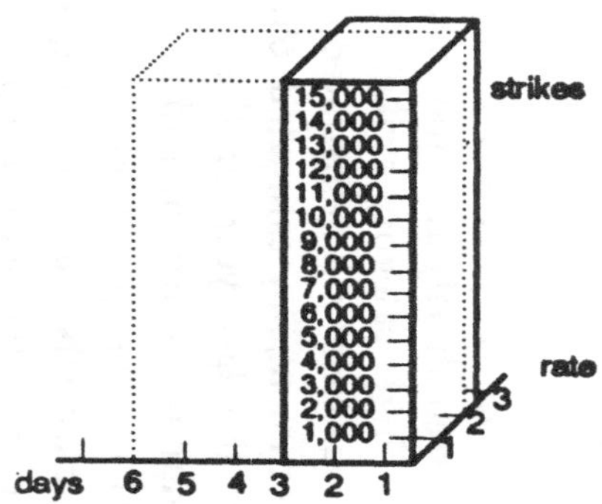

Figure -A
Castelo Branco Government
First Military Government
1964-1966

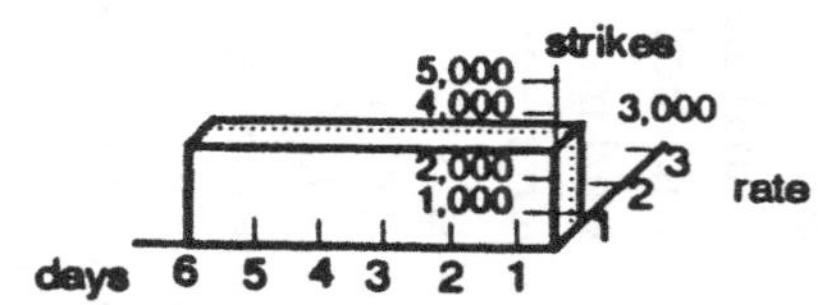

Figure -B
Costa e Silva Government
Second Military Government
1967-1968

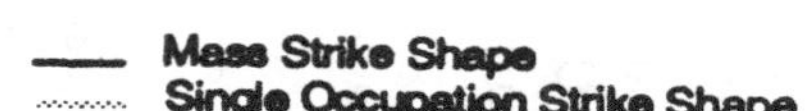

Table 4.4 – Ministerial Interventions in Unions According to Regions, 1964 and 1965

Region	*Nº Unions Affected*	*% of Interventions*	*Nº Existing Unions*	*% Affected in Region*
North	7	1.8	91	7.7
Northeast	102	26.0	492	20.7
Center-South	225	57.5	876	25.6
South	38	9.7	508	7.5
Center-West	19	4.9	67	28.5
Total	391	100.0	2,084	100.0

Source: Figueiredo, M. A., *Política Governamental e Funções Sindicais*, Master's Thesis, Universidade de São Paulo, 1975, cited in Candido Procopio Ferreira de Camargo, et alii. *São Paulo: Crescimento e Probreza 1975* (São Paulo: Edições Loyola, 1981), adapted from Table 31, p. 131.

who struck remained the same as during the Castelo Branco government, a period which had, in fact, the longest median strike duration since 1945. Those segments of the working class largely in the modern sector led the struggles against the regime, since the interventions had all but eliminated the militant leadership in the traditional sector unions. The brief flurry of strike activity among the metalworkers in 1968, which contributed in large measure to the average size of the strike shape and its duration, was systematically extinguished, ushering in the second major period under the dictatorship and the hardening of the regime.

The military governments of Castelo Branco and Costa e Silva were able to raze the populist organizations of labor leaders' inter-union networks which had served to command the immense mobilization of the pre-coup era. The interventions into the unions were concentrated in the center-south region, the heart of industrial militancy, and in the Northeast, the site of strong rural union activity (Table 4.4). Needless to say, the targets of the new regime were the combative nationalist leaders who were replaced by government protégés.

The available evidence with respect to the pattern of interventions shows that official repression focused to a large extent on the unions of the traditional industrial and service sectors, which had been in the forefront of strike activity since 1945. The effect was a drastic fall in the number of industrial strikes for both the traditional and modern sectors. The continuation of some strike actions during the first phase of the military regime evidenced differences in the strike activities of both sectors. As was understandable, the traditional sector workers were only able to mount single factory stoppages initiated primarily by some grass-roots organization. The modern sector workers, particularly the metalworkers, succeeded in organizing more strikes involving two or more factories, which indicates relatively greater resources to continue resisting the government's economic and political policies.

Worker Organization and Strikes in the Populist Era

Between 1945 and 1963, Brazilian workers had been largely unsuccessful in achieving substantial advances in their political or economic demands. Under the corporatist labor structure, which was originally inspired by the *Carta de Lavoro* of fascist Italy and survived intact the fall of the *Estado Novo*, working-class unions were firmly subjected to the tutelage of the state and dependent on government tolerance. As we have seen, industrial strike patterns varied according to the type of power relationship between the specific government and the organized segments of the working class. On the one hand, this dependence on state favor allowed for frequent manipulation of labor's support of politicians and factions within the polity in disputes against conservative military and economic elites. On the other hand, this dependence permitted organized labor to become an important actor in the political arena even under the shadow of the state.

The complexities of the challenge posed by a growing working class and its systematic analysis have often been obscured by the predominant notion that "populism is, in its essence, the exultation of public power: it is the state placing itself through its leaders in direct contact with individuals grouped in the masses."[13] This relationship is viewed as an atomizing one, "taking the form of a relationship between those in power and a mass of politically isolated individuals" readily "available" to be mobilized and manipulated in the interests of political elites.[14]

This Kornhauserean concept of mass politics[15] which describes the phenomenon of populism, current among many scholars of Latin American politics has more often than not ignored the ties between union and rank-and-file by unsubstantiated assertions of mass followings, while pointing to the large number of parallel organizations as evidence of elite organizational tendencies. Yet a review of the continuous changes in strike activities and the emergence of mass strikes as part of the repertoire of working-class collective actions, a repertoire which also included the local strike and the multiple factory strike, does not support the assumption that workers were 'individuals isolated in the mass'.

What is undeniable is the fact that labor leaders never attempted to reform the official union structure and thereby undo their subordination to the state, but rather assumed that these ties would facilitate the attainment of working-class objectives. The criticism that union leaders did not succeed in developing a strong rank-and-file base organization is not in itself sufficient to show a "mass politics" relationship.[16] In fact, the persistence of grass-roots commanded strikes and the varying importance of the union-led single category strikes demonstrate that workers' collective actions were not at all founded on a simple atomized mass-leader relationship. Future scholarly research on the forms of worker mobilization under the corporatist union structure will probably reveal that the Achilles' heel of the labor movement before 1964 was its sole reliance on the union structure for organizing workers in an authoritarian society. Unions achieved major political expression, especially during the more tolerant years; but when confronted with the power of the state, the interventions, and police repression, shop-floor organizers (*delegados sindicais*) and other committed workers were left adrift, without an alternative form of organizing and mobilizing resources.

Kenneth P. Erickson, in his study of working-class politics in Brazil, claimed that the timing of the mass strikes was dependent on economic deprivation of the workers and on military repression inasmuch as "union leaders called their workers off the job only when they believed that the workers' economic situation was grave enough to predispose them to strike. And they withheld the strike call when the military clearly planned to repress or undermine the stoppage".[17] A close examination of the strike data for the period 1961-1963 reveals that the conditions for frequent mass strikes were not primarily those of the workers' economic situation or the prospect of repression. Instead, the mass strike became the only form of collective action by the workers which was capable of pressuring the powerholders on a national level during a period of political and economic crises. Consequently, mass strikes were launched by the national coordinating organizations with the intention of obtaining political advantage as well as economic gains for the workers.

The mass strike developed over the decade of the 1950s and was a major feature of strike activity not only in the early 1960s but also marked the government of Getúlio Vargas (1950-1954). The mass strike emerged from organized labor's need to pressure the government on a variety of political and economic policy issues, since the legal single-category strikes were less effective in influencing national decision makers. In addition, the importance of the mass strike had varied over the years in accordance with the political conditions of the times and with labor's need to channel its demands from the local arena and into national politics. Thus, this form of strike activity had as its principal feature the dovetailing of political and economic claims directed to the governing elites.

In the period between 1961 and 1963, this type of collective action dominated strike activity. Even though the single category strikes were by far more numerous, mass strikes accounted for 90 percent of the strike participation at this time. The mobilizing issues were two-pronged. On the one hand, the mass strikes were called (1) to support political positions which challenged the conservative interests represented in the congress and by the military commanders, and (2) to demand fundamental changes in political arrangements, while proposing nationalist reforms in the economic structure of the country as a solution to the economic crisis. Coupled with these political demands were the economic ones, directed to a large extent at securing decrees for higher minimum wages, since the large majority of the workers' salaries were set in terms of the minimum wage.

Though the mass strikes intended to achieve economic benefits for the workers, in fact they were often called in times of political crisis to support the civilian president against the congress and military elites. Erickson's assertion that union leaders only chose moments of economic hardship to call strikes in order to obtain worker support seems an unlikely explanation, since most strikes were also motivated by political events. Furthermore, Erickson ignored the fact that a number of strikes were called in solidarity with other segments of the working class and did not imply any direct economic gains for many of the participants.

A more plausible interpretation is that the timing of mass strikes was partially explained by the timing of the political crises and by the existence of working-class organizations capable of successfully launching such large scale collective actions. The period between 1961 and 1963 was marked by a growing conflict of class interests, as economic crisis provoked increased political polarization. Because of this, mass strikes were generally called in support of the Goulart government in exchange for its patronage in the form of decrees increasing the official minimum wage and of access to the decision-making spheres in the government. In this respect, the pattern of strike activity for the period suggests that mass strikes were not only instruments in the contention for power, but were also a means of obtaining economic gains for workers.

Contrary to Erickson's analysis of the influence of military repression on the frequency of mass strikes, the data show that their frequency increased as the political crisis deepened, as did the frequency of military repression of strikers. The more important factor seems to have been President Goulart's growing dependency on labor's support to offset conservative forces. As time went on, the increased strength of labor displayed by these massive mobilizations drew greater opposition from both local and national elites. The heightening of repression of these actions was symptomatic of the polarization in class relations and of the disintegration of the multi-class alliance upon which the populist regime was based.

Mass strikes in the form of solidarity stoppages were occasionally used to pressure government to interfere in specific disputes when single category strikes proved ineffective. This use of the mass strike was less frequent, even though union leaders did use participation in mass strikes as a means of alerting workers and employers of forthcoming contract negotiations by displaying the union's capacity to mobilize workers and resources.[18] As a result, the gains from mass strike activity seem to have replaced to a large extent the need for large single category strikes.[19]

The single category strike at this time declined in importance among the industrial workers. About 70 percent of these strike actions were stoppages involving only one factory. This indicates that the single category strike became basically a weapon to be directed at local, individual establishments. The demands made by strikers were generally centered on such issues as the failure of employers to abide by contractual provisions. Few single category strikes involved all the members of the occupational category or most of the establishments in any specific geographical jurisdiction.

By and large, the period between 1961 and 1963 saw many unions capable of negotiating and winning benefits from employers. Because of participation in regional and national collective actions, unions were better able to negotiate with local employers without frequently resorting to strikes. This was possible through three mechanisms which enhanced their negotiating power. First, by engaging in the mass strikes, unions demonstrated to employers their capacity to mobilize workers and to stop production. Second, through their association with militant regional and national worker organizations, unions were able to pressure local employers both at the negotiation table and in the labor courts with the political, legal and technical assistance provided by the larger organizations. Finally, the receptivity of the government to the economic demands made in the mass strikes, especially with respect to the increases in minimum wages, attenuated to a certain extent the conflict between workers and employers, at least at the local level.

The data show unquestionably the unions' capacity to mobilize workers, at least between 1950 and 1963. These actions' frequency, duration, and size, ranging in the tens of thousands, indicate the level of rank-and-file participation which required more organization than the mere appeal to the masses suggested in mass politics theories. The Coup of 1964 exposed the danger of failing to develop parallel grass-roots linkages[20] which could have buttressed the politically vulnerable unions. Other societies in which worker unions overlap other forms of working-class social organization have shown greater resistance to authoritarian regimes.

It has also been argued by some that the mass populist nature of Brazilian unions was to be found in its extensive welfare role, thus enhancing the elite-mass relationship. In the later 1960s and early 1970s studies of working class attitudes often examined workers' views toward their unions which were largely non-combative and concluded that workers regard their unions as essentially welfare oriented.[21] Other scholars have shown, however, that workers involved in "militant unions" are indeed more politicized and see the organization as an important vehicle for pressing their demands, even though these unions have not reduced the welfare services they provide their members.[22]

While most critics of populist unionism point to this welfare aspect as exemplifying the hierarchical, dependent relationship established between leaders and workers, similar behavioral patterns have been observed in other less authoritarian societies. As Solomon Barkin, an experienced American labor scholar, pointed out many years ago in his study of textile workers in the American South:

> The influence of the established social patterns and of the social organization is visible in the operation of the unions themselves. The typical Southern textile union membership seeks and depends upon the union for leadership. Having been raised in a hierarchical society in which judgments have been provided from the top, they have introduced the same type of structure within the labor organization. The habits and practices of self-organization come very slowly. It takes patience and time to develop the people who would accept responsible union assignments requiring the making of independent judgments. Competition for positions of leadership tends to be rare. Local union officers tend to stay in their posts for years. The development of a sturdy democratic pattern of active participation takes years and years.[23]

It seems clear that many Brazilian unions have provided limited opportunities for extensive training in self-organization and democratic participation, especially considering the constraints imposed by the state. Dependent on the highly bureaucratized state, unions have been viewed by the dominant classes as necessary evils useful in checking the potential challenges of the working class. Unions are therefore constant objects of competition among the power contenders, both within the labor movement between competing ideological factions and outside it with other power groups. In the early 1960s the nationalist union leaders saw the corporatist structure as a channel for better pressing the state, while the ruling groups saw the unions escaping from the control of the state. The mobilizing facility under the civilian governments deceived labor leaders as to the extent of their strength.

In modern authoritarian regimes labor organizations are important institutions for controlling and monitoring the working class. Consequently, the workers' ability to adapt other forms of social organization to their need for mobilizing resources to challenge employers and an autocratic state will determine the strength of an independent labor movement. It was this lack of alternative forms of worker organization juxtaposed over the union structure which characterized the Brazilian labor movement of the populist era.

Notes

1. This graphic form of depicting strike patterns was developed by Edward Shorter and Charles Tilly and was first published in their article "The Shape of Strikes in France, 1830-1960," *Comparative Studies in Society and History* (13 January 1971):60-86. Other studies have subsequently used the same approach, see Edward Shorter and Charles Tilly, *Strikes in France 1830-1968* (Cambridge: Cambridge University Press,1974); Douglas A. Hibbs, Jr., "Industrial Conflict in Advanced Industrial Societies," *American Political Science Review,* 70 (1976): 1033-1058; Michael P. Hanagan, *The Logic of Solidarity* (Urbana: University of Illinois Press, 1980); P.K. Edwards, *Strikes in the United States 1881-1974* (Oxford: Basil Blackwell, 1981).

2. Following the criteria of Shorter and Tilly, the strike rate has been calculated as the number of strikes per 100,000 workers in the industrial labor force. For the purpose of this analysis of the Brazilian case, we have chosen to calculate the strike rate using the data from the *Censo Industrial, Produção Industrial, Transformação Industrial,* and *Pesquisa Industrial* - the

industrial censuses which have been conducted by the Brazilian census bureau, Fundação Instituto Brasileiro de Geografia e Estatística, on a yearly basis based on establishments of five or more employees. The use of these data, instead of the demographic census data which includes establishments smaller than five employees and consequently is approximately twice as large, was determined on the basis of two criteria: first, the economic studies of IBGE are the only source of yearly variation of the industrial labor force reported by branches of industry; second, studies have generally shown that small micro-establishments are not significantly strike prone, either in the advanced industrial countries or in the case of Brazil. As a result, the use of the data from the industrial economic census of IBGE did not distort the broad trends which our analysis presents in spite of the fact that the demographic census data present labor force employment figures about twice the size of the economic census data. The only study in Brazil demonstrating lower strike propensity among small establishments is Leôncio Martins Rodrigues, *Conflito Industrial e Sindicalismo no Brasil* (São Paulo: Difusão Europeia do Livro, 1966), pp. 49-100. For an analysis of the strike frequencies by establishment size in France, see Edward Shorter and Charles Tilly, *Strikes in France 1830-1968* (Cambridge: Cambridge University Press, 1978), pp. 227-235.

3. The Brazilian Communist Party, *Partido Comunista Brasileiro* (PCB) reached the apogee of its strength at the end of 1946 before the Dutra government repression, when the party had an estimated membership of 180,000. At this time, the party had eight newspapers in several cities and two publishing houses. For the presidential elections of 1946, the Communist candidate for president, Yeddo Fiuza, received approximately 600,000 votes out of 5,000,000 cast, and fifteen Congressmen and one Senator were elected from the PCB. In São Paulo, twenty-three communists were elected to the state legislature and in Rio de Janeiro, then federal capital, eighteen of the fifty city aldermen were from the Communist Party. Among the working class there was considerable support for the Communist Party. Working-class support for the PCB was also apparent in the São Paulo state legislature elections of 1946 as seen in the workers' electoral behavior. An analysis of the election districts, shows that there was a high positive correlation in any election district between the percentage of workers registered to vote and percentage of votes for the PCB and the Brazilian Labor Party (PTB). In general, workers preferred PCB over the PTB at a ratio to two to one. In addition to its electoral support, the PCB was regarded as being the

principal force in the labor movement in the major metropolitan areas of the country. While the Ministry of Labor controlled the state labor federations and the national confederations, the PCB had organized citywide union federations and was strongly supported by the naval and dock workers, the railroad workers, the seamen, bank workers, textile workers and, in Rio de Janeiro, also the metal workers. For more detailed analysis of the political importance of the Brazilian Communist Party at this time, see Ronald H. Chilcote, *The Brazilian Communist Party: Conflict and Integration* (New York: Oxford University Press, 1974); Timothy Fox Harding, "The Political History of Organized Labor in Brazil" (Ph.D. Dissertation, Stanford University, 1973); Jover Telles, *O Movimento Sindical no Brasil* (Rio de Janeiro: Editorial Vitoria, 1962).

4. Ronald H. Chilcote, *The Brazilian Communist Party*, p. 150; Timothy F. Harding, "The Political History of Organized Labor in Brazil," p. 194.

5. Francisco C. Weffort, "Democracia e Movimento Operário: Algumas Questões Para a História do Período 1945/1964," *Revista de Cultura Contemporânea*, 1:2 (January 1979): 4.

6. Raouf Kahil, *Inflation and Economic Development in Brazil 1946-1963* (Oxford: Clarendon Press, 1973), p. 64-66.

7. Leôncio Martins Rodrigues, "Tendências Futuras do Sindicalismo," *Revista da Administração de Empresas da Fundação Getúlio Vargas*, 19:4 (October-December 1979): 54, cf. 6.

8. Peter Flynn, *Brazil: A Political Analysis* (Boulder: Westview Press, 1978), pp. 256-258.

9. Hans Fuchtner, *Os Sindicatos Brasileiros: Organização e Função Política* (Rio de Janeiro: Editora Graal, 1980), pp. 208-209.

10. For a detailed study of the role of these parallel organizations in the political process, especially in the period 1960-1963, see Kenneth Paul Erickson, *The Brazilian Corporative State and Working-Class Politics* (Berkeley: University of California Press, 1977), Part III; Lucilia de Almeida Neves, *CGT no Brasil, 1961-1964* (Belo Horizonte: Editora Vega, 1981), chap. 3.

11. For a brief, interpretative discussion of this question with respect to the last general strike before the 1964 coup, see Marcia de Paula Leite and Syndey Sergio F. Solis, "O Ultimo Vendaval: A Greve dos 700,000," *Cara a Cara*, 1:2 (July-December 1978): 115-151.

12. Leôncio Martins Rodrigues, "Tendências Futuras....," p. 49.

13. Francisco C. Weffort, *O Populismo na Política Brasileira* (Rio de Janeiro: Editora Paz e Terra, 1978), p. 28.

14. Ibid., p. 27.

15. Arthur William Kornhauser, *The Politics of Mass Society* (New York: The Free Press, 1966).

16. John D. French and Sonia de Avelar provide two excellent and richly documented studies on the relationships between labor leaders and worker following during the populist era. In these pioneering works the authors largely disprove the alienation theories of populists leader-mass ties. See John D. French, *The Brazilian Workers' ABC: Class Conflict and Alliances in Modern São Paulo* (Chapel Hill: The University of North Carolina Press, 1992); Sonia Maria de Avelar, "The Basis of Workers' Solidarity: A Case Study of Textile Workers in São José dos Campos, Brazil" (Ph.D. Dissertation, The University of Michigan, 1985).

17. Kenneth Paul Erickson, *The Brazilian Corporative State and Working-Class Politics* (Berkeley: University of California Press, 1977), p. 116.

18. Interview with Francisco Moreno Ariza, textile worker union leader, 1945-1964, deposed from the presidency of the Textile Workers' Union of São José dos Campos by ministerial intervention in 1964 and held prisoner between 1964 to 1965. Interview held in São José dos Campos, São Paulo, October 1979. Francisco Ariza makes the point that the association of his union with the state and national labor organizations provided resources which enabled him to deal with local employers and resolve conflicts before resorting to calls for strike actions, see Sonia Maria de Avelar, "The Basis of Workers' Solidarity: A Case Study Of Textile Workers in São José dos Campos, Brazil" (Ph.D. Dissertation, The University of Michigan, 1985).

19. This finding is also corroborated by the case studies of union locals in the pre-1964 period, See Maria Andrea Loyola, *Os Sindicatos e o PTB: Estudo de um caso em Minas Gerais* (São Paulo: Editora Vozes e CEBRAP, 1980), p. 80; Sônia Maria de Avelar, "The Social Basis of Workers' Solidarity: A Case Study of Textile Workers in São José dos Campos, Brazil" (Ph.D. Dissertation, The University of Michigan, 1985); John D French, *The Brazilian Workers' ABC: Class Conflict and Alliances in Modern São Paulo* (Chapel Hill: The University of North Carolina Press, 1992).

20. Some key works in this area are E. P. Thompson, *The Making of the English Working Class* (London: Victor Gallancz Ltd., 1963) and Seymour Martin Lipset, Martin Trow and James Coleman, *Union Democracy* (New York: Doubleday Anchor Books, 1962); also see Michael P. Hanagan, *The Logic of Solidarity* (Urbana: University of Illinois Press, 1980); John R. Low-Beer, *Protest and Participation: The New Working Class in Italy* (Cambridge: Cambridge University Press, 1978), pp. 173-206; Joan M. Nelson, *Access to Power: Politics and the Urban Poor in Developing Nations* (Princeton: Princeton University Press, 1979), chap. 7; Sônia Maria de Avelar, "The Social Basis of Workers' Solidarity: A Case Study of Textile Workers in São José dos Campos, Brazil" (Ph.D. Dissertation, The University of Michigan, 1985); John D. French and Mary Lynn Pedersen, "Women and Working-Class Mobilization in Postwar São Paulo, 1945-1948," *Latin American Research Review*, 24:3 (1989) 99-125; John French, "Industrial Workers and the Origin of Populist Politics in the ABC Region of Greater São Paulo, Brazil 1900-1950" (Ph.D. Dissertation, Yale University, 1985); John D. French, *The Brazilian Workers' ABC: Class Conflict and Allliances in Modern São Paulo* (Chapel Hill: The University of North Carolina Press, 1992).

21. Youssef Cohen, "The Benevolent Leviathan: Political Consciousness among Urban Workers Under State Corportaism," *American Political Science Review*, 76 (1982): 46-59; Leôncio Martins Rodrigues, *Industrialização e Atitudes Operárias* (São Paulo: Editora Brasiliense, 1970), pp. 110-114; Amaury Guimarães de Souza, "The Nature of Corporatist Representation: Leaders and Members of Organized Labor in Brazil" (Ph.D. Dissertation, Massachusetts Institute of Technology, 1978) chap. 7; Juarez Rubens Brandão Lopes, *Crise do Brasil Arcaíco* (São Paulo: Difusão Europeia do Livro, 1967), pp. 107-127.

22. Maria Andrea Loyola, *Os Sindicatos e o PTB: Estudo de um caso em Minas Gerais* (São Paulo: Editora Vozes and CEBRAP, 1980), p. 99; Celso Frederico, *A Vanguarda Operária* (São Paulo: Editora Símbolo, 1979); Salvador A.M. Sandoval and Sônia Maria de Avelar, "Conciencia Obrera y la Negociación Coletiva en Brasil," *Revista Mexicana de Sociologia*, 1-3 (1983): 1027-1047; Sônia Maria de Avelar, "The Social Basis of Workers' Solidarity: A Case Study of Textile Workers in São José dos Campos, Brazil" (Ph.D. Dissertation, The University of Michigan, 1985).

23. Solomon Barkin, "The Personality Profile of Southern Textile Workers," *Labor Law Review*, 4:6 (1960): 471-472.

5

Working-Class Organizations During the Repressive Years: 1964-1977

The years after the 1964 coup were critical in the development of the Brazilian labor movement as a consequence of the harsh repression of labor militancy which forced committed workers to devise alternative forms of organization for political action other than the government controled unions. They also came to reject the corporatist ties which bound the labor unions to the state. These changes in workers' actions and thinking were fundamental for the development of a "new unionism" which emerged after fourteen years of military rule. To sketch the story of how workers pooled their resources to resist the authoritarianism of the regime is not an easy task because of the fragmented information available about labor militants' activities in the years of greatest repression. Nevertheless, the purpose of this chapter is to examine the alternative forms of working-class organizations developed to press for workers' demands and to analyze their contribution to the emergence of the "new union" movement.

Although unions had made rapid advances over the years preceding the 1964 coup, they failed to build sturdy organizations capable of withstanding the impact of repression and economic crisis. The massive mobilizations which marked the years between 1958 and 1963 gave the illusion of strong, well developed working-class organizations with the power to confront other political forces. But as seen in the previous chapter, labor unions in the populist era were unevenly developed. On the one hand, they were well structured bureaucratically, and their leaders participated in national politics through several parallel organizations independent of the official confederations controlled by the

Ministry of Labor. On the other hand, militant unions were founded on weak rank-and-file mobilization organization characterized by tenuous linkages with the workplace.

The contradiction between the better structured union leadership and the poorly organized base had serious consequences. In the first place, there appeared signs of divergence between the mass strike actions often favored by union leadership and the persistence of local grass-roots based stoppages. In periods when union leaders favored mass strikes, the proportion of local grass-roots based strikes increased. This was further aggravated by the leaders' apparent lack of concern with the level of rank-and-file organizational strength and their reliance on the patronage of the civilian governments as their major source of power, in spite of the past experiences of repression through the same patronage system. As a result, the advent of military rule exposed labor's weaknesses as workers were unable to resist widespread ministerial interventions and the dismantling of the militant parallel organizations.

The new regime set out to remove organized labor as a serious political contender by relegating the unions to the tasks of administering their social welfare programs and providing their members with judicial counselling. By tightening the strike regulations and prohibiting its use in disputes over wages, the military sought to severely limit the unions' capacity to attract and mobilize workers around one of their most important issues. Similarly, the introduction of a comprehensive wage policy in which all salary increases had to conform to the indices decreed by the Ministry of Finance seriously undermined the collective bargaining process by centralizing in the hands of the government the determination of the levels of annual wage increases. As a result, the nature of industrial relations was politicized even more as all wage disputes became automatic confrontations with the state.

Even against such barriers, groups of workers drawn largely from the skilled and experienced workers sought to bide their time in the beleaguered unions by seeking legal loopholes to advocate workers' demands. Beginning in 1965, some unions began to demand the creation of a base salary for their occupational groups. Through the struggle in the labor courts for recognition of the base salary, union leaders attempted to circumvent the government's role in setting wage increase indices by complementing these low salaries with increases in base pay. In addition, the base pay demands had three other important objectives: (1) to raise the wages of specific occupational groups to levels commensurate with the economic importance of certain industries, (2) to obstruct employers' tactic of firing workers on the eve of official wage increases only to rehire them later at the legal minimum wage, and (3) to guarantee that all new employees would benefit from the salary levels established by the annual raises. While the base pay was advocated by only a handful of unions in the late sixties, by 1973 it had become one of the major mobilizing issues of the labor movement.[1]

The demand for wage increases through base pay and fringe benefits issues did not preclude the unions from claiming wage increases higher than the official indices, though the labor courts were powerless to consider them. These demands were largely gestures against the rising cost of living and falling real wages as well as a legal way to protest the government's calculations of inflation and wages indices. The unions charged that the inflation rates were always underestimated, as were the rates of industrial productivity. In addition, unionists began to dispute many other fringe benefits as a judicial form of filling the void left by the weakening of collective bargaining and the courts. The uneasy position of the labor judiciary, caught between labor and employers, resulted in some justices' calls for a return to collective bargaining as early as 1975.[2]

In spite of the limited effectiveness of the judicial system, some unions continued to use the annual wage settlements as opportunities to organize campaigns among workers against low wages and the high cost of living and to reassert the unions' presence among the rank-and-file. In addition, this "new union" leadership assumed the various services of providing welfare and judicial assistance as another way of attracting workers to the union and of developing their commitment to the organization while biding for safer times for overt challenges to management and the state.

Of course, opposition to the weakening of the labor unions was far from universal. As Kenneth Mericle found in his study of the São Paulo union leadership, 25 percent of the union leaders did not feel that the wage setting mechanism needed to be changed. These leaders were largely the *pelegos* who, installed by the military regime, were comfortable with the unions' minimal role in wage disputes. Union *pelegos* opposed any situations which would increase conflict over real wages making them more vulnerable to workers' discontent and threatening their union positions. Thus, these union bosses were quite satisfied to leave the issue of wages in the hands of the finance ministry, thus dispensing with the need to mobilize workers. On the other hand, the *pelegos* also gave the more militant union activists a hard time within the labor movement in defense of their pro-government commitments and to avoid being overshadowed by the rising union opposition.[3]

After 1968 conditions for collective actions were no longer favorable; thus, workers were deprived of any firsthand conflict experiences. Unions which obstructed the execution of the government's economic policies could find themselves under intervention, and union leaders who were too politically militant might be jailed or "disappear". So the new leaders waited. Selective interventions taught them that indiscreet and unprepared militancy could land them in jail. The risks were very high, while the impact on the workers and the government might be slight, especially during the years of the "economic miracle". For this reason, the differences in behavior between committed union leaders and *pelegos* were often imperceptible to most workers. The leaders all performed their bureaucratic functions, though the militants aimed at turning efficient union services into activities for developing workers' union identification.

Among the rank-and-file, the precipitous decline of the unions did not extinguish the workers' aspiration for engaging in associations for economic improvement. In light of the unions' handicaps in attaining their demands, groups of workers turned to other forms of legally pressuring government for economic benefits. In addition to a whole array of sport and recreational clubs which developed within and outside the factories, neighborhood improvement associations and Church-based community groups provided the legal, and often Church protected, opportunity to assemble openly, to hold discussions with other workers, and to organize a variety of cultural, educational and pressure group activities.[4]

Neighborhood improvement efforts had existed for many years prior to the military takeover. Among the earliest of these were the *Sociedades Amigos de Bairro* (SABs) which marked their political importance at the beginning of the 1950s as the cornerstone of the popular mobilization to obtain municipal autonomy from the capital city for the cities of Osasco, Perituba, and São Caetano do Sul in the state of São Paulo.[5]

The SABs first appeared in their present neighborhood forms sometime between 1952 and 1953 as a consequence of populist election campaigns, especially the candidacy of Jânio Quadros who served for a few months as president in 1960. By 1970, 1,300 SABs were functioning in the state of São Paulo, of which 800 were located in the metropolitan area, and 500 of these in the city of São Paulo alone.[6]

As industrialization followed its path, the concomitant effects of rapid urbanization and the scarcity of housing and urban services fueled the rise of new SABs as pressure groups to obtain basic urban services. As of 1970, over 80 percent of the SABs represented the interests of residents who were migrants to the capital of São Paulo.

After the 1964 coup, with union channels of demand making effectively closed and with the worsening economic situation among the working population, urban workers turned to such associations as an alternative means of participation in expressing demands. By 1970, about 88 percent of the SABs in São Paulo had developed activities exclusively aimed at seeking neighborhood improvements from local authorities. These demands ranged in scope from better school facilities, neighborhood clinics, park and recreational facilities, light and potable water, sewage and other municipal services such as garbage collection and police protection to pressuring authorities to oblige private companies to attend to the neighborhood's needs in terms of better bus service, dumping and pollution control, and routing of heavy truck traffic.

In addition, over half the SABs had educational and recreational activities including literacy programs, sewing courses, and other short professional training courses which could help complement the reduced family income. In a similar vein, at least 41.3 percent of the associations had organized mutual assistance services for the neighborhoods, such as the donation of clothes, food and medicine as well as establishing food cooperatives.[7]

Municipal authorities, like all the rest of the state apparatus, were found to be largely unresponsive to the plight of the proletarian neighborhoods. This further politicized the SABs, which now represented primarily the interests of the residents in the working-class quarters of the cities. Though their origins were closely identified with electoral interests, by 1970 it appears that 96 percent of the associations were autonomous, free from any ties with political, judicial or financial entities,[8] which indicates a substantial break with the populist past.

Before 1964, attempts to create an umbrella organization which would unite the various SABs were unsuccessful, often because of political rivalries among the politicians and ideological groups. After 1964, the associations began to come together in regional groups within the metropolitan area; these groups continue to function today. The first meeting of SABs in the state of São Paulo was held in 1966, from which sprang the *Conselho de Sociedades Amigos de Bairro, Vilas e Cidades* with the task of coordinating the associations' campaigns. By the end of the 1970s, the *Conselho* had come to play an important role in extra-neighborhood activities of the associations, and its directors consciously tried to minimize the influence of the government party, the city officials, and the state government.[9]

Another important political area which opened up for working-class activists was within the programs of social action of the Catholic Church. As the repression heightened in the middle to late 1960s, the Catholic Church became another welcomed alternative. As Cândido Procópio F. de Camargo observed:

> The Catholic Church came to offer shelter and space to the student movement, worker groups and others, not affiliated to the religious institution, who made up the core of the resistance to the oppression of the state. Meetings and debates were held in its church buildings. No other institution could have the resources and independence to support these embryonic forms of civil defense.[10]

Thus, the Church presence in Brazilian politics changed after 1964, becoming strongly identified with the opposition to the autocratic regime. On the regional level, the Archdiocese of São Paulo expressed this political role in part through the Commission of Justice and Peace which undertook in the name of the Church the systematic and direct defense of human rights and the struggle against the repression, torture, and other abuses of the regime. On the grass-roots level, the *Comunidades Eclesiais de Base* (CEBs), the church's community base organizations, became the primary vehicles through which it was possible to mobilize popular resources and to continue the Church's social actions, especially after having also suffered the repression of its own youth and working-class organizations.[11]

The CEBs proliferated throughout the country and by 1980 were estimated at over 50,000 community groups which varied in the degree of politicization of their collective actions. Their political importance is best described by Cândido Procópio F. de Camargo in the following manner:

> They [the CEBs] constituted a web of experiences and the systematic exercise of new forms of popular associations for the discussion and searching for solutions to vital problems that afflict the working classes in the peripheries of the large cities and in rural areas.[12]

Furthermore, they provided the progressive clergy with a field of religious activities which penetrated the working-class neighborhoods and put them in direct contact with the needs of their members. The extensive organizational network of the Church, through its parish structure, provided an effective alternative form of organizing the population. This marked a break with the traditional ways of relating to the laity and introduced a more genuine democratic form of participation in Church affairs.[13]

Similarly, the CEBs provided dedicated working-class activists with a niche where they could continue to exercise the skills of organization, discuss the plight of the workers and their families, and encourage demand-making. For many other workers, the CEBs became an experience of consciousness-raising through learning the fundamental Christian exigencies of equality as the criteria for condemning the exploitation of the working class reflected in the whole of Brazilian society.[14] The political consequences of the new orientation were: the creation of a political consciousness which viewed demands as questions of social justice and rights, not as favors sought from public authorities or employers; the learning of organizational skills and the tactics of demand-making; and the involvement of CEB members in social movements of the poor.

The outcome of the Church's grass-root pastoral efforts is illustrated in the directives issued by the Third National Meeting of the CEBs in 1978 which expressed, among several items, the following:

> -In everything, we should look after our interests as the poor and to the interests of those who today are in power. All that oppression which befalls us has its roots in sin; the lands in the hands of those who do not need them; the workers subjected to earn shrinking wages, producing fruits like hunger, infant mortality, illiteracy. That great sin is now social and is called the capitalist system.

-Try to always be united and organized, doing our work within our communities so as to show our faith in the Lord that changes all things.
-Participate in all the instruments that will help us in our struggle for liberation, such as unions, associations, political parties and others which are ours and not just made for us.
-Assume our condition of an oppressed class, for we must work believing in one another, since our interests are the same.[15]

An indication of the extent of the CEBs' political consolidation and capacity to mobilize resources was their sponsorship of national protest movements beginning in the early 1970s. In 1973, the Mothers' Club of the parish of Vila Remo in the working-class district of south São Paulo wrote a letter to the authorities complaining about the high cost of living. The letter was soon published in the major newspapers, having escaped the eye of the government censors, and it became a banner of the opposition party in the 1974 elections for national Congress.

The following year, 1975, the residents of the same neighborhood organized a 2,000 questionnaire survey with the participation of 70 mothers' clubs of the periphery of the capital in order to determine the consequences of the deteriorating standard of living among working-class families. The data obtained were analyzed and served as the basis for the 1977 organization of the movement against the rising cost of living, the *Movimento Contra a Carestía da Vida*. The assembly which gathered to elect the first general coordinators of the movement was composed of delegates from 700 church base communities.[16]

After the launching of the movement, the action spread through the São Paulo metropolitan area, into the interior of the state, and finally to other states like Minas Gerais, Rio de Janeiro, Espirito Santo and Bahia. By 1978, the national assembly of the movement brought together over 5,000 delegates, representing associations from all over the country, which had gathered over the past year almost 1,300,000 signatures on a petition to the President of the Republic that called for a price freeze of basic foodstuffs.[17]

Even though the petition campaign had no positive effect on government policy and publically being rebuffed by the military president, it demonstrated the CEBs' capacity to organize a national campaign. More importantly, the effort provided thousands with both the experience of demand making after years of submission and with the experience of the President's rebuke. The final effects of this mobilization were to show up in the strike waves which erupted between 1978 and 1980 and in the bitter confrontations with the state and employers.

Another movement which began with the CEBs was in support of the rights of slum dwellers, the *Movimento de Loteamentos Clandestinos*, against the abuses of urban slumlords, resulting from the chaotic urban growth of São Paulo and from the disregard by the authorities of slum conditions. The *Movimento de Loteamentos Clandestinos* (MLC) was launched at the end of 1976 by the CEBs of four neighborhoods with the assistance of the Church's Pastoral Commission for the Periphery of Santo Amaro, which invited lawyers for legal counselling from the law students associations of the Pontificate Catholic University of São Paulo and the University of São Paulo.[18]

The main thrusts of the MLC were to define the legal situation of the residents and also to obtain urban services for the neighborhoods by pressing for municipal assistance. The MLC spread rapidly in São Paulo, and by 1978 over 50 associations of slum dwellers had joined forces to coordinate their political activities. These associations claimed to represent the interests of about 50,000 residents.[19]

After years of associative experience and cautious contention during the dark years of the repression, the workers had created alternative forms of organization for class mobilization which had been largely lacking in the pre-coup period. In 1978, the first year of massive strike activity since 1968, the CEBs launched the first community based centers for the defense of human rights in working-class neighborhoods. The center organization was intended to be a grass-roots response to the state's arbitrary repression, especially that against residents of the proletarian neighborhoods and the labor activists from the neighborhood associations. The Center for the Defense of Human Rights set as its objectives: (1) to diffuse information with respect to violations of human rights in their areas; (2) to expose these violations; (3) to organize files from newspaper reports; (4) to promote courses sponsored jointly with the regional commissions of the CEBs to teach residents legal "first aid" against police encroachment; (5) to provide legal assistance in cases of rights violations; and (6) to promote and support mobilizations and struggles for human rights, especially protest movements against the state's economic policies and political oppression. By 1979, with the assistance of university professors and students and the local chapter of the *Ordem dos Advogados* (OAB), the Brazilian attorneys' association, six centers were functioning and another six were being installed in the city of São Paulo.[20]

After 1964, the workers turned to the community associations and Church groups as havens where notions of new union action could be worked out based on rank-and-file organizing at the shop floor level and in the neighborhoods.[21] As early as 1965, the first factory commissions emerged from among the workers as the only way of circumventing the unions under state control and dealing directly with employers over workplace issues. By 1967 a new worker leadership with roots in the CEBs won the first of several union elections in the metalworkers union of Osasco. From this time on, the factory commission appeared in other industries and new, committed leaders gradually emerged from the rank-and-file.

The hardening of the repression in 1968, especially against the Osasco metalworkers strike, was a serious setback for the new union opposition forcing the workers to retreat to the day-to-day struggles of the workplace. From this time until 1978, resistance was organized through sporadic shop floor tactics of work stoppages, boycotts, slowdowns, and strict adherence to work norms as a hindrance to production. At the same time, the process of political education was conducted both in community organizations and in factories through the clandestine distribution of manifestos, pamphlets, and the use of rumors.[22]

There were, of course, great risks involved in engaging in such "subversion", especially after 1968 when activists were imprisoned, tortured, at times exiled, or killed. For this reason, little is known about worker opposition during the years of the worst repression (1968-1973); but, for certain, by 1974 the persistent and silent efforts of the union opposition groups bore results.

As early as 1972, there was labor unrest in some factories over the low rates of wage increases established by the government. A first re-appearance of strike activity occurred in 1973 in strike actions against the low wage differentials paid for overtime work in the Volkswagen, Mercedes Benz, Chrysler and Villares plants in São Bernardo do Campo. This unrest obliged the government to decree a 10 percent bonus to all workers.[23]

In January 1974, the Ford Motor Plant in São Bernardo do Campo was surrounded by military police called to prevent a workers' sit-down strike in protest of excessive overtime and low wages. Confronted with the pressure from the plant floor, the company agreed to sign the first negotiated contract since 1964. By midyear the victory of opposition workers in the metal worker union elections in Rio de Janeiro provoked an intervention by the Ministry of Labor and the annulment of the election. In São Paulo, the workers' movement to recover the unions from *pelego* control seems to have been more successful. In the General Motors plant there was widespread wildcat striking, and the Volkswagen workers boycotted overtime work at their plant for two weeks. Labor unrest spread from São Paulo to São José dos Campos where General Motor workers staged wildcat stoppages at the same time as similar actions occurred at the Chrysler and Mercedes Benz factories in São Bernardo do Campo. Pressured by these outbreaks of an organized rank-and-file, *pelego* labor leaders began to echo some of the demands expressed by the workers.[24]

These types of collective action continued in 1975, spreading to other regions of the country as in the case of the workers at the Wallig plant in Porto Alegre, Rio Grande do Sul, who stopped production for several hours to demand back pay and wage increases. The actions continued in the São Paulo area; stoppages halted production in another establishment in the capital and broke out again at the General Motors plant in São José dos Campos, this time followed by twenty days of sporadic slowdowns in protest of the low wage increase negotiated by the local union boss.[25]

The largest metalworkers union in the country, the São Paulo union, approved in late 1976 a demand for a 60 percent wage increase, about 20 percentage points above the official index. When the union only received a 43 percent increase, its opposition workers in the rank-and-file protested by further slowdowns in many establishments in the industrial belt of the capital. Meanwhile, in Rio de Janeiro, workers of the Fiat Motor Works brought down production by 60 percent in protest over unfair wages. In Rio Grande do Sul 100 trade union organizations sent a manifesto to the state legislature against press censorship and the lack of political freedom in the country.[26]

A new generation of union leaders was now in control of a few, but very strategic unions, especially the metalworkers union of the ABC (Santo André, São Bernardo do Campo, São Caetano do Sul) region of the São Paulo metropolitan area. They launched their 1978 wage increase campaign by demanding a 34.1 percent raise above the official index as restitution for lost wages resulting from the falsification of the 1973 inflation indices by the Minister of Finance, Antônio Delfim Neto.[27] The falsification issue was to become a major banner for worker mobilization and a source of "moral outrage" of the working classes against the government, thus accentuating the declining credibility of the military regime.

The year 1978 signaled the first indication that organized labor had regained some of its lost strength and under its new leadership was mobilizing resources to confront both the autocratic state and the employers. In May 1978, the first wave of widespread wildcat strike activity by São Paulo workers jolted the recently installed presidency of João Figueiredo by boldly breaking the strike law and paralyzing the industrial belt of São Paulo without the use of pickets.

The CEBs played an important role in the course of these strikes, for strikers received support in their neighborhood associations. One participant was quoted as saying that "without the neighborhood mothers' clubs it would not have been possible to mimeograph and distribute 240,000 daily bulletins on the progress of the strike actions".[28]

Backed by the Workers Pastoral, by the Pastoral of the World of Work, by the Young Catholic Workers, by the Catholic Workers' Action, and by the National Labor Front, a parallel organization of opposition unionists, the new working-class leaders took to the union halls their demands for restitution for lost income due to government adulterated inflation rates. The election tickets opposing incumbent union bosses always included workers who had been very active in various types of community organizations and in the worker pastorals. This was especially true for the opposition candidates in the major metallurgical unions of São Paulo, São Bernardo do Campo, Santo André, São Caetano do Sul, Osasco, and the important unions in the interior of the state of São Paulo such as São José dos Campos, Taubate, Campinas, Santos, and Jundiai.[29]

The "new unionism" leadership, which had grown in the shell of the archaic corporatist organizations with roots binding workplace and community, would play a leading role in the resurgence of strike activity in the late 1970s, as analyzed in the following chapter. Underlying the rise of a new generation of union militants was the expression of a strong sentiment for democratic participation of the workers and a sharper spirit of class antagonism than in the past - a consequence of the many years of exploitation and state oppression. Aware of the pitfalls and failures of the populist trade union movement and weary of the manipulation of vested political interest groups, the "new unionism" activists and workers were committed to: (1) the abrogation of the corporatist aspects of the system of industrial relations; (2) the total autonomy of the unions from the state; (3) the self-determination of the workers by minimizing the role of intellectuals, students and political groups; and 4) the strengthening of participation by rank-and-file workers in the union and in the factory through factory commissions and shop stewards (*delegados sindicais*).[30]

Notes

1. Cid José Sitrangulo, *Conteúdo dos Dissídios Coletivos de Trabalho* (São Paulo: Edições LTR, 1978), p. 81.

2. Ibid., p. 82.

3. Kenneth Scott Mericle, "Conflict Regulation in the Brazilian Industrial Relations System" (Ph.D. Dissertation, The University of Wisconsin, 1974), pp. 235-237.

4. Because of the important role which popular social movements played as expressions of working-class discontent during the years when labor unions were restrained from collective action, many studies have been conducted on this topic. Among these studies on current Brazilian social movements see Renato Raul Boschi, *A Arte da Associação* (Rio de Janeiro: Vertice, 1987); Renato Raul Boschi, (ed.) *Movimentos Coletivos no Brasil Urbano* (Rio de Janeiro: Editora Zahar, 1982); Maria da Gloria Marcondes Gohn, *A Força da Periferia: A Luta das Mulheres por Creches em São Paulo* (Petropolis: Editora Vozes, 1985); Maria da Gloria Marcondes Gohn, *Reinvindicações Populares Urbanas* (São Paulo: Cortez Editores, 1982); Pedro Jacobi, *Movimentos Sociais e Políticas Públicas* (São Paulo: Cortez Editores, 1989); Malori J. Pompermayer, (ed.) *Movimentos Sociais em Minas Gerais* (Belo Horizonte: Editora PROED, 1987); Marcia das Mercês G. Somarriba, Maria Gezica Valadares and Mariza Rezende Afonso, *Lutas Urbanas em Belo Horizonte* (Petropolis: Editora Vozes, 1984); Eder Sader, *Quando Novos Personagens Entraram em Cena: Experiências e Lutas dos Trabalhadores da Grande São Paulo 1970-1980* (Rio de Janeiro: Editora Paz e Terra, 1988).

5. José Álvaro Moisés, "Experiência de Mobilizações Populares em São Paulo," *Contraponto*, 3:3 (September 1978): pp. 70-72.

6. Ibid., pp. 75-80 passim.

7. Ibid., p. 83.

8. Ibid., pp. 83-84.

9. Ibid., p. 84.

10. Candido Procópio Ferreira de Camargo, Beatriz Muniz de Souza, and Antônio Flavio de Oliveira Pierucci, "Comunidades Eclesiais de Base," in Paul Singer and Vinicius Caldeira Brant, (eds.) *São Paulo: O Povo em Movimento,* (São Paulo: Editora Vozes-CEBRAP, 1980), pp. 60-61.

11. Scott P. Mainwaring, *The Catholic Church and Politics in Brazil, 1916-1985* (Stanford: Stanford University Press, 1986), Chapters 6 and 7.

12. Cândido Procópio Ferreira de Camargo et al., "Comunidades Eclesiais de Base," p. 62.

13. For other studies on the dynamics and functioning of the grass-roots church organizations see Thomas C. Bruneau, *The Church in Brazil: The Politics of Religion* (Austin: Latin American Monographs, No. 56, University of Texas Press, 1982); Thomas C. Bruneau, *The Political Transformation of the Brazilian Catholic Church* (New York: Oxford University Press, 1979); Scott P. Mainwaring, *The Catholic Church and Politics in Brazil, 1916-1985* (Stanford: Stanford University Press, 1986); Cândido Procópio Ferreira de Camargo, Beatriz Muniz de Souza and Antonio Flavio de Oliveira Pierucci, "Comunidades Eclesiais de Base," in Paul Singer and Vinicius Caldeira Brant, (eds.), *São Paulo: O Povo em Movimento,* (São Paulo: Editora Vozes-CEBRAP, 1980); Frei Betto, *O Que É Comunidade Eclesial de Base* (São Paulo: Editora Brasiliense, 1981).

14. Cândido Procópio F. de Camargo et al., "Comunidades Eclesiais de Base," p. 76.

15. Ibid.

16. Paul Singer, "Movimentos de Bairro," in Paul Singer and Vinicius Caldeira Brant, (eds.), *São Paulo: O Povo em Movimento* (São Paulo: Editora Vozes-CEBRAP, 1980), p. 98.

17. Ibid., p. 98.

18. Ibid., p. 94.

19. Ibid., p.95.

20. Ibid., p. 102.

21. "A Luta Por Um Sindicato de Base: Histórico da Oposição Sindical," *Cadernos do CEAS,* 63 (September-October 1979): p. 8.

22. Ibid., p. 9.

23. Lucia Lippi Oliveira, "O Movimento Operário em São Paulo 1970-1985" in Emir Sader, (ed.), *Movimentos Sociais na Transição Democrática,* (São Paulo: Editora Cortez, 1987), pp. 26-28.

24. "A Luta Por Um Sindicato de Base: Histórico da Oposição Sindical," *Cadernos do CEAS,* 63 (September-October 1979): p. 10.

25. Ibid.

26. Ibid.

27. "Greves...E há mais do que Isso," *Cadernos do CEAS,* 63 (September-October, 1979): p. 56.

28. "Comunidades Ecleciais de Base no Brasil," *Estudos da Conferência Nacional dos Bispos do Brasil,* 23 (São Paulo: Edições Paulinas, 1979), pp. 91-92.

29. Ibid., pp. 90-91.

30. "Pontos Básicos para uma Ação Sindical Unitária e Democrática," *Cadernos CEAS,* 63 (September-October 1979): pp. 19-24 passim.

6

The Revival of Industrial Strikes: 1978-1980

From the analyses in the preceding chapters some generalizations can be made about the transformations in strike activity over the three decades between 1945 and 1977. In the first place, it is clear that the level of strike activity largely depended on political conditions such as governmental tolerance and the conjunctural correlation of forces in the polity which facilitated or hindered the growth to the working-class movement. As was argued before, political factors have been intervening variables between those economic conditions which contributed to labor discontent and the actual mounting of collective actions to press for workers' claims. This was seen in the inconsistent correlations between strike frequency and business cycle indicators. The latter came to have more importance in periods of governmental tolerance toward working-class activity and were less significant in authoritarian periods when the weight of the state interfered with the workers' capacity to protest.

The importance of the political determinants was vividly illustrated in the transformation of the shape of strikes over the different political periods. Though to a certain extent strikes increased because of the growth of the work force during the past decades, in general each period produced strike patterns with distinct shapes as a consequence of changes in the dimensions of the strikes brought about by political factors.

These transformations in strike activity demonstrated the working class' response to the political environment. Because political power was perceived as a key factor in attaining their goals, workers' organizations developed in the direction of facilitating interest representation and of coordination of collective actions on a national level where they could better press government for their demands instead of concentrating on workplace bargaining in the manner of business unionism.

A second point is that worker organizational innovation was prompted by governmental repression and by the need to create effective national entities which could coordinate the unions in their struggles. As repression demonstrated the importance of acquiring political power and access to the centers of decision-making, union leaders turned to creating organizations which would enable them to act jointly. In addition, the official regional and national worker organizations dominated by pro-government unionists, or *pelegos,* led independent union leaders to rely on "parallel organizations" which would bypass these union bosses and their constraints on militant activities. Consequently, during periods of relative governmental tolerance the new parallel organizations came to have a significant impact on strike activity as strikes reached regional and national proportions. After the coup of 1964, the parallel organizations were dismantled by the government, and the workers turned to other forms of organization to resist the repression.

A third fact to be drawn from the strike activities of the period prior to 1978 is that political and organizational developments led to changes in the loci of worker contention. During the repressive governments workers tended to direct their organizational efforts to local, single category work stoppages and other forms of seeking economic redress, since their access to the national power structure was blocked by the character of the regime. In more tolerant periods, workers demonstrated their capacity to influence national politics through large mass strikes which pressed for policy changes and higher minimum wages. These shifts from national contention to local protests reflected workers' responses to changes in the correlation of forces in the polity.

A fourth major conclusion from the examination of the impact of politics on industrial conflict is that changes in the sectorial distribution of strikers were also partially a result of political factors. Since 1945 strike activity had been dominated to a large extent by workers from the traditional industries because of their earlier labor movement tradition, organizational experience and relative importance in the industrial economy in Brazil prior to the Second World War. Through the decade of the 1950s this pattern persisted, while the number of workers employed in the modern capital-intensive industries grew as a result of rapid industrialization. By the beginning of the 1960s, they had reached a level of militance similar to that of the older traditional sector. Though the workers of the modern sector became more strike-prone because of economic factors like falling wages in the face of increasing productivity and profits, their collective actions soon aimed at contending for political power. After all, the economically based causes of workers' discontent were soon transformed into political issues because of the central role of the state in industrial relations. After the great labor agitations of 1961-1963, the military government which took over in the coup of 1964 proceeded to destroy labor's encroachment into the polity, particularly by targeting its efforts against the unions in the traditional sector which spearheaded the populist labor movement. Unions in the capital-intensive industries appeared to have suffered less damaging effects from the military's initial repression. This, in turn, allowed the workers of this sector to gradually recover their control over the unions during the years of repression. Meanwhile, the traditional sector unions remained largely in the hands of pro-government bosses, and the workers were unable to recuperate their past mobilization capacity.

In analyzing the resurgence of industrial conflict between 1978 and 1980, we find that the generalizations taken from the events of the previous thirty years are also valid for the revival of working-class unrest in the late 1970s. As this chapter shows, political factors continued to have a strong impact on shaping strike patterns. Workers continued to respond to governmental repression of their collective protests through new forms of organization. Led primarily by modern sector workers, strikes continued to be struggles for power between the workers on the side and employers and government on the other.[1]

Even before the metalworkers of the ABC region[2] of the São Paulo metropolitan area disrupted the already uneasy political atmosphere, signs of a new era appeared. The steady erosion of the military regime had become apparent since the elections of 1974 when the government party, *Aliança Renovadora Nacional* (ARENA), suffered parliamentary defeats in the more industrialized states. By 1977 the growing appeal of the opposition party, *Movimento Democrático Brasileiro* (MDB), forced the outgoing president, General Ernesto Geisel, to make use of the *Fifth Institutional Act* which empowered the chief executive to suspend the Congress and to legislate reforms. At this time Geisel, anticipating a possible defeat in the Electoral College of his candidate for presidency, decreed drastic reforms in the composition of the college to assure the succession; he also altered the composition of the Senate by creating a third appointed senator from each state in order to guarantee the next government a majority in the upper house.[3]

The imposition of congressional recess and changes by decree of the structure of presidential elections clearly evidenced the deterioration of the regime's political base and revealed to the country the limits of the Geisel initiated "democratic opening". In addition, these maneuvers by the Geisel government only served to stigmatize the incoming Figueiredo administration.[4]

The workers and the progressive factions within the Church were not the only groups articulating their activities against the autocratic regime. In addition, there was increasing middle class opposition, and by 1977 important segments of the industrial bourgeoisie declared their support for the re-democratization of the political institutions as a necessary requisite for further economic development. Faced with demands for reforms and plagued by growing tensions within the government's supporting alliance, authorities again promised that the new administration of General João Figueiredo would direct the process of restoring democratic institutions.[5]

The calm which pervaded the first months of the Figueiredo government was soon disrupted by the outburst of wildcat strikes in the industrial belt of the city of São Paulo. After nine years of systematic repression, workers stopped the machines in protest against the low wages and high cost of living. These demands embodied not only the discontent with the economic situation of the workers, but, more importantly, they expressed the workers' deep seated opposition to the regime and the deterioration of its legitimacy. By year's end, an estimated 581,150 industrial and service workers had struck. The following two years confirmed the revival of working-class militancy and the appearance of the "new unionism", as 1,424,400 and 662,260 workers struck in 1979 and 1980, respectively.

The strikes of 1978 were evidently a prelude to the more extensive actions of the following years as the strike shapes in Figure 6.1 illustrate. The considerably smaller size of the rectangular figure in comparison to the ones for 1979 and 1980 certainly demonstrates that the characteristics of the strike changed substantially from this initial year. The 1978 shape reflects the first steps in strike activities, through many small strikes, largely of single establishments and of relatively short duration, suggesting the cautious restraint on the part of the workers and progressive labor leaders.

Figure 6.1 National Strike Shapes, 1978-1980

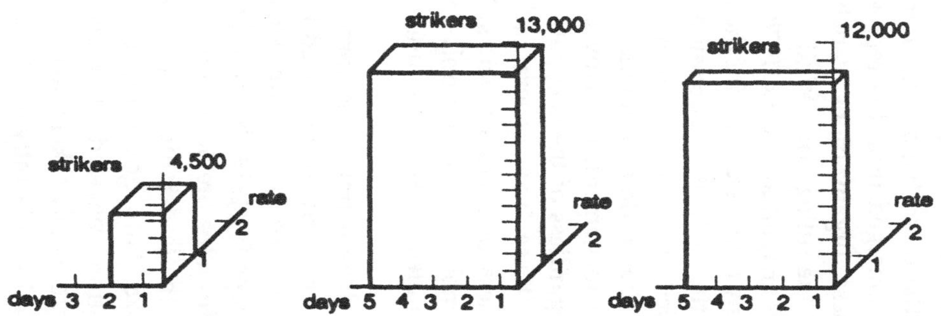

Figure -A: 1978 Figure -B: 1979 Figure -C: 1980

Confronted with this first wave of strike activity after many years of repressed labor discontent, the government and the employers were not prepared to meet an unanticipated challenge of the workers. The ruling elites were faced with a dilemma. They had sustained the corporatist union structure, which congregated workers of broadly defined occupational categories in a single geographically delimited union, because its provisions facilitated controls over the various segments of the working class. On the other hand, under the effects of industrial expansion, these unions emerged from the repressive years as massive, strategically located class organizations capable of waging strong opposition to rulers and the ruling class. While there were laws enough to prosecute workers, the magnitude of the 1978 strikes and the unions' frequent disclaimers of any responsibilities for the seemingly spontaneous work stoppages made the task of suppression impossible. Thus, the authorities were compelled under pressure from the industrialists to turn to the "new generation" labor leaders for mediation between the workers' strike committees and management. In many cases, even in 1979 and 1980, wildcat strikers, regardless of the occupational group, would only accept the mediation of these "new generation" leaders, especially in situations where the strikers' own unions were still controlled by *pelegos*. Consequently, the 1978 mobilizations not only resumed the practice of striking, but also catapulted these "new union" leaders to national prominence.

The strikes of 1979 demonstrated the force and intensity of labor agitation; the total number of strikes decreased from 104, in 1978, to 77, in 1979, while the number of strikers doubled to almost a million workers. As the strike shape for 1979 shows in Figure 6.1-B, the average size of the strike tripled from the previous year because the more militant unions openly assumed the leadership of the major strike movements. After the events of 1978, both government and management were prepared in 1979 to confront renewed strike actions and, in particular, planned to defeat the large metalworkers unions. As a result, the strikes' median duration increased significantly in 1979 as employers, backed by government, became more intransigent, refusing to negotiate with the unions, and determined to break the workers' resistance.

This time a large number of strikes were declared illegal, and the Ministry of Labor intervened in important opposition unions. The strength of the grass-roots organizations, as confirmed in the strikes of the ABC region, was clear when the strikers refused to return to work even after the unions were occupied by military police and their leaders were jailed. Yet the employers were concerned with bringing back into the factories workers who demonstrated a strong spirit of class antagonism and who were reasonably organized inside the plants, for they feared the prospects of introducing the turmoil of the strike actions into the workplace. Because of this, employers' associations began to pressure the government for the release of the deposed union leaders and the lifting of the interventions as a guarantee for a calm resumption of work.

By the end of 1979 workers had scored more political points than their adversaries. Though the economic gains were moderate, the labor movement had tested its strength; other segments of the working class rose to a new militancy, as strikes spread out from the metropolitan areas into the interior. The agitation had succeeded in widening the cracks in the government-bourgeois alliance while mobilizing other sectors of society around the issues of union democracy, the right to strike, and the right to bargain collectively with employers without state interference. The agitation of 1979 also succeeded in changing the stringent wage laws so that union and management could negotiate wage adjustments resulting from the increase in the workers' productivity. This law reform on wage determination was an attempt to introduce very restricted collective bargaining over wages with the expectation that labor unrest would subside.

Quite the contrary, the situation at the beginning of 1980 was one of uneasiness throughout the country, as the metalworkers of the ABC and interior regions of São Paulo launched their wage increase campaign. In late 1979, the unions had begun to prepare for another major conflict. The lessons of past strikes indicated that this year would be a landmark in Brazilian labor opposition. For the metalworkers in the ABC region and several unions in the interior of the state, it was all too clear that their wage increase campaign would be the first test of the "new unionism". For the first time the unions created strike funds, and plans to safeguard the movement in case of another intervention were made by setting up several coordinating committees of workers which would assume, in turn, the leadership of the strikes in case of more repression.

The confrontation between the ABC metalworkers, and the employers and the state lasted 41 days, though most of the other unions involved in this series of strikes returned to work much earlier. The massive use of the military police against the strikers, the imprisonment of their leaders accused of breaking the national security law, and the occupation of the union headquarters reverberated in a decline of strikes throughout the later part of the year. The total number of strikers decreased by two thirds from the 1979 level, even though the average size of the strike was not much reduced and the duration remained the same. As is illustrated in Figure 6.1-C, the strike shape for 1980 maintained the characteristic shape of strikes under autocratic regimes, i.e., large in size, long in duration, and narrow in depth given the low strike rate. This peculiar strike shape is typical of those during more authoritarian governments, as in the clientelistic period and the first years of the military government after 1964. The exception to this pattern is the repressive populism of 1947-1950 which was a period of demobilization resulting from state repression and self-imposed by caution on the part of communist labor leaders who sought to avoid confrontation with the conservative Dutra government.

During the years of 1978 to 1980, strike activities followed a yearly pattern indicative of the growing unrest among the working population. At the beginning, strikes were almost entirely concentrated in the São Paulo metropolitan area, principally in the ABC region of the industrial belt. The strike proneness in this area sheds some light on why the articulation of grass-roots groups was possible, considering the intense associational activities in the proletarian neighborhoods of the region.

But 1979 also was marked by the spread of strikes in the cities of the interior of the state of São Paulo and in the state of Minas Gerais (Table 6.1). Rio de Janeiro remained a weak center of strike activities, probably because of the less active neighborhood associations in highly industrialized areas, the more conservative mentality of the local Church hierarchy, and the general economic slump which had resulted from deindustrialization of the former national capital. On the other hand, the state of Rio Grande do Sul accounted for 10 percent of the industrial strikes in this year, marking the resurgence of its union militancy since the 1964 coup.

Finally, by 1980, strike actions again occurred in all regions of the country. Though the city of São Paulo and its industrial belt continued to lead in the larger proportion of strikes, and the incidence of strikes in the larger cities of the interior increased. Similarly, the stoppages spread to other states, as worker discontent erupted in outer waves of wildcat strikes, especially among the service workers. Of the industrial stoppages, the metalworkers played the predominant role in the agitations. Over the

Table 6.1 - Distribution of Strikes by Geographical Regions, 1978-1980

Region	*1978*	*1979*	*1980*	*Total*
NORTHEAST	---	---	3.1 (1)	.5 (1)
CENTER-SOUTH				
Minas Gerais	2.0 (2)	31.6 (22)	3.1 (1)	12.4 (25)
Rio de Janeiro	---	1.4 (1)	6.3 (2)	1.5 (3)
São Paulo State	1.0 (1)	11.4 (8)	18.8 (6)	7.4 (15)
Metro São Paulo	52.0 (52)	10.0 (7)	9.4 (3)	30.7 (62)
ABCD Region	42.0 (42)	27.1 (19)	21.8 (7)	33.7 (68)
Santos-SP	---	1.4 (1)	3.1 (1)	1.0 (2)
Campinas-SP	2.0 (2)	5.7 (4)	6.3 (2)	4.0 (8)
Vale do Paraiba-SP	---	1.4 (1)	12.5 (4)	2.5 (5)
SOUTH				
Parana & Santa Catarina	---	---	3.1 (1)	.5 (1)
Rio Grande do Sul	1.0 (1)	10.0 (7)	12.5 (4)	5.9 (12)
Total	100 (100)	100 (70)	100 (32)	100 (202)

Note: Absolute number of strikes in parentheses. SP = São Paulo

three-year period, 71.6 percent of the strikes involved workers of all the various branches of the metal work industry. Among the more militant were the automobile and electrical appliance and equipment workers, who each year led the annual round of industrial conflict, both in São Paulo and in other states.

As shown in Table 6.2, approximately 90 percent of the strikers were metalworkers. Of course, this was not unexpected since by then these industries accounted for about 42 percent of the industrial labor force. Within the metalworkers unions, strike experience became widespread during this period, since about 55 percent of all metalworkers had been involved, sometime between 1978 and 1980, in a work stoppage. Only rubber, chemical and construction workers demonstrated any other noticeable levels of unrest, but even these cases never exceeded 2 percent of the total number of workers employed in the respective industries.

Generally speaking in the period between 1978 and 1980, we find that worker participation in strikes peaked in 1979 because of the growing threat of governmental repression. Yet the actions certainly had their impact on the political arena, where opposition groups were hammering out future power relations with the armed forces and the dominant groups in society. In the past, before the 1964 coup, strike movements had involved large numbers of workers when the labor unions contended for political power. To what extent the revival of labor conflict was indeed a touchstone separating the more populist era from a not-yet fully emerged but certainly new and different form of unionism can be found in the type of worker organization underlying the work stoppages of these three years.

The hallmark of the new labor movement was the type of organization which developed among the workers and juxtaposed the organizational ties of the occupational union with the interpersonal networks of the residential community. Further, the nature of the claims being made expressed a greater sense of class self-determination in dealing with the employers and the state.

With respect to the occupational changes evidenced in these strikes, there was a clear shift from the traditional sector occupations which dominated the populist trade union movement (textiles, leathers, ceramics) to the metalworking groups which were less expressive in populist politics of the pre-1964 vintage. As Table 6.3 illustrates, the traditional sector occupations were largely absent from the 1978-1980 agitations. In the few cases for which we have any data, traditional sector

Table 6.2 - Number of Strikes and Strikers as a Percentage of the the Industrial Labor Force in Selected Industries, 1978-1980

Industrial Sector and Industries	*1978*	*1979*	*1980*
TRADITIONAL SECTOR:			
Textiles	5,490 (1.5)	6,000 (1.6)	3,000 (.8)
Leathers	---	---	---
Foods	1,000 (.2)	3,386 (.6)	---
Printing	1,200 (.9)	80 (.0008)	---
Non-Metalic	---	1,150 (.4)	---
INTERMEDIATE SECTOR:			
Rubber	4,300 (7.9)	1,500 (2.7)	---
Paper	---	---	---
MODERN SECTOR:			
Metalworks	391,130 (27.3)	820,620 (55.0)	325,590 (21.0)
Chemical	2,342 (.7)	10,445 (2.9)	7,000 (2.0)
OTHERS			
	488	6,969 (1.7)	---
Total	405,950 (9.7)	954,150 (21,8)	342,080 (7.2)

Note: Percentages in parentheses are the number of strikes as a percentage of the total number of workers employed in the specific industry for the year in establishments employing five or more persons.

strikes were undertaken by grass-roots organizations in all instances, and the rank-and-file based strikes accounted for the larger average number of strikers. This was to be expected, since to a large extent the unions in this sector continued to be in the hands of the pro-government bosses, many of whom assumed control of the unions as a consequence of the interventions in the middle 1960s.

Among the modern sector workers, mainly the metalworkers, strike organizational patterns, as indicated in Table 6.3, were strongly based on union leadership, especially after the 1978 strike wave when the metalworkers unions began to challenge openly the corporatist institutions. In 1978 the majority of the strikes were grass-roots initiated in the form of wildcat actions but always looked to the union leadership for mediation between the workers and their employers. The two largest strikes in this year were union-led and averaged about 127,000 workers. These two large collective actions occurred toward the end of the year. The contrasts between the shapes of the strike patterns for 1978, 1979, and 1980 also reflect this wary behavior on the part of union activists in the first year of confrontations with employers and government. By the end of 1978, and certainly afterward, the union-led strike became the predominant pattern at least among the workers in the metropolitan areas. The new strikes, which arose in other areas of the Center-South, were many times grass-roots based as workers began to revolt against their own complacent union leadership.

As the previous chapter pointed out, the 1978 strikes had their precursors during the darker years of the repression, when working-class struggles occurred only in the confines of the workplace as scattered episodes of work stoppages and slowdowns organized by shop militants. Because of this, in 1978 many of the strikes, especially in the ABC region, were wildcat in appearance, while in essence they had been groomed by the new generations of activists. Their wildcat form was quite likely a tactical option to safeguard the union from possible interventions.[6]

By late 1978, it was apparent that both the government and the employers were concerned over the workers' unrest and the potential threat posed by the large metalworkers unions. Employers began to increase production and to stockpile as a cushion against a new wave of work stoppages. The government, while encouraging collective bargaining, declared its intention of enforcing the labor laws against "illegal" strikes.

Table 6.3 - Average Number of Workers per Strike According to Industrial Sector and Type of Strike Organization, 1978, 1979, 1980

Industrial Sector	*1978*	*1979*	*1980*
TRADITIONAL INDUSTRIES:	1,219 (10)*	4,998 (27)	1,900 (5)
Worker Organizations	1,200 (2)	13,016 (6)	3,500 (1)
Union Organizations	---	2,838 (2)	1,500 (2)
None Mentioned	1,221 (8)	2,948 (19)	1,500 (2)
MODERN INDUSTRIES:	4,809 (92)	18,888 (46)	14,460 (24)
Worker Organizations	1,676 (26)	6,733 (10)	3,003 (3)
Union Organizations	127,000 (2)	41,184 (10)	26,147 (11)
None Mentioned	1,785 (64)	13,761 (26)	3,995 (10)
INTERMEDIATE INDUSTRIES:	2,150 (2)	786 (4)	---
Worker Organizations	---	1,030 (2)	---
Union Organizations	---	---	---
None Mentioned	2,150 (2)	560 (2)	---
ALL INDUSTRIAL STRIKES:	4,510 (104)	13,252 (77)	12,217 (29)
Worker Organizations	1,642 (28)	8,193 (18)	3,127 (4)
Union Organizations	127,000 (2)	34,793 (12)	22,355 (13)
None Mentioned	1,619 (74)	8,828 (47)	1,123 (12)
TOTAL Nº STRIKERS:	405,950	954,150	342,080

* Number of strikes in parentheses.

In light of these developments, the militant unionists began to lay out plans for a more prolonged confrontation. As is apparent from the data in Table 6.3, the number of strikes in the modern sector decreased from 1978 to 1979, while the number of union-led strikes and their average size increased, indicating the change in tactics from wildcat strikes to union-led ones. Furthermore, the intensity of the confrontation with employers and government was also evidenced by the leap in the median strike duration from the previous year. As Table 6.4 indicates, strikes more than doubled in duration, raising significantly the number of man-days lost due to employers' intransigence and workers' resistance. Interestingly, the increase in median duration was not limited either to union-led strikes or to strikes in the modern sector. In fact, both modern sector grass-roots strikes and traditional sector ones increased their duration in the same measure, which suggests the diffusion of a spirit of resistance as class antagonisms became "moral outrage".[7]

During the time that the metalworkers unions in the ABC region of São Paulo assumed the leadership of their strikes, wildcat strikes continued to erupt elsewhere as more workers, encouraged by the events of 1978 and early 1979, joined in the swell which extended to every region of the country and eventually involved 21.8 percent of the industrial workers and an equally large number of service workers. This growth stemmed from the persistence of the grass-root strikes, not only among previously passive modern sector workers, but also among those in the traditional and intermediate industries as well. A good indicator of the strength of these strikes was their median duration. With regards to each sector, modern and traditional, the median duration was four to five days in the traditional sector and six to seven days in the modern sector industries, depending on the type of organization which initiated the strike action (Table 6.4).

As a result of the magnitude of the 1979 strikes, though they did not attain the higher levels of strike activity as in the populist era, fifteen years earlier, the military government and the larger industrialists led by the multinational corporations were determined to turn the tide of working-class protest by breaking the power of the metalworkers unions. After the widespread labor unrest of 1979, the offensive feature of strike activities remained the keynote of class relations during 1980. Viewed from the vantage point of the shape of the strike pattern for this year (Figure 6.1-C), the frequency of work stoppages fell about 50 percent after the long and bitter forty-one day strike of the ABC metalworkers in the

Table 6.4 – Median Duration of Strikes According to Industrial Sector and Type of Strike Organization, 1978, 1979, 1980
(in days)

Industrial Sector and Type of Organization	*1978*	*1979*	*1980*
TRADITIONAL INDUSTRIES:			
Workers Organizations	1	5	3
Union Organization	—	4	1
None Mentioned	1	5	1
MODERN INDUSTRIES:			
Workers Organizations	2	6	6
Union Organization	3	7	6
None Mentioned	2	3	3
ALL INDUSTRIAL STRIKES	2	5	5

beginning of the year. This strike movement was marked by considerable violence, military occupation of the region, government seizure of the unions, and imprisonment of the leaders in an effort to break the workers' resistance. The strikes in this year generally assumed the narrow rectangular shape though slightly smaller in average size, as many other occupational groups refrained from overt collective actions after the forty-one day conflict in the ABC region.

The reduction in strike frequency affected the average size slightly, but left the median duration unaltered. Strikes continued to last about five days because of the determination on the part of the strikers to resist in spite of the heightened risks of repression by the state and reprisals from employers. The level of repression and intensity of the conflict between the workers (this time supported by the Catholic Church and the opposition party) and the employers (under the protection of the government) strongly influenced the 62 percent decline of strikes that year. As a result, the total number of strikers in 1980 fell from 954,150 industrial strikers in 1979 to an estimated 342,080 in 1980 (Table 6.3).

Among the traditional industries, few workers struck in comparison to the 1978 and 1979 (Table 6.2), and the median duration of these actions decreased, even though those initiated by grass-roots organizations were the most enduring among the sector's strikes (Table 6.4). As the disposition of the state to use coercion to control labor unrest became more evident, union-led strikes came to dominate the scene, and grass-roots activities gave way to the better organized union mobilizations.

In 1980, the authorities, pressured by the more conservative military factions, took steps to curb labor unrest through a concerted assault against the first major strikes of the strong metalworkers unions in the ABC. Yet it was clear that governmental repression and employers' intransigence would not satisfactorily provide a long-term solution to the institutional crisis in industrial relations. Confronted by a strong revival of the labor movement with the support of the Catholic Church and with the employers seriously divided over a wide range of political and economic issues, the government groped for appropriate measures to reduce popular discontent, to restore industrial "peace", and to buttress the declining authority of the regime.

The experience of the São Bernardo do Campo metalworkers exemplifies the extent of the political crisis and the transformations which the new unionism had undergone. On April 1, 1980, the day after the

ABC metalworkers began their strike, the Regional Labor Court declared itself incompetent to pass judgment on the legality of the strike.[8] This decision was disconcerting for the government, which expected the movement to be declared illegal as a first step to its suppression and intervention in the unions. The court's decision not only delayed any repressive actions, but also signaled the growing problems which the government was having in controlling the intermediate institutions in charge of handling popular unrest.

Two weeks later and after much pressure, the court reversed its decision, but the reversal further showed the tensions between the government and the judicial system inasmuch as the new ruling was approved by a narrow vote of fifteen to eleven, indicating the resistance by some judges to providing legal justification for the government's repression of the strikers[9] and to using the judiciary as an instrument for the arbitrary policies of the regime.[10] The two-week setback for the government's plans to force the strikers back to work was sufficient time to allow the strike to spread from São Bernardo to other cities in the interior of São Paulo. Then, the union leaders refused to abide by the new court ruling and questioned the legitimacy of the judicial procedures. A few days after the declaration of the strike's illegality, the Minister of Labor ordered interventions in the ABC unions, and the following day the deposed union leaders were arrested.

In order to secure the termination of strike activities, military police occupied the union headquarters, prohibited the use of the local stadiums for assemblies by the more than 200,000 striking workers, and assigned a large contingent of the military police to virtually occupy the region. With the growing agitation and confrontation in the city squares between workers and police contributing to the radicalization of the movement, the auxiliary bishop of the ABC region offered the Church's support for the strikers and placed at their disposal the use of the cathedral and parish churches for union strike meetings.[11]

The institutional support offered by the Church reflected the deep roots which the new unionism had within the ecclesiastic base communities (CEBs) of the region. In fact, since late 1979 the São Bernardo do Campo and Diadema activists had discussed the need to consolidate a new form of organization of the rank-and-file through articulation of the workplace with the neighborhood associations in the working-class districts. Therefore, even before the salary campaign which preceded the 1980 strike action, the union had organized a 400 member committee to go into the neighborhoods and to approach the workers in the SABs and CEBs to begin the formation of union nuclei. The activists held meetings with the community groups to discuss the need to mobilize the workers through the neighborhood associations and to debate with the workers and their families the importance of the union's demands. These discussions centered around a union drafted booklet which explained the various claims and a slide show focusing on the political education of the working-class family. The objective of the union's effort to enlist the support of the rank-and-file through the neighborhood groups was to forge a tie between the worker's commitment to the unions and his commitment to his community and family, while developing an alternative form of maintaining the workers mobilized during periods of government control of the unions.[12] These efforts at grass-roots organizing resulted in an elaborate web of intermediate worker networks created initially for the 1979 strike and extended into the community during the strike actions of 1980.[13]

The possibility of looking to the community associations as a haven for the unions was facilitated by the relatively large number of neighborhood groups found in the ABC region. At the time of the 1980 strike in São Bernardo do Campo alone, there were about forty *Sociedades Amigos de Bairro* (SABs) functioning in the city. They had already formed their municipal federation of SABs which was presided over by a former metal worker. In addition, the city had over sixty parish churches, each of which claimed a number of *Comunidades Eclesiais de Base* (CEBs).[14]

The union's outreach to the community could not, however, be restricted to the city of São Bernardo, the union's jurisdiction, since a large number of the metalworkers commuted from the surrounding cities which make up the industrial belt of the São Paulo metropolitan area. If the mobilization through the neighborhoods was to prove effective as a buttress to the union structure, it was necessary to extend the efforts beyond the municipality to other areas such as Diadema, São Caetano do Sul, Santo André, Maua, and São Paulo. Thus, the union sent organizers into the proletarian neighborhoods of the other cities where large contingents of metalworkers lived. This extension of the union beyond the immediate São Bernardo area is illustrated by the fact that during the strike it established strike fund central distribution posts, not only at the São Bernardo cathedral, but also in other regions of the metropolitan area of São Paulo. It was through these centers that basic foodstuffs and strike bulletins were distributed daily to workers, and regional coordination was made for meetings of strikers coming from the local neighborhood associations.[15]

The effect of appealing to the community associations was demonstrated during the strike, when the workers were able to hold out for thirty days after the intervention of the union in spite of intense police repression. Needless to say, the support of the Catholic Church in providing meeting facilities and offering its network of church organizations to gather contributions for the strike fund proved invaluable in maintaining solidarity among the workers in the face of the repression.

The reliance on the community associations as alternative bases of organization also facilitated the gauging of the strikers' morale. The neighborhood and regional meetings permitted the substitute strike leaders to have a more accurate measure of the willingness of the workers to continue to hold out. This was extremely important, given the difficulty of canvassing the workers because of the repression. As a result, the ties to the associations provided the besieged militants with a reliable link to the rank-and-file for obtaining information as to the level of commitment and the material needs of the strikers.[16]

The development of close ties with the community associations reflected not only a tactical concern on the part of the workers' leaders in their struggle against the employers and the government, but more importantly, it represented a deliberate effort to create solid grass-roots organizations capable of penetrating the factories and wresting from management some of the prerogatives related to the control of the work process. From the start of the strike activities, the militant unions advanced pro-active claims which openly challenged many of the bases upon which the corporatist state rested, especially with respect to its control over the labor organizations. The union opposition advocated two radical changes in the area of industrial relations: (1) the institutionalization of rank-and-file factory commissions and union representation in the procedures for dealing with workplace decision-making, and (2) the union's right to collectively bargain with employers and, if necessary, to strike with a minimum of state interference.

The concept of collective bargaining had always been accepted, though it was little practiced in industrial relations, especially after 1964, because of the state's intent in averting class conflicts through the use of its preponderate powers in labor affairs. Workers had often been denied the right to negotiate with management who, in turn, looked to the state for safeguards against "uncooperative" workers and "subversives". Consequently, as a result of the abuses by both employers and government over the years since 1964, the demands for greater control over decisions affecting the workers, both as an occupational group and at the factory, became an intrinsic feature of the demands made in the late 1970s.

The São Bernardo do Campo metalworkers union led the revival of class conflict and spearheaded the drive for fundamental reforms in the institutions mediating the relations between capital and labor. Of the several demands made by metalworkers over the three year period of strike actions, the more important were those calling for the re-democratization of the system of industrial relations and, in a broader sense, the re-democratization of the political system.

The cornerstone of the changes in employer-worker relations was the factory commission.[17] Some form of workplace union representation had long existed as a form of organizing nuclei of workers in the factories, but their importance increased after 1964 when the unions virtually ceased being a form of channeling workers' demands. As a result of the repression against union activism, workers looked to the workplace as the focal point of articulation in defense of more immediate interests. In many factories informal groups were formed to deal with management. The beginnings of these groups are diverse: some arose from soccer clubs organized in the factories;[18] others evolved as older, more respected workers became intermediaries between the rank-and-file and the managers;[19] still others began in the factory safety committees which employers were obliged by law to create;[20] some arose from among workers active in neighborhood and community associations;[21] and finally, others were formed by workers active in union activities.

The work of the commissions was centered primarily around the day-to-day problems of the workplace and supervision of the compliance with the labor laws and contracts. The commissions were instrumental in offering the rank-and-file the support necessary to win union elections and thereby to gradually ease out pro-government union bosses. Often they negotiated informally with management, and by 1978 they were sufficiently prepared to assume the leadership of many of the wildcat strikes.[22]

The new unionism viewed the factory commissions as an indispensable aspect of weakening the authoritarian union structure and changing the absolutist mentality of the employers. Their presence in the major establishments of São Paulo and Minas Gerais led many employers to adopt measures to deal with the commissions. While a large majority of the employers continued to resist the recognition of the commissions, some such as Ford do Brasil[23] and Embraer, the Brazilian aircraft industry,[24] agreed to their institutionalization. Others, such as Volkswagen do Brasil, attempted to create its own version of the commissions under employer control.[25]

A second demand by the unions aimed at weakening the employers' authority and strengthening rank-and-file organization was the legal recognition of the union representative (*delegado sindical*) within the factory. The figure of the *delegado sindical* was not new to the labor movement. In the past, union delegates were chosen from among the more stable workers in order to better resist management's intimidations. To a very large extent, it seems that grass-roots organizing was dependent on the union delegate and his clandestine activities since labor unions in Brazil never had legal access to the factories prior to 1988.[26] The demand for the legal recognition of the union delegate was aimed at institutionalizing existing union practices and providing a formal link between the factory commissions and the union.

Essential to bridging the call for sweeping reforms of the institutions and the "bread and butter" demands of workers was the government's falsification of the inflation indices in 1973 and the unions' subsequent clamor for restitution of lost wages due to government corruption. Since the adulteration of the inflation rates affected large segments of the salaried population, this issue served to arouse what Barrington Moore has called "moral outrage" among the workers, both in industry and in the various branches of services.

The main claims for a rapid re-democratization of the institutions quickly pervaded the other movements as they struck a common cord not only among the industrial workers, but among the service workers as well. By 1979, under the initiative of the metalworkers of the metropolitan area of São Paulo plans were being made for a national meeting of union representatives to elaborate a project of basic reforms in the labor laws in response to government's plan for superficial changes. *The Basic Principles of the Labor Code* was elaborated by forty union leaders and thirty labor attorneys and served as a starting point in the discussion with the over one-hundred union leaders participating in the meeting. The document was based on the demands advocated in past years at the annual congresses of various occupational categories such as the metalworkers, carpenters, printers, bank workers, doctors, architects, journalists and others.[27]

The main proposals for reforming the labor laws centered on excluding the state from interference in labor affairs, on providing for shop floor representation of the workers through union delegates and factory commissions, and on returning to the labor courts greater power of arbitration. In addition, the unionists' project would deny the state the power to interfere in union elections or registration of unions and would gradually abolish the union tax. These last proposals would mean the virtual demise of the support mechanisms of union bossism which had flourished under government patronage. The three pronged attack against the corporatist state explicit in the unionists' document was also aimed at reducing the prerogatives of management by calling for a greater role by the workers in the decision-making process at the workplace and for institutionalization of worker representation.[28] Even though none of the demands had materialized by 1981, from the very nature and tone of the unionists' proposal, it was evident that the labor movement now represented a clear rupture with the past dependence on the state.

Several circumstances conjoined to restrain the hard-line factions within the ruling elites from reverting to the severe repression of the previous decade. The strong upsurge of the labor movement got under way with the open support of the Catholic Church and in the midst of the deterioration of the regime's social base. The revival of working-class militancy and the strength of the labor unions seem to have left the government unprepared to deal with the emergence of labor as a power contender. The government's pretense of re-democratizing the political institutions permitted not only rising expectations as to the pace of the process, but also opened up sufficient space in the public debate to allow for a rapid consolidation of a definite anti-regime consciousness among many sectors of the population. The vacillations by the newly inaugurated Figueiredo administration in dealing with the first great upsurge of strikes in 1978, and its apparent abandonment of the repressive policies relentlessly applied against the working class by many earlier military presidencies, signaled the opportunity for many segments of the industrial and service workers to advance their claims not only against employers and the inequalities of the distribution of the benefits of economic development, but also against the autocratic state.

As the government attempted to incorporate the challenge of the new union movement into its long-range plans for gradual democratization of some institutions, events dictated major changes in the political process. In the first place, this new generation of union leaders assumed the more militant stance among the opposition groups in Brazilian society and tacitly took as their banner the demands for an immediate return to democracy while other opposition factions advocated compromise and gradual re-democratization. Second, unlike other opposition groups, the labor leaders were the first major segment of society, other than the university students, to openly defy the regime through mass mobilizations and paralyzations of strategic economic activities. Until the strikes of 1978-1979, the opposition party and the Church had largely conducted their efforts to accelerate the process of re-democratization through negotiations with political representatives of the regime. The outburst of the strikes definitely altered the political scene.

For the first time since the beginning of the "democratic opening" under the Geisel government, a contender made use of direct actions to press for its demands. This had three major effects on the dynamic of re-democratization. First, the open confrontation of the workers with the state forced other opposition groups, particularly the Church and the politicians of the opposition party, the *Movimento Democrático Brasileiro* (MDB), to take a stand with regard to the legitimacy of collective actions that confront the state. While the government frequently warned that labor unrest could endanger the "democratic opening," labor unions continued to strike at the autocratic regime through their struggles for better economic conditions. By 1980, during the long metalworkers' strike in the ABC, both the Church and the MDB were compelled to openly support the "illegal" strikes.

The second impact of the working class strikes on the political process was the introduction of the unions as serious contenders in the political arena. Until this time, the process of bargaining a new "social contract" with the military government had been restricted to the politicians, the Church and the more progressive industrialists. The emergence of the "new unionism" not only introduced into the domain of the political opposition working-class claims to be attained by the liberalization of the institutions, but unsettled the tacit alliance between Church, politicians and industrialists.

Third, the demands for political rights for unions to conduct their affairs in the interests of the workers, i.e. free from interference by the state and the right to a larger share of the fruits of industrialization, had as a consequence the challenging of the government's timetable for the complete return to elected civilian rule. Through agitation and demands for higher wages, shop stewards, factory commissions, and union autonomy workers were anticipating institutional changes which were not included in the designs of the regime's political planners and the goals of many of the opposition politicians. The constant questioning of the authorities' gradualist approach to re-democratization brought to the opposition camp a new source of political initiative, and broadened the forms of action beyond the parliamentary negotiations to which the opposition party had largely restricted itself.

The military governments after 1964 created the conditions for a substantial change in the nature and composition of labor militancy. The relentless repression of union activism and the imposition of pro-government labor leaders precluded the possibility of mobilizing workers through the unions. The suppression of organized labor strike activities did not extinguish the workers' desires to associate and to collectively act on behalf of their interests. Thus, during the repressive years while unions carried out their judicial and welfare functions, committed workers attempted to use other legal forms of organizing to resolve their problems. A large number of them became especially active in the neighborhood improvement and religious associations which proliferated in the proletarian districts of the large cities. These organizations attracted workers seeking a place in which they could engage in collective efforts for economic betterment and express their criticisms of the regime.

Under the auspices of the Catholic Church and other civil institutions, workers active in the neighborhood groups established contacts with intellectuals who were invited to provide assistance in the committees' endeavors to pressure local governments for improvements. As a result, this interaction contributed to the development of organizing skills and political consciousness of the importance of grass-roots organization, an aspect of the labor movement which was largely absent prior to 1964.

Despite the presence of pro-government union bosses in the union directorships, worker activists, drawn largely from the ranks of the skilled and younger workers, turned to the task of winning back the unions. Gradually they managed to be elected to union posts and to assume leadership of the organization as in the case of São Bernardo do Campo, São Caetano, Santo André and Osasco; or to form coalitions with moderate bosses as was the case of the São Paulo metalworkers union and several of the unions in the interior of the state.[29]

The increased repression, specifically after the strike by the metalworkers in Osasco in 1968, obliged the new leaders to follow a more cautious approach to labor problems in order to avoid the risk of intervention and possible imprisonment. The impossibility of the unions' leading the struggles for economic betterment forced labor activists to focus their energies on the development of strong workplace organizations which could press for demands inside the factories and build worker solidarity through extra-union associations. The strategy led to the consolidation of shop floor and factory committees which became substitutes for the unions in representing workers' interests within the factories. This capacity to mobilize the workers was evidenced by workplace skirmishes which characterized industrial conflicts from 1969-1977.

When the long awaited opportunity to renew strike activities came in 1978, the efforts of the new leadership produced consequences few of them had expected. The first metalworkers' strikes in the ABC ignited a wave of working-class protest not seen since the pre-coup period. The government, facing pressure for democratic reforms and disunited internally over the appropriate response to labor unrest, adopted a vacillating stand toward the "new" labor movement. Employers mounted resistance to the workers' demands and refused to accept their insistence to negotiate collective agreements.

A new working-class reality was reflected in the magnitude of the labor agitation. The intense and pervasive repression of the dictatorship had obscured the political potential of an urban working class which had grown extraordinarily over the fourteen years of military rule. The marginalization of the unions from the state and the re-enforcement of corporatist controls contributed to the development of a grass-roots based working-class movement independent of the state apparatus.

The workers emerged from their strike experiences more conscious of the interdependence of attaining economic improvements and the democratization of industrial relations. Their varied associational activities provided the necessary innovative experiences to create strong grass-roots ties among the workers and helped shape their critical conceptions of themselves and their relationship with those who ruled them, employers and authorities. The overlapping of class interests expressed through the opposition unions and interpersonal ties among the networks of workers formed in community groups and workplace activities served as the bases for the solidarity underlying the new unionism and the workers' militance. Their new views of society, influenced by the authoritarianism of employers and the state, were expressed in unprecedented demands for fundamental reforms and opposition to the regime. The strikes led by the "new union" movement nurtured a new mode of working-class consciousness which, in contrast to the populist-paternalism of the past, was characterized by clear sentiments of exclusion from the socially produced wealth of the country and the need to place several of management's prerogatives under worker control. The "new unionism," in representing working-class interests in society, also held a distrust in politicians, espousing independence from political patronage and clientelism while expressing its sharp opposition to the autocratic state.

Notes

1. Some case studies which analyze the strikes of 1978, 1979 and 1980 from diverse theoretical and ideological perspectives are: Lais Abramo, "O Resgate da Dignidade (A Greve de 1978 em São Bernardo)," (São Paulo: Master's thesis, Universidade de São Paulo, 1986); Ricardo Antunes, *A Rebeldia do Trabalho: O Confronto Operário no ABC Paulista - As Greves de 1978/80* (São Paulo: Editora Ensaio-UNICAMP, 1988); Hercules Corrêa, *O ABC de 1980* (São Paulo: Civilização Brasileira, 1980); Hamilton José Barreto Faria, "A Experiência Operária dos Anos de Resistência: A Oposição Sindical Metalúrgica de São Paulo e a Dinamica do Movimento Operário: 1964-1978," (Master's thesis, Pontíficia Universidade Católica de São Paulo, 1986); John Humphrey, *Fazendo o 'Milagre': Controle Capitalista e Luta Operário na Industria Automobilistica Brasileira* (Petropolis: Editora Vozes, 1982); Octavio Ianni, *O ABC da Classe Operária* (São Paulo: Editora Huicitec, 1980); Amneris Maroni, *A Estrategia da Recusa: Analise das Greves de Maio 1978* (São Paulo: Brasiliense Editora, 1982); Luis Flavio Rainha, *Os Peões do Grande ABC* (Petropolis: Editora Vozes, 1980); Luis Flavio Rainha and Osvaldo Martines Bargas, *São Bernardo: As Lutas Operárias e Sindicais dos Metalurgicos 1977-1979* (São Paulo: Editora FC, Associação Beneficiente e Cultural dos Metalurgicos de São Bernardo e Diadema, 1983); Eder Sader, *Quando Novos Personagens Entraram em Cena: Experiências e Lutas dos Trabalhadores da Grande São Paulo 1970-1980* (Rio

de Janeiro: Editora Paz e Terra, 1988); Eder Sader and Paulo Sandroni, "Lutas Operárias e Tacticas Burguesas: 1978-1980," *Cadernos da PUC*, 7 (1981).

2. The ABC region of the metropolitan area of São Paulo consists primarily of the cities of Santo André, São Bernardo do Campo, São Caetano do Sul and Diadema, but is often used to refer to the industrial belt surrounding the city of São Paulo,

3. Robert Wesson and David V. Fleischer, *Brazil in Transition* (New York: Praeger Publishers, 1983), pp. 106-108.

4. Ibid.

5. Ibid., p. 108.

6. Francisco C. Weffort makes a similar argument in his analysis of the metal workers' strikes of Contagem and Osasco in 1968 when he compares the strategy of a union-led strike versus a wildcat strike at the time of governmental repression. See Francisco C. Weffort, *Participação e Conflito Industrial: Contagem e Osasco, 1968* (São Paulo: Cadernos de CEBRAP, No. 5, 1972).

7. Barrington Moore has observed how various aspects of people's lack of trust in governing elites and discontent over perceived unwarranted injustices coalesce into a psychological disposition to challenge authority. This he has coined as "moral outrage", see Barrington Moore, Jr., *Injustice: The Social Bases of Obedience and Revolt* (White Plains: M.E. Sharpe, 1978).

8. Octavio Ianni, *O ABC da Classe Operária* (São Paulo: Editora Huicitec, 1980), p. 17.

9. *41 Dias de Resistência e Luta*, (São Paulo: Instituto de Planejamento Regional e Urbano da Pontifícia Universidade Católica de São Paulo, 1980), p. 11.

10. This observation about the previous use of the judicial system to legitimize repressive policies is noted by Cid José Sitrangulo, *Conteúdo dos Dissidios Coletivos de Trabalho* (São Paulo: Edições LTR, 1978).

11. "Puebla Começa pelo ABC," *Folhetim Republica de São Bernardo, Folha de São Paulo*, 11 May 11, 1980, no. 173, p. 6.

12. *41 Dias de Resistência e Luta* (São Paulo: Instituto de Planejamento Regional e Urbano da Pontifícia Universidade Católica de São Paulo, 1980), pp. 21-23.

13. Maria Helena Moreira Alves, *Estado e Oposição no Brasil (1964-1984)* (Petropolis: Editora Vozes, 1984), p. 260.

14. "De Bairro em Bairro," *Folhetim - Republica de São Bernardo, Folha de São Paulo,* 11 May 1980, no. 173, p. 10.

15. *41 Dias de Resistência e Luta,* p. 29.

16. Ibid., pp. 28-29.

17. Some studies on the rise of factory worker commissions in Brazil, are Iram Jacome Rodrigues, *Comissão de Fábrica e Trabalhadores na Industria* (São Paulo: Editora Cortez and FASE, 1990); José Carlos Aguiar Brito, *A Tomada da Ford: O Nascimento de um Sindicato Livre* (Petropolis: Editora Vozes, 1983); Oposição Sindical Metalurgica (São Paulo), *Comissão de Fábrica: Uma Forma de Organização Operária* (Petropolis: Editora Vozes, 1981).

18. Interview with an executive of Chrysler do Brasil, São Paulo, Brazil, 1 November 1979.

19. Interview General Electric do Brasil sales manager, Belo Horizonte, Minas Gerais, 22 December 1979.

20. Interview with skilled worker of EMBRAER, São José dos Campos, 12 February 1980.

21. Interview with workers of General Motors do Brasil, São José dos Campos, June 1980 to February 1981.

22. Oposição Sindical Metalurgica (São Paulo), *Comissão de Fábrica: Uma Forma de Organização Operária* (Petropolis: Editora Vozes, 1981).

23. Roque Aparecido da Silva, "A Comissão da Ford," *Revista de Cultura e Política,* 8 (June 1982): 125-138.

24. *Acordo Coletivo de Trabalho - 1983* (São José dos Campos: Sindicato dos Metalurgicos de São José dos Campos, 1983), p. 7.

25. "Documento: A Representação dos Empregados da Volkswagen do Brasil S/A," *Revista de Cultura e Política,* 3 (November-January, 1981): 95-102.

26. The new Constitution of 1988 granted workers the right to elect their workplace representatives, though its provisions does not state that these representatives need be union delegates.

27. "Sindicatos Propõem Codigo de Trabalho," *Folha de São Paulo,* 25 July 1979, p. 20.

28. John Humphrey, *Controle Capitalista e Luta Operária na Industria Automobilistica Brasileira* (Petropolis: Editora Vozes-Cebrap, 1982), p. 201.

29. "Comunidades Eclesiais de Base do Brasil," *Estudos do Conselho Nacional dos Bispos do Brasil,* no. 23 (São Paulo: Edições Paulinas, 1979), p. 91.

7

Labor Unrest in the 1980s

The strike actions that ended the decade of the 1970s not only marked a resurgence of labor as a political force in Brazilian society but also contributed decisively to deteriorating the legitimacy of the military dictatorship. Mid-March of 1979 saw a second year of worker unrest as hundreds of thousands of metalworkers in the ABC region of the São Paulo metropolitan area struck for better wages. Military police repression of pickets and demonstrators was violent throughout the region while metalworkers in other cities in the interior of the state joined the strike wave that was accompanied by police repression in these localities.

By the eleventh day of the strike movement the Ministry of Labor declared federal intervention in the striking unions, canceled the union leaders' mandates, and imposed appointees to head the unions and bring the strike actions to an end. The striking workers refused to return to work, unless their leaders were reinstated. The region was occupied by large contingents of the military police riot squads. Union headquarters were closed down in the expectation, on the part of both government and employers, that the strike could be broken. In spite of government repression, the workers continued to look to the deposed leaders as their representatives in the negotiations with employers. After fifteen days of striking, the workers returned to their jobs through a negotiated truce and by May 15th federal interventions were lifted and the union leaders reinstated.

A year later, on March 30, 1980, a third round of major confrontations began between the metalworkers and their employers and the government. This time, the strike actions were planned to coordinate worker contention in the ABC region and other major industrial cities of the interior. Once again hundreds of thousands of metalworkers stopped their machines in the industrial heartland of Brazil, openly supported by the Catholic Church and hundreds of working-class community organizations. This time the workers' determination exceeded that of previous years as the strike lasted forty-one days. Once again the government resorted to the use of military police supported by military air surveillance to repress pickets and demonstrators.

Soon union headquarters were seized and labor leaders were imprisoned and accused of acts threatening national security by the *Departamento de Ordem Política Social* (DOPS), the national political police. The showdown between the workers and the dictatorship focused on the large São Bernardo metallurgical workers union. The city was occupied by military police, workers' meetings were prohibited and leaders imprisoned while the workers refused to return to work. Public manifestations in other cities, especially in the capital of São Paulo, demonstrated increasing support among the population for the striking metalworkers and gave evidence of widespread opposition to the military regime.

On May 1, thirty-three days after the strike began, Labor Day celebrations in São Bernardo do Campo were forbidden by police authorities. The city's bishop celebrated a Labor Day mass that was attended by striking workers and prominent national opposition politicians, intellectuals, and clergymen. By the end of the ceremony the city cathedral was surrounded by approximately 100,000 demonstrators whose massive presence forced police to retreat from the city's central square as the multitude, waving national flags and singing the national anthem while under close surveillance by military helicopters, made its way over two kilometers to the municipal stadium where the metalworkers once again assembled to vote for the continuation of the strike.

In light of the continued repression of workers' demonstrations, on May 9, imprisoned labor leaders went on a hunger strike to pressure for the resumption of negotiations with employers and an end to police violence. Two days later, a mass meeting of striking workers in São Bernardo decided to suspend the movement and call for an end to the hunger strike of their imprisoned leaders. The metalworkers returned to their factories intent on obtaining the liberation of their leaders and the lifting of federal intervention in the unions. These goals were finally achieved by May 25th, fifty-six days after the beginning of the conflict.

A decade later, on March 8, 1989, General Leonidas Pires Gonçalves, Minister of the Army of the government of President José Sarney, in an interview after a meeting with the other military ministers, expressed his disbelief that the forthcoming general strike called by the national labor organizations, the *Central Unica dos Trabalhadores* (CUT) and the *Central Geral dos Trabalhadores* (CGT), would reach the dimensions expected by the labor leaders. Nevertheless, according to the general, the military ministers were alert to the situation and would enforce the constitution. He denied that the armed forces had been mobilized for the general strike and pointedly recommended prudence on the part of striking workers.

The following day, the Minister of Justice sent out a telex to all the state secretaries of public security instructing them to adopt preventive measures to maintain order during the general strike planned for the 14th and 15th of March. In his message the minister reminded the state governors and public security secretaries of their responsibilities and of the seriousness of the situation, claiming that the general strike would not contribute to the solution of any problem and most likely would aggravate the national situation if normalcy were not maintained. The central government would not permit the strike movement to become violent. For this reason, the justice minister was requesting that the states mobilize their contingents of military police for eventual action.

Representatives of employers' associations called for rigorous governmental response to the "illegal and politically motivated" general strike that threatened the stability of the process of re-democratization and the plans of the economic elites to bring the hyperinflation under control. National newspapers were prompt to classify the general strike as a failure. As was to be expected, government and employers' estimates claimed weak support for the mass action while union leaders acclaimed moderate success. One national newspaper estimated that there were approximately six million strikers among the industries in sixteen major cities. In addition, public transport in the capital cities largely stopped for the two day mobilization, as did other public services. Regardless of the battle over statistics, the March 1989 general strike, in light of its size and national dimensions, marked a new phase in working-class mobilization that was significantly different from those beleaguered days at the beginning of the decade when police repression characterized governmental response to labor unrest.

During the ten years since the 1978-1980 strikes there has been a significant increase in the level of strike activity in Brazilian society. As can be seen from the data depicted in Figure 7.1, the number of strikes remained relatively small during the first years of the Figueiredo government, when strike actions rarely rose above the 1978-1979 levels. Beginning in 1983, labor unrest began its upward climb as strike actions almost tripled in number in comparison to the previous five years. In this respect, the 1983 annual strike rate[1] rose to 1.86 from the .74 rate of the year before. From this time on labor disputes set a pattern of yearly increases for the rest of the decade.

As Figure 7.1 illustrates, strike activity took an upward turn toward the end of the last military government and then made its most impressive increases in the final years of the civilian government of President Sarney when 3,164 strike actions occurred in 1989 as compared to the 144 strikes in 1980. Needless to say, one of the causes of the increased strike activity can be attributed to the process of re-democratization under the *Nova Republica*[2] when there was certainly greater tolerance for worker protest than in the years under military rule. In spite of the low percentage of unionization, estimated at around 20 percent between 1986 and 1988,[3] labor unrest grew as a response of workers to the rising inflation and as a result of unions' increased organizational capacity to mobilize protest against government economic policies.

One indicator of the rise of the organizational potential of the Brazilian working class was the increase in the number of labor unions during the last two decades, which accompanied the accelerated industrialization and the concomitant growth of the urban working class. Of the non-agricultural workers' unions, 42.7 percent were founded after 1960, raising the number of labor unions from 1,670 before 1960 to 2,916 in 1988. Of this 42.7 percent, the large majority, 69 percent, were created between 1971 and 1988. Breaking down these broad percentages to specific types of labor unions, we find that 40.5 percent of the industrial workers' unions were founded in the period after 1960. Similarly, among the service workers, 46 percent of the bank workers' unions and 65 percent of teacher, health and other service workers' unions were founded after 1960. Thus, during the years since 1960, there has been a significant expansion of working-class union organizations throughout the country, many of which would rise in militancy in the 1980s and contribute to the emergence of a genuinely national labor movement.

Figure 7.1 Strike Activity in Brazil, 1978-1989

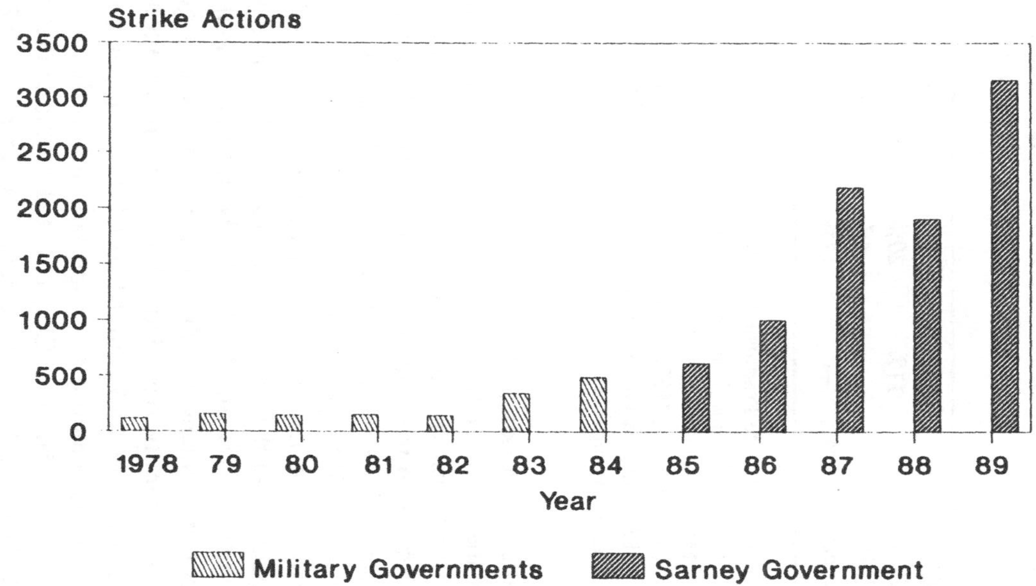

Source: S. Sandoval, *"Strikes in Brazil"* (1978-1979); NEPP-UNICAMP (1980-1987); SIGREV-Ministerio do Trabalho (1988-89).

Table 7.1
Distribution of Unions by National Confederation Affiliation and Type of Company - 1989 (percentages)

National Entity	*State Enterprises*	*National Enterprises*	*Multinational Enterprises*
CUT	*89%*	*51%*	*56%*
CGT	*11%*	*20%*	*18%*
USI	*—*	*4%*	*—*
Independentes	*—*	*14%*	*18%*

Source: Centro de Pesquisa de Relações no Trabalho, as cited in "Trunfo Sindical: Pesquisa Mostra CUT Mais Forte e CGT Menor" *VEJA*, 22, no. 44 (November 8, 1989), adapted from table on page 108. Study based on sample of 157 of the 500 largest enterprises.

This evolution in working-class organization is further demonstrated by the rise in the 1980s of the first national labor organizations with widespread union bases. The first steps in forming such an organization took place in 1981 with the convening of the national conference of the working classes (*Conferência Nacional das Classes Trabalhadoras - CONCLAT*) which in 1983 gave way over ideological cleavages to the founding of two major national confederations: the *Central Única dos Trabalhadores* (CUT) and the *Central Geral dos Trabalhadores* (CGT).[4] Since then, the activities of CUT and CGT have been fundamental in forging a national labor movement. Of the two, employers and government authorities have generally regarded CUT as the more aggressive and strike-prone. A study[5] in 1989 found that CUT was faster growing and more strategically based among the important unions than was the CGT. This was shown by the fact that CUT counted on the affiliation of 1,400 unions while CGT had 1,340. In addition, in a sample of 157 of the 500 major companies in the Brazilian economy, CUT counted on the support of 65.3 percent of the unions in these companies as opposed to only 16.3 percent for the CGT. This strategic importance of the pro-CUT unions is evidenced by the data in Table 7.1.

Among all three types of enterprises studied (public owned, national private owned and multinationals), the influence of the CUT far outweighted that of the CGT inasmuch as the large majority of the unions in each category were pro-CUT. Thus it is possible to conclude that CUT has succeeded over the years in attracting the support not only of a larger number of unions but in particular those that represent workers in the largest companies in the economy. On the other hand, CGT congregated almost a similar number of unions, but the data suggest that its presence among the workers of the largest corporations was more restricted than that of its rival. In spite of the differences in ideology and numerical strength of each organization, the fact remains that over the past ten years the labor movement has built up national organizations with the capacity of mobilizing and supporting workers in thousands of stoppages, three strike waves, and four general strikes, which together account for the significant increase in working-class protest during the 1980s.

Changes in the Composition of Strike Activity

In the forty-five years of strike history with which this book is concerned, the first major change in the working-class composition of strike activity occurred during the late 1950s when the workers of the traditional sector industries gradually declined in strike activities while there was a concomitant rise in the militance of the workers employed in the modern sector industries, as we discussed in Chapter 3. This inversion of the sectorial composition came to mark strike mobilization through the decades that followed.

During the decade of the 1980s there emerged another major change in the sectorial composition of strikes with the rise of militancy among the service sector workers. Even though the terciary sector has accounted for just over 60 percent of the labor force in the formal sector, the strike militancy of this segment of the working class has only emerged in the mid-1980s. From the information on the strike rates per year,[6] we find that the service workers only equalled the industrial workers in strike rate by 1987: the industrial workers had a strike rate of 11.86, the service workers' strike rate was 10.35 and the overall national strike rate was 10.76 (Table 7.2, Column B).

If the service workers strike rate grew slowly over the decade, the

Table 7.2 - Strike Rates and Man-Days Lost in the Industrial and Service Sectors, 1980-1987

Year and Sector	*(A) Number of Strikes*	*(B) Strike Rate*	*(C) Percent of Work Force*	*(D) Percent Man-Days Lost*	*(E) Total Number of Man-Days Lost*	*(F) Man-Days Lost Per Worker*	*(G) Proportion Strikers to Workers*
1980	144	.72	100.0	100.0	24 225 695	1.21	6.1
INDUSTRY	62	.92	33.7	47.0	11 499 659	1.71	8.3
SERVICES	82	.66	62.1	50.0	12 233 136	.99	4.0
1981	150	.77	100.0	100.0	6 545 003	.33	4.9
INDUSTRY	48	.78	31.9	24.0	1 609 056	.26	2.4
SERVICES	102	.82	63.9	58.0	3 850 769	.31	5.1
1982	144	.74	100.0	100.0	6 967 215	.35	3.8
INDUSTRY	77	1.28	30.9	20.0	1 405 825	.23	2.5
SERVICES	67	.53	64.6	78.0	5 471 653	.43	4.6
1983	347	1.85	100.0	100.0	28 407 743	1.52	9.9
INDUSTRY	199	3.71	28.5	5.0	1 571 255	.29	4.5
SERVICES	148	1.20	65.8	94.0	26 825 850	2.18	13.7
1984	492	2.54	100.0	100.0	13 311 365	.68	8.4
INDUSTRY	335	6.03	28.6	21.0	2 795 780	.50	8.7
SERVICES	157	1.23	65.8	78.0	10 480 133	.82	9.0
1985	619	3.28	100.0	100.0	90 637 512	4.81	38.2
INDUSTRY	269	4.28	33.3	23.0	21 138 232	3.36	30.7
SERVICES	350	2.83	65.5	76.0	68 908 500	5.58	38.3
1986	1004	5.05	100.0	100.0	49 525 864	2.49	21.9
INDUSTRY	579	8.49	34.3	16.0	8 274 391	1.21	14.9
SERVICES	425	3.31	64.5	83.0	41 246 292	3.21	26.0
1987	2193	10.76	100.0	100.0	132 445 423	6.49	45.7
INDUSTRY	832	11.86	34.4	9.0	12 285 119	1.75	23.3
SERVICES	1361	10.34	64.5	90.0	120 089 918	9.12	57.9

Source: Nucleo de Estudos de Políticas Públicas-NEPP, *Relatório Sobre a Situação Social do Pais, 1986*; *Relatório Sobre a Situação Social do Pais, 1987*. Percentages and rates calculated.

importance of these mobilizations in terms of strike strength was extraordinary after 1982. This accelerated rise in militancy can be measured by three indicators: (1) the percentage distribution between the two sectors of the total number of man-days lost in strikes in comparison to the percentage distribution of the work force between both sectors; (2) the proportion of man-days lost in each sector in relation to the total number of workers employed in each sector as a measure of the number of man-days lost per worker; (3) the proportion of strikers in each sector in relation to the total number of workers employed in each sector as a measure of worker mobilization by sector.

In examining the data, comparing the percentage distributions of man-days lost and of the work force between the service and industrial sectors (Table 7.2, Columns C and D), we find that the service workers as of 1982 began to account for higher proportions of man-days lost than their corresponding participation in the work force. In 1982, 78 percent of the man-days lost were due to service sector strikes while service workers accounted for 64.4 percent of the formal work force. Since then, this has become a tendency and many times exceeding the 1982 proportions as in the case of 1987 when 90 percent of the man-days lost were among service workers while they continued to represent only 64.5 percent of the work force. Thus the 1980s has been a decade in which service workers strikes have proportionately outnumbered industrial workers in the number of man-days lost.

Another indicator of the growing strength of service workers' strikes is the yearly rates of man-days lost in each sector (Table 7.2, Column F). Since 1982, service workers' strikes have rated a higher proportion of days lost per worker employed in the sector than has been the case for the industrial sector. More important is the fact that this rate has grown rapidly over the years to the point that, by 1987, the service sector had a rate of 9.12 compared to 1.75 in the industrial sector. In other words, service workers had about 5.2 times more man-days lost per worker in that year than did industrial workers. In this respect, the service workers' strikes were more intense in terms of duration than were industrial strikes.

Finally, in analyzing the proportion between the number of strikers and the number of workers employed for each sector as a measure of worker mobilization, we find that in 1981 service workers strikes were mobilizing about 5.1 percent of the sectorial work force as compared to 2.4 percent in industry and civil construction. Since then, the service workers have been able to mobilize a larger contingency of strikers in proportion to their size in the sector than have the industrial workers. Though both sectors have grown in proportionate mobilization, the highest rates are to be found among the service workers as in 1989 when about 57.9 percent of the service workers went out on strike compared to only 23.3 percent of industrial and construction workers (Table 7.2, Column G).

Judging from the data of these three indicators of strike activity, we find that the service workers have come to overshadow their industrial comrades in terms of strike intensity and consequently have emerged as an important force not only in the labor relations field but also in the political arena as well.

In spite of the rapid growth of the service sector in strike activity, a closer look at the strike data reveals that service sector militancy has been almost exclusively restricted to a few occupational categories whose structural employment characteristics allow for their greater capacity for organizing and mobilizing workers. These categories have been by and large civil servants, public school teachers and health workers, bank workers, and city transport workers. A major determining characteristic of these categories is the monopolistic or oligopolistic employer structure: one or few employers for a large number of workers within each branch. Thus organization and mobilization of workers are facilitated inasmuch as workers confront a few employers and similiar working conditions in each branch of activity. For this reason, the rise of service sector militancy has been mainly based in those branches of the service sector, either public or private owned, which are dominated by monopolies and oligopolies: bank workers organize and mobilize against the major national banks; bus drivers, subway employees and suburban railway workers strike against a few city transport companies; civil servants, public school teachers and health care professionals mobilize against federal, state and municipal authorities. On the other hand, workers employed in the highly decentralized and heterogeneous branches of the service sector, such as in commerce and business or the personal service activities, have been noticeably absent in their participation in strikes.

The data on Table 7.3 show the changes in strike rates of the main occupational groups which have participated in strikes for the period between 1985 and 1989. Among public sector workers, educational and health workers were by far the most strike prone over the period, attaining the highest strike rates in 1987 with 139.5 and 70.9 respectively,

Table 7.3
Strike Rates for Public and Private Sector and Selected Occupational Categories, 1985-1989

	1985	1986	1987	1989
Sector:				
Public Sector	5.6	6.7	24.9	31.2
Private Sector	2.6	4.6	8.0	10.6
Occupation:				
Metal Workers	23.5	53.3	48.3	n
Chemical Workers	6.4	6.4	10.1	n
Food Workers	n	n	6.7	n
Construction	2.6	4.8	12.5	n
Civil Service	1.7	2.0	9.5	n
School Teachers	30.5	33.6	139.5	n
Health Care Workers	n	n	70.9	n
Bank Workers	n	n	5.6	n
City Bus Drivers	4.8	6.3	13.7	n
Commerce Workers	n	n	5.4	n

Source: Strike data for 1985-1987 see NEPP, 1989; strike data for 1989 see Ministerio do Trabalho-SIGREV, 1990.
(n) Strike data by occupational categories not available for 1988 and 1989.

much higher than any other occupational groups either in the private or public sectors. Workers employed in public administration were much less strike prone in comparison to their co-workers in education and health.

Among the private sector workers there was little change in the ranking of occupational categories with respect to their strike rates. In industry, the metalworkers, chemical workers and construction workers continued to dominate the strike movement in the decade, while workers in the traditional industries remained much less active. Bank workers and urban transit workers have risen in their militancy as indicated by the growing strike rates up to 1987, thus contributing to the emergence of service worker militancy in the 1980s.

If among the service workers as a whole, strike activity was found primarily among a few branches of the sector, the data show that even among these workers the bulk of strike efforts is found among those workers employed in the public sector, as evidenced by the rapidly growing strike rates of the public sector as compared to the private sector (Table 7.3). By 1989 the public sector had a strike rate of 31.2 compared to 10.6 for the private sector. Over the years between 1960 and 1970, the growth of the role of the public sector in Brazilian society was a keynote to the type of economic development espoused by the military regime. The presence of the state through its direct administration or indirectly through its public enterprises came to play a pivotal role in the economic life of the country. In terms of employment of the work force, the public sector represented by the federal, state, municipal governments and the public enterprises came to employ, in 1982, 18.3 percent of the workers of the formal sector, a percentage which increased to 20.5 percent in 1985. In the same period, the public sector accounted for 59.3 percent of the jobs generated in the formal economy.[7] Thus by the middle of the decade the public sector not only accounted for approximately 20 percent of the work force in the formal sector but also demonstrated significant vitality in generating new jobs in the economy.

As a result, we find that in this decade the workers in the sector entered the political arena as new and important actors in the labor movement. Viewed from the perspective of their strike activities, the rise of the public sector workers militance is vividly illustrated in Figure 7.2 in which strike actions are differentiated by public and private sectors. As depicted, the private sector contributed the bulk of the strike actions throughout the period. Between 1978 and 1984, during the last military government, public workers had a much lower number of strike actions than those in the private sector. In 1985, during the first year of the Sarney government, the public sector workers began their upward tendency in strike activity and marked the take-off point in 1987 when public sector worker strikes were 38.2 percent of all labor disputes. Since then, the public sector has come to represent a large proportion of collective actions in each year, though the private sector still accounts for the majority of worker mobilizations.[8]

In looking at the differences between the two sectors, as in the case of 1989, we find that 36.7 percent of the strikes occurred among the public sector workers and 63 percent in the private sector and .3 percent of the strikes involved both public and private sectores. As Figure 7.2 shows, there are important differences in the variation of strike frequencies between the two sectors pointing to differences in the forces

Figure 7.2 Annual Public and Private Sector Strikes, 1978-1989

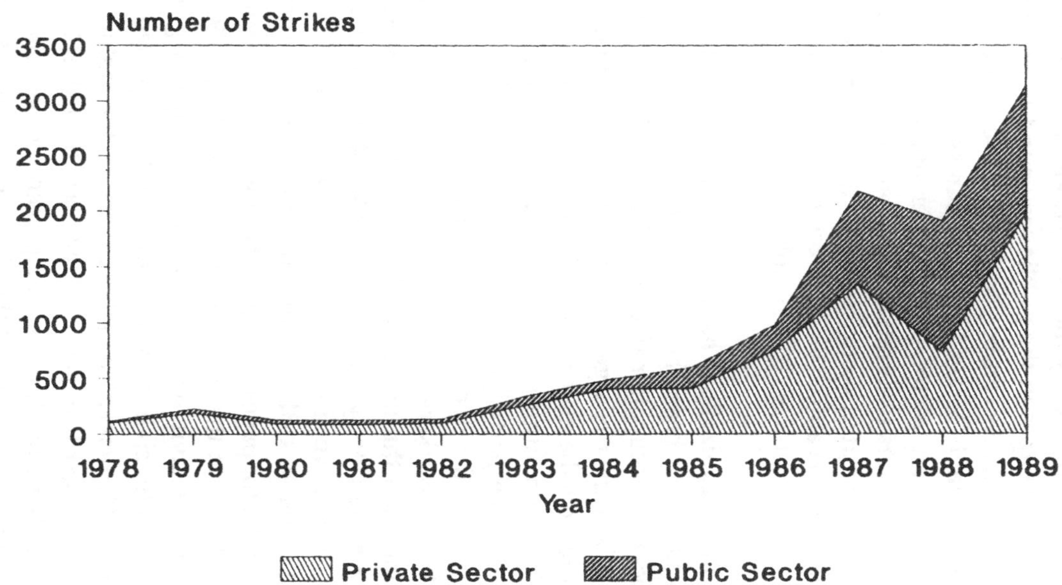

Source: S. Sandoval, *"Strikes in Brazil"* (1978-1979); NEPP-UNICAMP (1980-1987); SIGREV-Ministerio do Trabalho (1988-89).

influencing sectorial strike behavior. Even though this chapter will not analyze in depth these forces, the aggregate strike data available allow us to observe some relevant features of public sector strikes.

In comparing strike activity in the public and private sectors, let us return to the shapes formed by the three strike dimensions.[9] Figure 7.3 illustrates the strike shapes in the public sector and in the private sector between 1986 and 1989. As can be seen from these figures, public sector strikes were considerably larger in their volumes than were the private sector ones. The private sector had a larger number of strikes, but in terms of strike rate, average duration and average size, the public sector strikes were by far greater, contributing to the larger volume of strike activity among civil servants. This can be visualized from the larger size of the strike shape volumes in the public sector as compared to the private sector.

Civil servants organizations have been more successful in mobilizing workers than has often been the case for the private sector, in general, except for the few occupational categories mentioned above. In this respect, we see how the upsurge of a strong government employee strike movement represents the major change in strike composition in the 1980s and whose effects on future labor mobilization is undeniable. This is readily seen from the participation of the public service workers in the strike waves and in the general strikes of the 1980s as well as in the pressures that these workers exerted on the national congress to legalize civil service unionism through provisions in the new 1988 Constitution.

Examining more closely the data in Table 7.4 on the composition of public sector strikes, we find that the state government civil servants were the most prone to strike activity in 1989, not only indicated by the frequency of work stoppages in which these workers accounted for 40.3 percent of the strikes in the sector as well as mobilizing 49.4 percent of the total number of civil servant strikers. The high degree of strike activity among state civil servants was to be expected since they represent about 60.2 percent of all workers in the public sector.[10] In second place, with regards to strike activity, are the federal civil servants who in spite of only accounting for 24.3 percent of the strikes, succeeded in mobilizing about 33.2 percent of the civil servants that struck that year, or approximately one and a half times their proportion in the public sector work force. Finally, the municipal workers were the less militant in spite of the fact that 34.7 percent of the strikes were among municipal workers. Municipal employees accounted for only 12.3 percent of the

Figure 7.3 Public Sector and Private Sector Strike Shapes, 1986, 1987, 1989

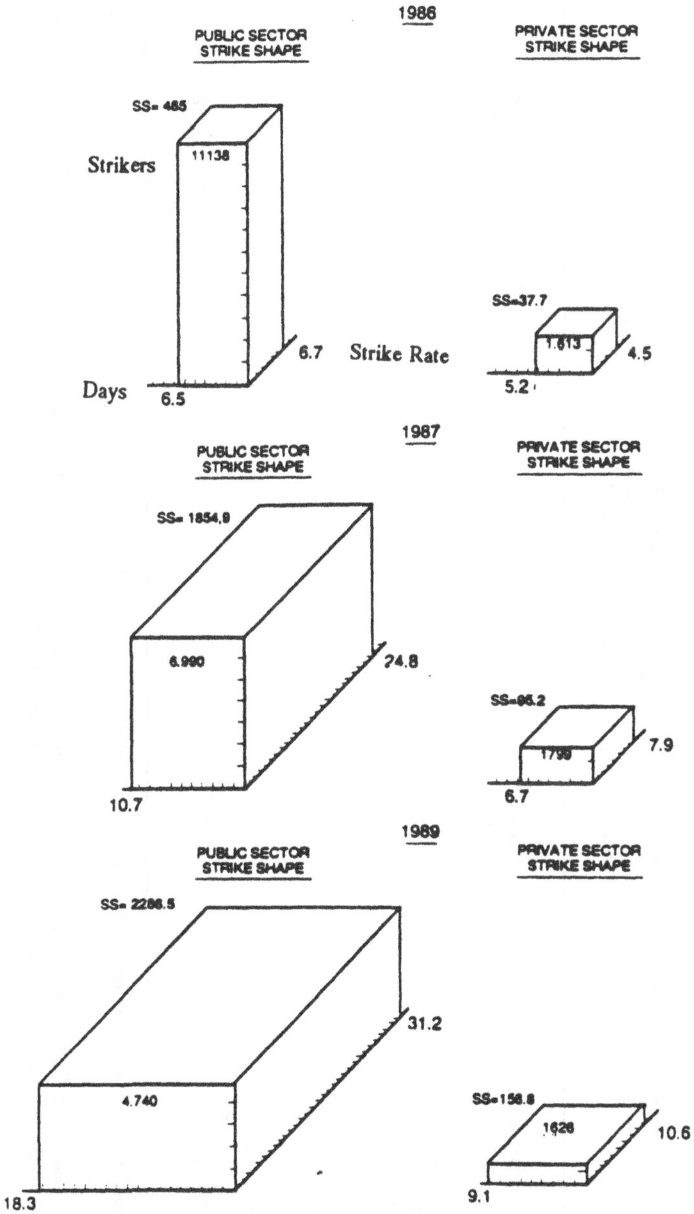

Table 7.4 - Strike Dimensions for Public Sector Strikes, 1989

	Municipal Workers	*State Workers*	*Federal Workers*	*Federal Enterprises*	*Others (a)*	*Total*
Number of Strikes	401 34.7%	464 40.3%	184 15.9%	97 8.4%	8 .7%	1154 100%
Percentage of Workers on Strike	12.3%	49.4%	22.9%	10.3%	2.1%	100%
Average Duration (days)	12.5	17.0	19.5	10.7	15.4	15.3
Average Number of Strikers per Strike	1703	5895	6892	5885	14,797	4790

(a) These are joint strikes involving various branches of the public sector.

Source: Data for Table 7.4 based on Rosane Maia, "As Greves em 1989: Os Trabalhadores na Corda-Bamba da Hiperinflação." (Brasilia: Ministerio do Trabalho, Texto de Discussão nº 22, February, 1990), Table 7, p. 23.

strikers in the sector in comparison to the fact that they comprise 22 percent of the public employees. This lower number of strikers but larger number of stoppages is indicative of a segment of civil servants very much dispersed among a large number of local government units which makes regional and national organizational efforts more difficult.

On the other hand those civil servants employed in the more centralized and larger regional governments, such as the state or federal governments, have better conditions for more effective organizing and collective action by larger numbers of workers. This is certainly the case with regards to the federal employees in which there are a smaller number of strikes but proportionately the largest average number of strikers per stoppage. Similarly is the case of the state public workers who also mobilized a large contingency of strikers in proportion to their work force and had the largest number of strikes because, in part, of the larger number of state governments.

In looking at average duration of public sector strikes (Table 7.4) we find that federal government workers' strikes have the longest duration, of approximately 19.5 days, highest for any group, closely followed by the state workers' strikes of seventeen days duration and finally the municipal workers that averaged about 12.5 days. Judging from the relatively longer average duration of public sector strikes in comparison to the private sector, especially in the case of federal and state employees' strikes, it is evident that the government is a more intransigent employer in confronting strike negotiations than are the capitalists in the private sector, in as much as public sector workers are obliged to stay out on strike for longer periods of time. This is clear when we compare the significantly longer durations of state and federal employees strikes of seventeen days and 19.5 days, respectively, and the much shorter duration of 10.7 days for the federal enterprise workers' strikes. The fact that the public coorporation strikes' average duration is almost half that of the federal and state government workers' strikes suggests that the state owned enterprises are more prone to enter into dispute resolution negotiations with their employees because of market and other economic pressures, thus resulting in earlier strike terminations. In fact in 1989, the average duration of these enterprise strikes was more similar to the average duration of the private sector strikes than to the other types of public sector strikes (Table 7.5).

In general, the data show that state government workers tend to be more strike active given the long duration of the stoppages, the average

Table 7.5 - Strike Dimensions for Public Sector and Private Sector Strikes, 1989

Strike Dimensions	*Private Sector*	*Public Sector*	*Joint [a] Sectors*	*No Information*	*Total*
Number of Strikes	1987 62.8%	1154 36.5%	11 .4%	12 .4%	3164 100%
Average Number of Strikers per Strike	1626	4790	b	219	3179
Average Duration in days	9.1	15.3	6.8	11.8	11.3
Man-Days Lost	34,166.7	109,353.7	b	24.1	146,695.3

[a] Including the General Strike of 1989.

[b] The data on the number of strikers from the original table suggest some distortions given the underestimation of the number of strikers in the General Strike of this year. Consequently the indicators calculated with the data on strikers are probably inaccurate.

Source: Data for Table 7.5 based on Rosane Maia, "As Greves em 1989: Os trabalhadores na Corda Bamba da Hiperinflacão." (Brasilia: Ministerio do Trabalho, Texto de Discussão nº 22, February, 1990) Table 6, p. 22.

size of each strike and the high frequency of strike actions. Federal employees are second in strike strength with the municipal strikes considerably less intense than either the state or federal ones. From these trends in civil servant militancy, certainly this segment of the working class will continue to exert its influence on the labor movement whether through its strike actions or through political and organizational pressures as public employees unions become more active in the large national labor organizations such as in the CUT.[11]

The Evolution of the Strength of National Strike Activity

The year-to-year variation in the national patterns of strike actions clearly reflect the political and economic factors which characterized the transition from dictatorship to civilian rule.[12] In examining the strike shapes for each year in the decade one finds that between 1980 and 1984 there was in fact a gradual decline in the volume of strike activity when considering not only the number of work stoppages but also the average strike size and duration. In terms of strike frequency, the number of strikes remained the same between 1980 and 1982, as noted above, increasing significantly for the years 1983 and 1984 as indicated by the respective strike rates.

Yet with respect to the size of strike actions, there was definitely a sharp decline in the number of workers striking each year. In 1980 the average number of strikers per stoppage was 9,012, but by 1984 this number had fallen to 2,946. In part the decrease in the average size of the strike can be attributed to the increased number of strikes in 1983 and 1984, even though the falling size also occurred in 1981 and 1982. The decline in strike strength can also be noted in the significantly yearly decrease in the average duration from 7.4 days in 1980 to 3.9 days in 1984. This shortening of the strike duration further contributed to the reduction of the volumes of the strike shapes for each year.

Two patterns of strike activity can be identified, through the strike shapes, in the years of the Figueiredo government. The first one characterized the years 1980, 1981, 1982 when strike activity was restricted to a few strike actions most likely due to governmental controls and a lower mobilization capacity of workers organizations under the military government. Strikes in these years typically involved large numbers of workers per strike from among the better organized and

Figure 7.4 National Strike Shapes, 1980-1989

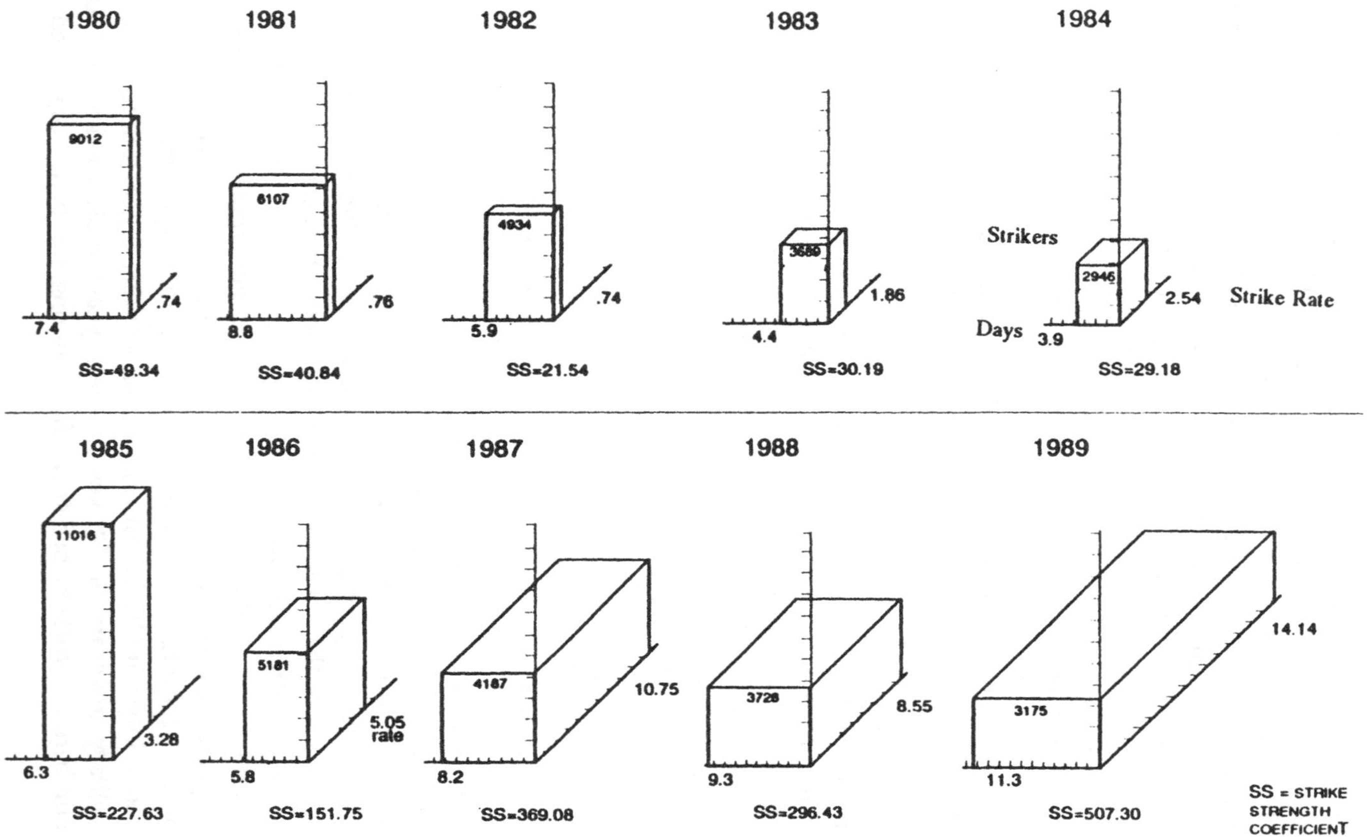

employed in the larger enterprises. These work stoppages were marked by a longer average duration which reflects not only the capacity of these workers to mobilize but also resist against the intransigence of employers and the pressures of the autocratic authorities. This pattern characteristic of strike activity in periods of greater governmental intolerance for working-class mobilization, is depicted by the slim tall rectangular strike shape illustrated in Figure 7.4 for the years 1980, 1981 and 1982 and is similar to other strike shapes found in previous periods of increased government repression of strike actions. One can observe that over these three years, the annual strike shapes do not alter their basic form but gradually decreased in volume. This decrease in the volume represents a decline in the strength of strike activity under the last military government.

The year of 1983 marked the beginning of an important change in the patterns of strike activity which continued through the rest of the decade. Even though the strength of strike actions continued to decline as seen by the decrease in the volume of the strike shapes in 1983 and 1984, there was certainly an increase in the strike rates three and four times greater than for the 1980-1982 period. But this increased number of mobilizations does not offset the fact that the average size and duration of the strike decreased significantly from the 1980 levels.

Despite this decline, the changes in the strike dimensions represent a second type of strike pattern characterized by a shape that forms wider based rectangles in contrast to the ones found in the autocratic periods. These broader based shapes reflect the spread of strike activity in geographical terms as well as to other segments of the working class in addition to those already active in previous years. This tendency is repeated in the 1984 strike shape, though there is again a decline in the overall volume of the rectangle (see Figure 7.4).

If one takes the combination of the three dimensions of strike actions as an indicator of the strength of strike activity for each year,[13] we find that between 1980 and 1984, strike strength declined from a coefficient of 49.34 in 1980 to 29.18 in 1984. This represents a decrease in the intensity of strikes actions in spite of the fact that there was indeed an important increase in the number of work stoppages which most likely meant an introduction of new workers to the experiences of labor disputes. Between 1980 and 1984, this mixed variation of the strike dimensions points to an overall decline in the strength of strike activities characteristic of the Figueiredo years.

In fact the resurgence in labor militancy, after the memorable years of 1978-1980, only occurred in 1985, the first year of the civilian government, when labor unrest attained a major increase in all of the three dimensions of strike activity, as shown in the 1985 strike shape figure. At this time, strikes not only became more frequent with the strike rate rising to 3.28 over the 1984 rate of 2.54, but, in addition, strike duration increased from 3.9 days in 1984 to 6.3 days while the average size of strike actions rose almost four times that of the previous year, from 2,946 in 1984 to 11,016 in 1985. The significance of the changes in strike activity can best be visualized in the comparison of the shapes for these years. When considering the strength of strike actions, as represented by the volume of the strike shape, one finds that 1985 was a year in which strike intensity surpassed all other years since 1978: in 1985 the strike strength coefficient was 227.63 as compared to 49.34 in 1980 and 29.18 in 1984. Thus 1985 can be defined as a strike wave year.[14]

After the 1985 strike wave, 1986 was a year in which work stoppages again increased in frequency but decreased in both average size and duration. In comparison to the previous year, the strength of strike activity in 1986 showed a decline whereby the strike strength coefficient went from 227.63 in 1985 to 151.75 in 1986. This is easily seen in the reduced size of the volume of the strike shape for 1986 (Figure 7.4). Certainly one factor that led to a decline in strike activity was the reduction of the inflation rate from the 235.11 percent in 1985 to 65.03 percent in 1986, with the introduction of the economic program, *Plano Cruzado*. Though strike strength on an average was lower than in 1985, in fact, strike activity accelerated through the year as inflation rose. Since the strike shapes are averages for the year, changes within the period are not readily apparent. In this respect, it is worth noting that the decline in the overall strike shape in 1986 only represented a prelude to greater strike activity in 1987 as strike actions gained momentum through the year.

1987 witnessed the second major strike wave in the decade after the 1985 one. The annual strike rate more than doubled from the previous year and reached a historical new height. Similarly, strike duration returned to an average of 8.2 days, reminiscent of the 1978-1980 period, as employers were more resistant to negotiation. At the same time, the average number of participants per strike declined slightly from the 1985 size, suggesting that more workers in smaller establishments entered the ranks of strikers protesting the then record annual inflation rate of 415.83

percent. This marked increase in strike activity is illustrated in the doubling of the strike shape volume over the 1986 year and its increase by 1.6 times the level of strike strength of the previous 1985 strike wave.

The recurrence of another strike wave two years after the 1985 wave is indicative of the increasing capacity of worker mobilization as attested to by the high number of work stoppages. In this regard, more workers became involved in labor disputes motivated by the uncontrolled inflation spiral, demonstrating their increased resistance to employers by holding out for longer periods of time. Thus the strike wave of 1987 marked a new trend in strike activity represented by the significant change in the strike shape from the previous years. From this year until the end of the decade, yearly strike activity was characterized by a greater number of strike events with a lower average number of participants but a longer duration, as opposed to the prior pattern which was dominated by the larger average number of participants per strike and proportionately fewer work stoppages.

While the tall, short based strike shape has been characteristic of strike activity in years of greater government intolerance, the shorter, broad based strike shape has been more typical of periods in which there has been less government interference and repression, allowing for an increase in strike actions among a broader range of workers and establishment sizes. In addition, the strike wave of 1987 not only represented an upsurge of labor discontent expressing its conjunctural protest against deteriorating economic conditions, but also established a new phase in the labor movement when work stoppages reached a new plateau in scope and strength.

The 1987 strike wave established a new level of strike activity over the previous years, but as generally happens in years following strike waves, 1988 was one of less intense strike activity represented by a reduction in strike strength as compared to the levels of the strike wave of 1987. Nevertheless, the 1988 strike shape volume remained larger than in other years, even when compared to the 1985 strike wave. In this respect, we find that each strike wave ushered in successively higher levels of strike activity throughout the decade.

In 1988, in spite of the inflation rate reaching record heights (1037.62 percent for the year), strike activity did not reach the levels of the year before. In fact the 1988 strike rate and average number of strikers slightly decreased from 1987 while duration only slightly increased. Consequently, the combination of this year's strike dimensions resulted in a strike strength coefficient of 296.43, a decline from the 1987 one of 369.08, but certainly higher than any other year.

The final year of the Sarney government, 1989, was marked by yet another wave of work stoppages which significantly expanded the levels of strike activity. This third strike wave in the decade was the working-class' response to the hyperinflation which gripped the society, threatening economic chaos to the working man. Labor disputes increased almost twofold from the previous year (1988) and almost 1.5 times from the prior strike wave year of 1987. While average duration increased to 11.3 days, larger than at any other time for national strike averages, the average number of strikers per stoppage decreased slightly from before. This new peak in labor unrest can be visualized in the change in the volume of the strike shape of 1989 compared to the previous ones. The volume represents a strike strength coefficient of 507.30; 1.7 times greater than the previous year; 1.37 times greater than the 1987 strike wave year; 2.2 times greater than the 1985 strike wave and 10.28 times greater than the strike activity in 1978-1980, at the time of the *abertura política* (the political opening).

This pattern of increasing strike activity through a series of strike waves can also be seen in another indicator: the annual numbers of man-days lost in strikes. As depicted in Figure 7.5, there are almost identical patterns in the fluctuations of strike strength coefficients and the yearly number of man-days lost throughout the decade. This similarity was to be expected inasmuch as strike wave years also had disproportionate increases in man-days lost. Thus each year in which strike strength peaked corresponds to a rise in man-days lost. Similarly, in those years between strike waves, when strike strength fell, the number of man-days lost also fell in the same proportion. The only year in which strike strength does not correspond to the number of man-days lost was in 1983 when man-days lost increased but the strike strength coefficient remained as low as in previous years. This lack of correlation between the two measures can be attributed to the fact that the man-days lost indicator is strongly affected by those strikes which are large in size and long in duration as in 1983 when a large number of the man-days lost was due to a few strikes, such as the 38-day strike of 240,000 federal employees, and not the result of an expansion of strike actions. Thus the data lead us to conclude that 1983 can not be characterized as a strike wave because of its small number of strike actions. Since the strike strength coefficient takes into account not only strike size and strike

Figure 7.5 Strike Strengths and Total Man-Days Lost, 1980-1989

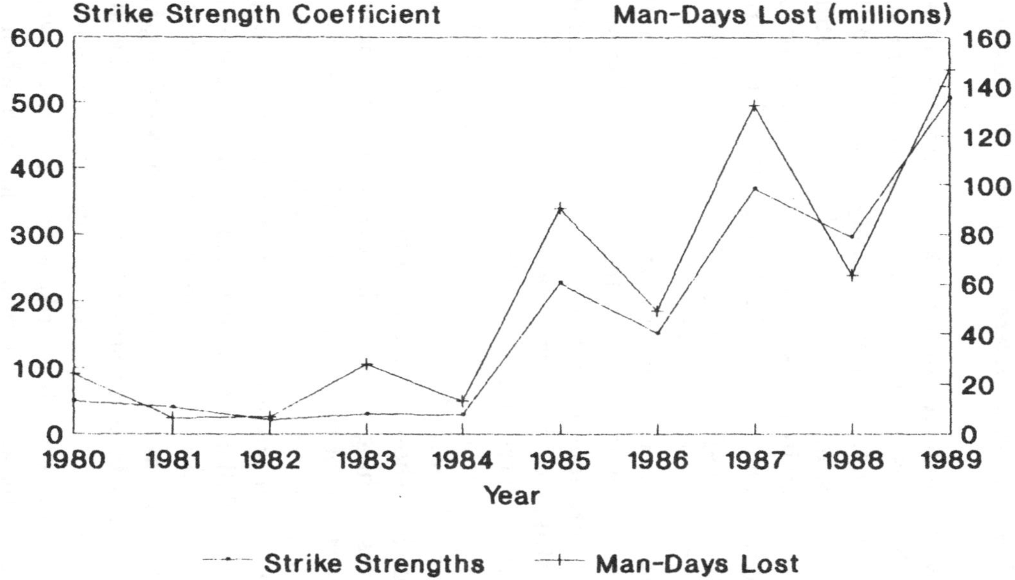

Source: Data on man-days lost: NEPP-UNICAMP (1980-1987); SIGREV-Ministerio do Trabalho (1988-1989).

duration, as in the man-days lost indicator, but also strike frequency, the coefficient is a more accurate indicator of strike activity and of strike waves as in the case of 1985, 1987 and 1989.

The Economic Determinants of Strike Activity

In reviewing the decade of the 1980s, one important feature of strike activity which stands out is the continuous growth in strike strength throughout the period. While many analysts have noted the increasing frequency of strikes, none have observed the fact that strike activity in fact grew punctuated by periodic strike waves, which shot strike activity to increasingly higher levels. The importance of the strike waves in pushing strike levels up was clearly seen in the year-to-year variation of the strike shapes where some years stood out above the rest in terms of their increased strike dimensions. 1980, 1985, 1987, and 1989 not only accounted for major increases in their volume of strike activities in comparison to previous years but also marked the years in the decade from which strike activity rose to new heights in strike intensity. This zig-zag pattern of increasing strike strength over the 1980s can best be illustrated by Figure 7.6 which depicts the evolution of strike activity in terms of the coefficients of strike strength in relation to annual inflation rates. As the chart shows, strike activity in fact evolved through cycles of strike waves pushing strike levels upward in each succeeding phase.

The importance of strike waves in understanding the evolution of strike activity in the 1980s can also be seen in analyzing the relationship of strike activity to inflation over the period. Even though a relation between rising inflation rates and increased strike actions is evident, in fact workers' responses to constantly increasing inflation was not as direct a relationship as one might imagine. In examining Figure 7.7, we find few anomalies between strike frequencies and the inflation curve which point to a more complex relationship between inflation and worker protest, such as in 1986 when strike actions increased even though the inflation rate decreased significantly, or in 1988 when strike actions decreased when inflation took another of its yearly leaps, and yet again in 1987 when strikes increased at a much higher rate than would be comparably expected, judging from the inflation for that year. In general, inflation was undoubtedly an important determinant of labor unrest, but the pattern of strike activity also illustrates the complexity of explaining

Figure 7.6 Annual Strike Strengths and Inflation Rates, 1980-1989

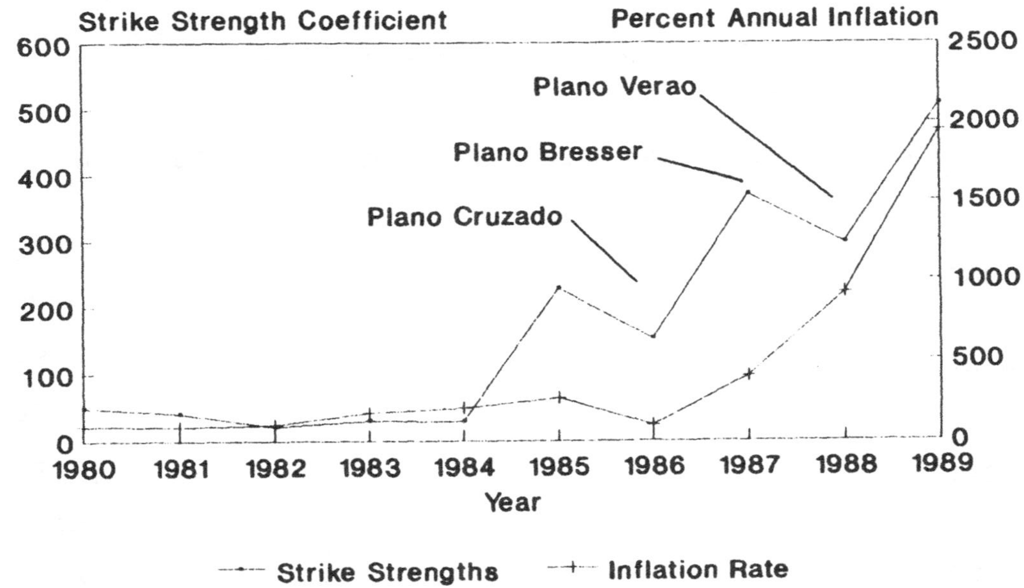

Source: Inflation data: FIPE-USP; Strike data: NEPP-UNICAMP and SIGREV-MTb. Coef=Strike Duration x Size/1000 x Rate.

Figure 7.7 Annual Strike Activity and Inflation Rates, 1980-1989

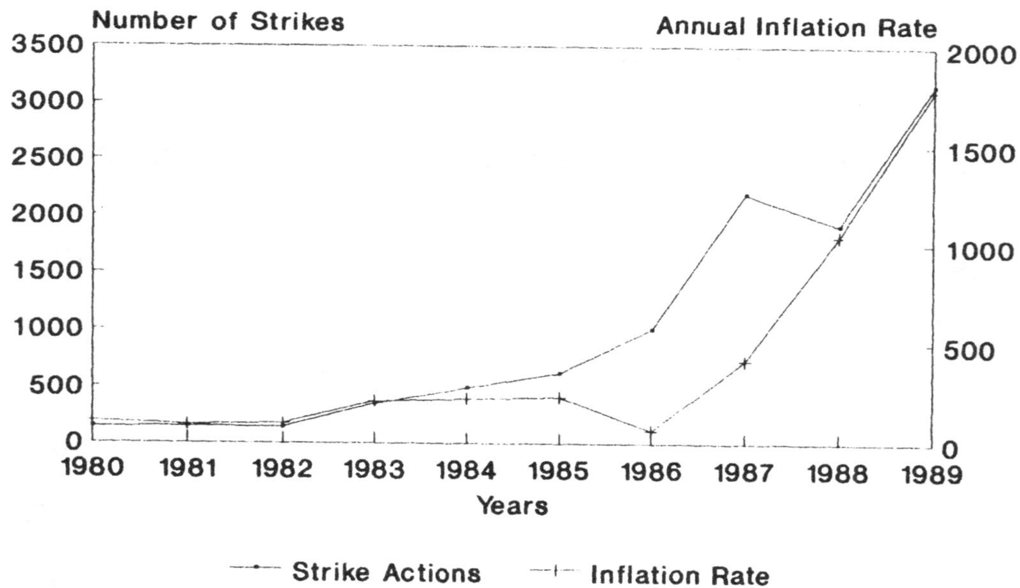

Source: Strike Data: NEPP-Universidade Estadual de Campinas; SIGREV-Ministerio do Trabalho; Inflation data: FIPE-USP.

working-class mobilizations during these years of political transition and economic instability.

If one focuses, instead, on the relationship between annual inflation and strike strength coefficients, as depicted in Figure 7.6, we see that labor's cyclical outbursts in strike waves in years when inflation rates increased, as in 1985, 1987 and 1989, were followed each time by corresponding years of reduced strike activity, the effects on labor discontent of the various economic stabilization programs implemented by the federal government in its attempts to bring inflation under control. This evolution of strike activity is illustrated in the zig-zag curve formed by the yearly strike strengths. Strike strength coefficients declined in years following strike waves which were also years of new government stablization programs, as was the case in 1986 with the *Plano Cruzado,* and in 1988 with the decline in strike strength with the implementation of another economic stabilization program, the *Plano Bresser,* even though in this case inflation in fact rose in spite of the objectives of the plan. Only 1989 escaped this pattern. The rocketing inflation and the failure of the *Plan Verão* of 1989 to hold inflation down and thus reduce working-class discontent made 1989 another strike wave year, which in turn was followed by yet another stabilization program, the *Plano Collor,* and an expected relative decline in strike activity in 1990.

Looking at the fluctuation of strike intensity in relation to income variation in this decade, we also find a very close correlation between changes in real median earnings and strike strength, as depicted in Figure 7.8. Through the 1980s there was heightened strike activity in those years of declining earnings, such as in 1985 and 1987 which were defined as strike wave years. Though earnings fell between 1983 and 1985, it was not until 1985 that workers protested through the first outburst of a strike wave suggesting the importance of strike control by government threats of repression in the final years of the military regime.

On the other hand, there was a decline in strike activities in those years when earnings increased as in 1986 and 1988 which followed strike waves and economic stabilization plans. In 1989 we see that strike strength increased in this third strike wave even though earnings apparently remained stable due to monthly salary increases and in response to the high inflation, but the levels of economic instability in a situation of near hyperinflation certainly had strong effects on worker discontent with authorities and planners as they engaged in another outburst of strike actions.

Figure 7.8 Strike Strength Coefficients and Real Average Earnings (base=1986), 1980-1989

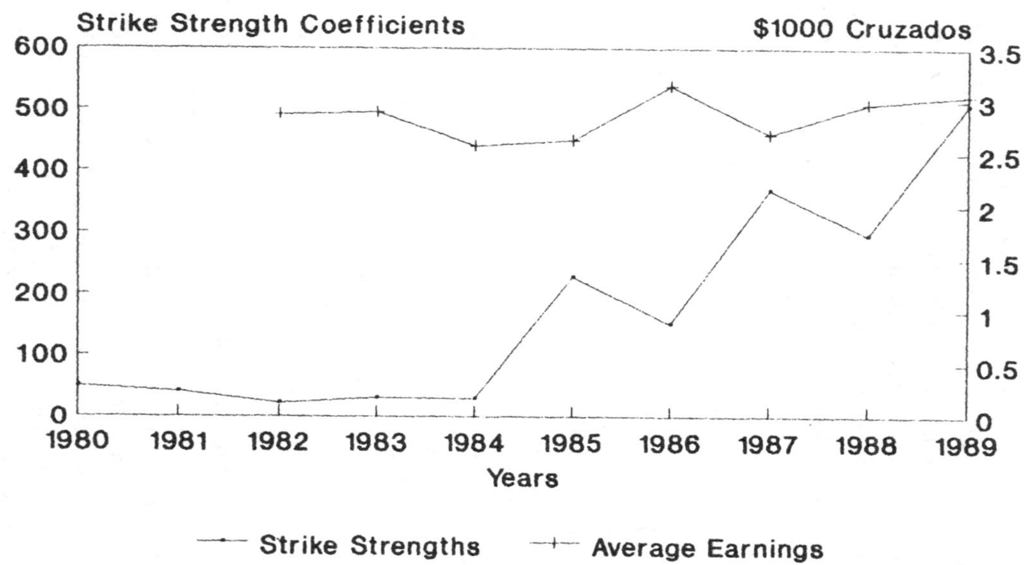

Source: IBGE, "Rendimento dos Empregados com Carteira Assinada", deflated by INPC Indice Nacional de Precos ao Consumidor.

While the analysis of yearly strike strengths reveals another perspective on how workers protested, in cycles of strike waves, we also find that each strike wave established a new plateau of strike activity in terms of the increased dimensions of strikes for each year. Thus the strength of labor protest grew over the decade in a rising staircase-like fashion with increasing successive yearly strike strengths led by the strike wave years.

The identification of years of strike waves through the analysis of all three dimensions of strikes, instead of focusing only on strike frequency, reveals that the growth of labor unrest followed this particular pattern. Each wave brought into the political arena new contingents of workers, exposing them to the experiences of protest organization and activities as well as transmitting to them a sense of class solidarity in an atmosphere of widespread working-class discontent with political and economic elites. Each strike wave period forced workers to test their resistance levels as they were confronted by the instransigence of employers and the ineptitude of governmental authorities in finding solutions to the deteriorating economic situation of the working class. Governmental responses to the threats of economic instability and political popular unrest resulted in economic plans offering temporary relief from the pressures of inflation and in a relative decline in working-class strike activity though never a return to previous lower levels of worker protest strength. Thus each strike wave taught more workers how to protest and the failure of each new plan taught them to distrust authorities and showed them that through working-class mobilization economic and political elites could be forced to respond to workers demands.

This cyclical pattern of labor mobilization suggests a more complex explanation as to why, how and when workers engage in protest than has often been presented by more superficial, economicistic interpretations. Without a doubt economic factors are important ingredients, but organizational capacity, work and strike experiences and conjunctural political conditions also play a significant role in the process of worker mobilization. The analysis of strike activity focusing on strike strength and strike waves highlights the complex dynamics of fluctuating currents of working-class political behavior often ignored by many scholars of popular movements in Brazil.[15] Working-class protest is determined first and foremost by the workers' capacity and disposition to organize and mobilize in collective actions. The development of organizational resources is not only evident in the progressive growth of the strike strength coefficient, but also in the recurrence of strike waves and the resurgence of the general strike tactic through out this decade.

The General Strikes in the 1980s

The resurgence of general strikes in the 1980s serves as another indicator of the rapid capacity of the labor movement to recuperate its strength in undertaking concerted collective actions in protest against government policies and continuous economic crisis. In this sense, this analysis of the four general strikes of 1983, 1986, 1987 and 1989 focuses comparatively on aspects of each strike which indicate the growth of the labor movement's ability to mobilize large national protest actions.

The issues around which workers mobilized in general strike actions reflected the political and economic circumstances of a decade of political transition under conditions of economic instability. In the case of the four general strikes, we find that the protest against high inflation was the constant feature over the period. In July of 1983, when the first general strike of the decade occurred, the month's inflation rate was at 11.77 percent, amounting to an annual accumulated rate of 211 percent. Thus, the issues which mobilized workers in the 1983 general strike were workers' discontent with the rising cost of living and the government's incapacity to take effective measures, opposition to proposals to pay the foreign debt, and protests against the threats of holding down wages and government's interventions in the unions.[16]

As time passed, economic crisis continued and the national government resorted to the first recessive economic stabilization program, the *Plano Cruzado* 2, which reduced purchasing power and lowered working-class incomes as a form of controlling inflation. At this time, a second general strike was called for December 1986 when inflation reached an accumulated annual rate of 152.4 percent. The aims of the general strike movement included, in addition to manifesting discontent with inflation, protests against the economic plan through demands for the recuperation of lost wages and against payment of the foreign debt.[17]

Once again, the 1987 general strike occurred in response to the implementation of another economic program, the *Plano Bresser*, which proposed to halt the inflation spiral through economic policies which again included wage controls. The general strike was called for August when inflation was at a monthly rate of 9.24 percent and came to an accumulated annual rate of 415.83 percent. This new high in the rise of the cost of living again reflected the failure of governmental economic planning. The increased level of conflict between labor and capital was reflected in the more politicized demands of the 1987 general strike: demands for 37.74 percent salary increase to recuperate lost wages due to inflation and government policies, protest against payment of the foreign debt, demands for job stability and a 40-hour week, and support for agrarian reform. As can be seen from these demands, the political nature of the economic crisis was clearly reflected in the demands of the 1987 movement.[18] The increase in the number of demands from the previous general strike is indicative of the growing politicization of the general strikes over the period.

Finally, a fourth general strike was called for March of 1989 to protest against another economic stabilization plan, the *Plano Verão,* and at a time when the monthly inflation rate had reached 14 percent in February contributing to a record annual accumulated rate of 1037.6 percent. The federal government's new economic plan was again characterized by wage reductions and recessive measures.[19] The 1989 general strike closed a decade of intensive strike activity, expressed labor's struggles against government policies of income reduction, economic recession and continued failure to lower the accelerated inflation and signaled the consolidation of a national labor movement.

In examining the size of each general strike a preliminary word of warning should be mentioned about data on these events. In Brazil governmental and non-governmental agencies have only recently begun to systematically collect strike statistics.[20] Because of the politically charged nature of the general strike in Brazil and its explicit, though temporary, challenge to the governing and entrepreneurial elites and their economic policies, the political interests of each actor (labor, government and employers) weigh heavily over the reporting of general strike data where the predominating concern is in demonstrating success or failure of the action, thus making estimates of general strike participation a difficult task. Consequently, our analysis of these general strikes relies on data from several sources such as national labor union organizations, Ministry of Labor, patronate organizations, newspapers, etc. in attempting to ascertain a reasonably realistic estimate of the force of each collective action by examining varied estimates of worker participation, accounts of the regional extension of the work stoppages, reports of the number and type of occupational groups involved, as well as contextual factors such as the level of strike activity at the time of a particular general strike. Through these indicators we have been able to arrive at an approximation of the comparative size of each of the four general strikes and examine some aspects indicative of growing union strength over the decade.

All the four general strikes were led by national labor organizations representing rare coordinated efforts among an ideologically and politically divided trade union movement. The 1983 general strike was organized by the *Comissão Pró-CUT* of the *CONCLAT,* the first post-dictatorship national labor organization which later was to break-up into the two main national labor confederations: the *CUT* and the *CGT.* The 1986 and 1987 general strikes were planned initially by the *Central Única dos Trabalhadores* (CUT) and subsequently supported by the *Central Geral do Trabalhadores* (CGT). In 1989 the general strike was organized by the coordinated efforts of the CUT and CGT, but this time the mobilization was also supported by the opposition party, the *Partido dos Trabalhadores* (PT) and its city mayors as well as other opposition parties' mayors which together controlled important state capitals and large industrial cities. It was in part the support of these city governments which contributed to the impact of the 1989 general strike.

With respect to the estimates of worker participation in the four general strikes, we find a very clear and significant tendency of increased worker adherence to successive strike calls. Worker support for the 1983 general strike ranged between two million[21] to three million workers;[22] the 1986 movement increased about fivefold, to 10 million, the number of strikers;[23] in the 1987 general strike the number of strikers remained at the previous general strike level of 10 million strikers to the much reported deception of union leaders and elation of government and employers;[24] finally the 1989 general strike dramatically doubled in participation size from the previous general strikes affecting about 22 million workers.[25]

Furthermore, it should be noted that the 1989 general strike was a two day stoppage. On the first day the number of strikers was about 22 million, falling to approximately half that on the second day. In spite of the sharp drop of worker adherence on the second day of the action and in light of the concerted efforts by government and employers against the movement, the participation of 10 million strikers on the second day evidenced the growth of the mobilization capacity of the labor movement.

In looking at the regional extension of the four general strikes, we find that there was also a progressive increase in the number of states and cities which reported strong worker involvement in the stoppages. This regional support for the general strikes meant to a large extent the adherence of the workers in the major urban industrial areas and the state capitals and an observably lesser support in the cities of the interior. Nevertheless, the data indicate a group of states with strong general strike participation (São Paulo, Rio Grande do Sul, Rio de Janeiro, Santa Catarina, Bahia, Federal District, Goias, Espirito Santo, Paraiba, Maranhão, Pernambuco), and another group with a lower level of involvement. Over the four general strike actions, we find accounts of strike activities in states that were previously unreported, indicating an expansion of support from one strike to another. In 1983 eleven states reported general strike mobilizations of which four states were considered as having widespread stoppages. In 1986, fifteen states were reported to have worker involvement in that general strike. Of these fifteen states, accounts indicated that ten states had strong worker adherence. In the 1987 general strike, twenty-two states reported worker involvement in the protest and of these fourteen were regarded as having strong worker mobilization. Finally in the 1989 general strike, nineteen states were reported to have paralyzations. Of these states, fifteen were strongly affected by the general strike. Thus the experiences of the four general strikes point out a marked tendency of increased participation on a regional bases. As was to be expected, the strongest support was in state capitals and other large and medium size industrial centers with much less support in the small towns and among the rural population.

Analyzing the bases of working-class support for general strike actions from the point of view of the occupational categories which adhered to them we can identify, in general terms, a nucleus of occupational groups which have been steady supporters of the four general strikes and representing the trade union backbone of the general strike movements. These occupational groups are the following: metal and automotive workers, chemical and petroleum workers, construction workers, state and federal civil servants, public schoolteachers, city transit workers, doctors and health care workers, and bank employees.

In addition to these core supporters, over the decade there has been a progressive increase, through each successive general strike action, in the involvement of other occupational groups reported to have participated, indicating the increasing support for the general strike tactic beyond the more militant segments of the labor movement. Among these later supporters are such occupational categories as textile workers, sales clerks, railroad workers, air transport workers, electrical workers, and shoe and leather goods workers.

With respect to the relationship between the upsurge of general strike activities and political and economic contexts, we find that the increase in the strength of each successive general strike closely accompanies the constant rise in yearly strike strengths over the decade. At the same time the size of each general strike has increased in a concomitant manner in relation to the pattern of strike waves.

The first general strike in 1983 was the weakest in number of participants at the same time when overall strike strength was among the lowest for the decade, as seen in Figure 7.9. The 1986 and 1987 general strikes occurred at a time of rapid increase in strike activities thus corresponding to the fivefold increase in general strike participation in comparison to the 1983 movement. Again, the 1986 general strike was called the year following the first strike wave of the decade in 1985. It is difficult to ascertain just what influence the 1985 strike wave had on participation levels in the 1986 general strike but certainly the effects of increased strike activity led the way to support for the 1986 protest.

The 1987 general strike occurred during another year of strike wave activity, but apparently the serious divisions within the labor movement which failed to mobilize large contingents of workers in important industrial cities in the states of São Paulo and Minas Gerias contributed to the repetition of 1986 general strike participation level in spite of the strike wave atmosphere that marked that year and strike leaders expectations and efforts in obtaining greater support. Finally we see that the 1989 general strike reached a higher level of worker stoppage of about 22 million at a time when strike activity for the decade reached its highest point with a 2097 percent increase in strike actions over the beginning of the ten year period and marking the third strike wave in which strike strength was at its highest for the decade.

From Figure 7.9 we see that general strike participation has clearly accompanied the evolution of annual national strike strength throughout the decade. In this respect, the estimates of the number of workers supporting each general strike appear to be relatively reliable in as much as the levels of worker involvement in each general strike closely follows

Figure 7.9 Strike Strengths and General Strike Size, 1980-1989

the growing tendency of strike strength as workers quickly adopted the tactic of the general strike in addition to other strike actions as a means of expressing their demands in this period of economic instability and institutional transition.

Over the decade of the 1980's, the resurgence of the general strike as an important form of working-class contention can be understood within the context of rising discontent with the decade long economic crisis of stagnation and inflation, and aggravated by the declining credibility in government and economic elites. The 1983, 1986, 1987 and 1989 general strikes represent tips of icebergs of popular protest which mark this critical period in Brazilian economic and political development. Underlying these four national mobilizations was a process of accelerated labor unrest which characterized strike activities in the 1980s as a decade of strike waves.

The occurrence of these strike waves and general strikes against socio-economic inequalities are forms of redressing power imbalances between workers, capitalists and the state. All strike waves and general strikes, as indeed all strikes, necessarily involve aspects of protest and confrontation, but the changes in the intensity and patterns of labor unrest are determined by the characteristics of industrial development and, especially, by the structure of power relations.[26]

Consequently, the strike waves and the general strikes of the 1980s reflected the process of de-institutionalization of the power relations between the classes resulting from major changes in the economy and the unwillingness of the dominant groups in society to accept the legitimacy of working-class demands of access to the polity and a share in the power and benefits of economic growth through the re-institutionalization of different power relations. In this sense the outburst of strike waves and general strikes depended on the timing of political and economic crises which magnified these imbalances in a context which combined several key factors such as: (1) the existence of local and national working-class organizations capable of mobilizing workers; (2) the presence of a cadre of working-class leaders intent on nationalizing the labor movement; (3) the inability of the dominant groups to resolve critical structural impasses; (4) the identification of the national government as the relevant target of labor protest; and (5) widespread popular distrust and discontent with political and economic elites.

Notes

1. The annual strike rate is the proportion of the number of strikes per one hundred thousand workers in the non-agricultural work force. Quantitative strike data for this chapter were taken from the following sources: for the strike analysis for the period 1981 to 1987 data were taken from the strike reports in *Brasil 1986: Relatório Sobre a Situação Social do Pais* (Campinas: Nucleo de Estudos de Políticas Públicas, Universidade Estadual de Campinas, 1987) pp. 54-86; and *Brasil 1987: Relatório Sobre a Situação Social do Pais* (Campinas: Nucleo de Estudos de Políticas Públicas, Universidade Estadual de Campinas, 1989) pp. 111-145; 1988 and 1989 strike data were taken from Ministério do Trabalho, Sistema de Greves, "Acompanhamento de Indicadores de Greves, 1988-1989," mimeographs (Brasilia) and Rosane Maia, *As Greves em 1989: Os Trabalhadores na Corda-Bamba da Hiperinflação* (Brasilia: Ministério do Trabalho, Secretaria de Emprego e Salários, Texto para Discussão no. 22, February 1990).

2. The *Nova Republica* is the name given to the first civilian government, the José Sarney Administration 1985-1989, following the military dictatorship.

3. IBGE - Instituto Brasileiro de Geografia e Estatística, *Pesquisa Nacional por Amostra de Domicilios, Suplemento no. 1, Associativismo* (Rio de Janeiro: Fundação Instituto Brasileiro de Geografia e Estatística, Departamento de Emprego e Rendimento, 1986) Table 3, p. 46; IBGE, *Participação Político-Social, 1988: Brasil e Grandes Regiões* (Rio de Janeiro: Fundação Instituto Brasileiro de Geografia e Estatística, Departamento de Estatísticas e Indicadores Sociais, 1990) Table 4.1, p. 8.

4. For a more detailed discussion of the initial rise of the CUT and CGT, see CEDI-Centro Ecumenico de Documentação e Informação, *Trabalhadores Urbanos no Brasil/82-84*, (São Paulo: CEDI, Aconteceu Especial 16, 1986) pp. 41-47; Margaret E. Keck, "The 'New Unionism' in the Brazilian Transition," in Alfred Stepan, (ed.), *Democratizing Brazil* (New York: Columbia University Press, 1990).

5. "Trunfo Sindical: Pesquisa Mostra CUT Mais Forte e CGT Menor," *Veja*, 22, no. 44, November 8, 1989, p. 108.

6. The sector strike rate is defined as the proportion of strikes in a specific sector per 100.000 workers employed in the sector.

7. Rosane Maia and Rosangela Saldanha, *Abrindo a Caixa Preta... (Estudo sobre a Evolução do Emprego na Administração Pública Estadual e Municipal)* (Brasilia: Ministério do Trabalho, Secretaria de Emprego e Salário, Mercado de Trabalho, Texto Para Discussão No. 12, December 1988) p. 14, Table 1.

8. For a descriptive analysis of public sector strikes in 1986 and 1987 see, *Brasil 1987: Relatório sobre a Situação Social do Pais* (Campinas: Nucleo de Estudos de Políticas Públicas, 1989) pp. 119-128.

9. The three strike dimensions are calculated in the following manner: Average Duration (D) = the total number of days on strike divided by the total number of strikes; Average Strike Size (W) = the total number of strikers divided by the total number of strikes; Strike Rate (S) = the number of strikes for every 100,000 non-agricultural workers. In the case of strike rates for different sectors or occupational categories, the rate is calculated by 100,000 workers employed in either the sector or the occupational group, whichever is the case. See Chapter 4 for the discussion of the strike shape.

10. Data for employment in the public sector are based on 1982 and 1985 data since more recent information was not available. In spite of this, the analysis in this chapter allows us to illustrate the tendencies indicated in these data. See Rosane Maia and Rosangela Saldanha, *Abrindo a Caixa Preta...*, p. 14.

11. To date the only study of the CUT is Lêoncio Martins Rodrigues, *CUT: Os Militantes e a Ideologia* (Rio de Janeiro: Editora Paz e Terra, 1990) especially pp. 43-53.

12. Two partial but informative analyses of strike activity for the period between 1982 and 1985 are CEDI-Centro Ecumenico de Documentação e Informação, *Trabalhadores Urbanos no Brasil/82-84*, (São Paulo: CEDI, Aconteceu Especial 16, 1986); Marcia de Paula Leite, "Tres Anos de Greves em São Paulo 1983-1985," *Revista São Paulo em Perspectiva*, 1 (2) (July-September 1987): 50-64; For a brief description of the situational circumstances around which this strike activity occurred for the period 1980 to 1986, see *Brasil 1986: Relatório sobre a Situação Social do Pais* (Campinas: Nucleo de Estudos de Políticas Públicas, Universidade Estadual de Campinas, 1987), pp. 54-86; for 1987 see *Brasil 1987: Relatório sobre a Situação Social do Pais* (Campinas: Nucleo de Estudos de Políticas Públicas, Universidade Estadual de Campinas, 1989) pp. 111-145.

13. The combination of the three dimensions of strike activity can be represented by the area of each strike shape as presented in Chapter 4. In addition, the calculation of the area of the volume of each shape provides a numerical indicator of the average strength of strike activity for each year and allows for comparative analyses. This indicator of strike strength, which we have called the **coefficient of strike strength**, is the area of the strike shape divided by 1000: volume or strike strength coefficient is equal to the product of average duration (D) multiplied by average size (W) multiplied by strike rate (S), divided by 1000. Strike Strength Coefficient = (D x W x S)/1000. For a discussion of strike dimension indicators see P.K Edwards, *Strikes in the United States 1881-1974* (Oxford: Basil Blackwell, 1981) Appendix C: The Statistical Description of Strike Activity, pp. 316-320.

14. According to Shorter and Tilly a "strike wave occurs when both the number of strikes and the number of strikers in a given year exceed the means of the previous five years by more than 50 percent," See Edward Shorter and Charles Tilly, *Strikes in France, 1830-1968*, pp.106-107. We have defined strike waves as being periods when the number of strikes and the number of strikers exceed the means of the previous five years by more than 50 per cent, as Shorter and Tilly, and, in addition, when the size of the strike shape volume (the coefficient of strike strength) also exceeds the means of the previous five years by 50 per cent.

15. Adam Przeworski, "Marxismo e Escolha Racional," *Revista Brasileira de Ciências Sociais* (February 1988); Salvador A. M. Sandoval, "A Crise Sociologica e a Contribuição da Psicologia Social ao Estudo dos Movimentos Sociais," *Educação e Sociedade*, 34 (December 1989): 122-129.

16. "A Greve Geral do Dia 21," *Boletim DIEESE* (July 1983) p. 17. For a more detailed report of the 1983 General Strike see CEDI-Centro Ecumenico de Documentação e Informação, *Trabalhadores Urbanos no Brasil/82-84* (São Paulo: CEDI, Aconteceu Especial 16, 1986), pp. 37-40.

17. "Greve Nacional," *Boletim DIEESE* (January 1987) p. 27.

18. "Greve Geral," *Boletim DIEESE* (August 1987): p. 37.

19. "Greve Geral," *Boletim DIEESE*, appendix, 8 (April 1989) p. 3.

20. The Departamento Intersindical de Estatística e Estudos Socio-Economicos began in 1983 to systematically collect and report strike information based on a combination of union reporting and newspaper

information; the Ministry of Labor through its unit SIGREV, Sistema de Greves, began in 1985 to collect and report strike data based on strike information briefs provided by the ministry's regional labor offices; the Nucleo de Estudos de Políticas Públicas of the Universidade Estadual de Campinas began in the mid-1980s to record strike data basically from DIEESE and newspapers sources. Strike data prior to 1978 was not systematically collected by any institution, consequently the data for this book, for this period, is based on original collection in major national newspapers, see Salvador Antonio Mireles Sandoval, "Strike in Brazil 1945-1980" (Ph.D. dissertation, The University of Michigan, 1984).

21. "Dez Milhões Pararam," *Senhor* no. 300, December 16, 1986: p. 36.

22. "As Greves em Julho de 1983," *Boletim do DIEESE* (São Paulo: August 1983): p. 17.

23. "Dez Milhões Pararam," *Senhor,* no. 300, December 16, 1986, p. 36.

24. "Estimates of the 1987 general strike participation are varied. SNI authorities (national intelligence agency) calculated about 10 million workers; the major newspapers reported around 9 million and the CUT, 25 million," see Eduardo Garuti Noronha and Marisa R. Ribeiro de Almeida, "Relações Trabalhistas," *Brasil 1987: Relatório sobre a Situação Social do Pais* (Campinas: Nucleo de Estudos de Políticas Públicas, Universidade Estdual de Campinas, 1989), p.113, cf. 4. We have chosen to estimate the general strike size as being around 10 million strikers because of the correspondence of estimates of two sources, the SNI and newspapers, as well as considering that the national stoppage was less effective in the states of São Paulo and Minas Gerais, two of the most industrialized states of the country.

25. The *O Estado de São Paulo* on March 15, 1989 surveyed 16 major cities finding that 37 percent of the workers failed to show up to work on the first day of the general strike. Considering the fact that the press reported support for the strike not only in the large industrial cities but also in the middle range cities of the interior of the states and that the strike was greater than in the case of the 1986 general strike, as well as considering the effects of the stoppages of the municipal transit systems in most major cities of the country, it is safe to estimate the degree of worker stoppage at about 37 percent of the urban work force or around 22 million workers. See "O X do Problema," *Veja,* 22, no. 12, March 22, 1989, p. 28.

26. For excellent analyses of the relation between strike waves and political crises see Leopold Haimson and Charles Tilly, (eds.), *Strikes, Wars and Revolutions in an International Perspective: Strike Waves in the Late Nineteenth and Early Twentieth Centuries* (Cambridge: Cambridge University Press, 1989); Edward Shorter and Charles Tilly, *Strikes in France 1830-1968* (Cambridge: Cambridge University Press, 1978), especially Chapter 5.

8

Conclusion: A Note on Theories of Strike Activity

In this study we set out to accomplish three different things: (1) to provide an overview and quantitative description of Brazilian strike activity between 1945 and 1989, which depicts more precisely what industrial conflict was like over these forty-five years; (2) to examine the patterns of work stoppages in order to bring to light empirical evidence about some widely speculated questions on the nature of working-class political participation; (3) to explore the importance of political and organizational processes in the generation of industrial strikes.

In the previous chapters we have made some assertions with respect to the major factors affecting the characteristics of strikes and the transformation of strike patterns over the years. The first assertion is that the struggles for power between groups of workers, employers, and authorities have a strong influence on the frequency, intensity, and nature of strike activity, particularly because of the corporatist structure regulating industrial relations. Our analysis has shown that the shape of strike patterns varies considerably as a result of the politicizing effects of the state's central role in resolving industrial disputes.

A second assertion is against a purely economic interpretation of labor conflict in favor of an alternative in which economic circumstances, mediated by conjunctural political factors, influence short-term fluctuations of strike activity, while long-term changes depend more on political transformations. We have presented evidence to demonstrate that, depending on the type of political rule, strike frequency does indeed vary in its association to economic factors. In authoritarian periods there is a much weaker relationship between economic indicators and strike frequency than in periods of more governmental tolerance, when economic factors assume more importance. To be sure, workers in general have struck over real economic grievances such as low wages, bad working conditions, and the rising cost of living, but the fluctuations in frequency of strikes and in other strike dimensions depend more on existing political conditions.

Third, we have argued that the intensity, scale, and form of strike activity also are dependent on the availability of organizational resources capable of channeling workers' grievances and of facilitating strike actions. We have shown how workers developed alternative forms of organization and collective action in response to changes in power relations. This was reflected in the shaping of strike patterns which, in turn, had its effect on the struggle for workers' access to the polity.

Our fourth assertion is with respect to the impact of accelerated industrial expansion and the subsequent rise in prominence of the modern sector workers in strike movements. Since 1950, industrial growth has brought about major changes in Brazilian society, particularly in the size, composition and importance of the urban working class. The effects of these changes were two fold. First, the growth of the industrial working class and the diversification of the economy made existing corporatist institutions obsolete even though the dominant groups in society persisted in sustaining them. Second, the rise of the capital intensive industries of the modern sector had as a counterpart a similar increase of strike activity among its workers. Nevertheless, the prominence of these workers in strike movements after 1961 was to a large extent explained by the government's suppression of the traditional sectors' militant workers and their organizations, and not a consequence of the economic performance of the modern sector.

In this concluding chapter, these generalizations and other findings will be discussed in light of the three main theoretical approaches to the study of industrial conflict: the economic model, the industrial relations perspective, and the political organizational approach. Since analyses of strikes have been largely confined to the experiences of the advanced industrial nations, comparisons across countries with wider differences in industrialization, political regimes, and industrial relations systems provide an opportunity to assess the explanatory contribution of each approach for the case of a late-industrializing country like Brazil.

The Economic Interpretation of Strikes

Generally speaking, the economic approach has viewed changes in strike activity as determined by the structure of the production process and fluctuations in the state of the economy. This approach has a long history of research and has been most successful in demonstrating that strike frequency varies with fluctuations of some business cycle indicators. Though much quantitative research has been devoted to exploring the economic determinants of strikes, advocates of the model have only been able to account for strike frequency, while the other components of the strike such as size and duration have been shown to be less dependent on economic fluctuations.[1] Indeed, as P. K. Edwards found in his study of ninety-four years of strike activity in the United States, the relationship between economic variables and strikes appears to be 'unstable' over the long run.[2] Similarly, Edward Shorter and Charles Tilly in their study *Strikes in France 1830-1968* found the relationship between economic variables and strike activity to be stronger in the short-term than in the long-term, when it appears that political and organizational factors assume greater importance.[3]

In the Brazilian case, for the overall period of 1945 to 1968 fluctuations in real industrial product and real wages showed moderate correlations with strike frequency. On the other hand, when the twenty-four year span was subdivided into three periods according to the predominant type of political rule, the relationship between the variables presented contrasting results.

Similar to the findings of Edwards and of Shorter and Tilly, the relationship between economic factors and strikes was likewise unstable. As in the case of France, the correlations changed substantially from one period to another. We found that each political period presents a set of correlations whose values and inferences are entirely different. The analysis of each reveals a dynamic of strike determination more complex than suggested by the economic model. The varying influence of economic factors is only understandable when examined within the political context of each period. Even though the correlational evidence for Brazil lends support to the conclusions of Edwards and of Shorter and Tilly, the changing values of the coefficients over time suggest that in the short run political factors have a strong effect on strike frequency as well. Two characteristics of contemporary industrializing countries are salient. First, in countries like Brazil, the state occupies a key position as central planner and regulator of the economy. Because of its role in economic planning, the state exercises considerable power over the various sectors of the economy through its fiscal and investment policies. As a regulatory agency, it can set wage and price ceilings and other conditions in the marketplace. Through this planning and regulatory role, governing elites can manipulate business cycle factors to a certain extent so as to attenuate or delay their effects on the working population. For example, in Brazil the state, through its' price setting mechanisms, can pressure employers to either give workers larger wage increases or to resist workers' demands. As a result, strikes can either be avoided by early resolution of the conflicts or provoked and prolonged according to the interests of the governing groups.

Second, the need for an active and aggressive state in late industrialization as an imperative of rapid economic growth led to the expansion of state-owned enterprises. The development of a strong and pervasive system of state capitalism is illustrated in the Brazilian case by the fact that by 1978 the state controlled 29 percent of the sales of the 500 largest firms operating in the country, while national private firms and multinational corporations controlled 36 percent and 35 percent, respectively. These public enterprises dominate in the production of raw materials, infra-structure items, and basic industrial goods.[4]

As an entrepreneur, the state exerts other influences through its enterprises which permit it to interfere with the short run effects of the market on strike activity. Governments can determine wage levels, working conditions, and other worker related issues in those branches of industry in which it predominates by setting policies for its own companies which serve as unofficial standards for other employers to follow, even if this involves financial loss for the public sector enterprises or is the result of politician pressures in place of union worker mobilizations. In this manner, the government can impose ceilings to labor's demands without officially intervening in the disputes.

Another form of interference with the market forces is through public enterprise employment and investment policies, which can modify the immediate consequences of fluctuations in the business cycle. For example, the government can implement employment policies which delay in the short-run the effects of economic recessions and avoid popular unrest. In addition, public enterprises can create internal divisions among workers in an occupational group by providing greater or fewer economic benefits for its employees compared to those employed by private firms, which may affect the mobilization capacity of workers.

The economic role of the state has made it an important actor in industrial relations far beyond its traditional role of institutional mediator, and as Douglas Hibbs observed for advanced industrial societies, this active participation in determining wages, working conditions, etc. has resulted in strikes becoming more politicized, as workers use the strike weapon to pressure the government for concessions.[5] In late industrializing countries, this role is enhanced by its more aggressive and interventionist position in the economy. Consequently, the politicization of strikes is commonplace, since workers must deal with the state and its policies in pressing for their demands.

The Industrial Relations Approach

A second perspective to the study of industrial conflict, the industrial relations approach, views strikes as disputes over economic and workplace issues in which workers' and employers' claims are contained by the institutional mechanisms of collective bargaining. This emphasis on the forms of collectively negotiating settlements of disputes identifies workplace issues as the primary cause of industrial conflict.[6] Thus, strikes are regarded as actions somewhat isolated from other forces within society, and their analysis focuses mainly on the several dimensions of collective bargaining which have an impact on strike activity.

The size of strikes, it is argued, is affected by the bargaining structure, since it will vary according to whether negotiations are at plant, regional, or national level. Similarly, the number of strikes will also vary. More recently it has been noted that the approach does not adequately account for long-term trends in strike patterns, since it focuses on the current impact which bargaining structures have on strikes.[7]

Because of this limitation of the industrial relations approach, P. K. Edwards, in his study of the United States, attempts to develop an interpretation of long-term changes in strike activity consistent with this perspective. To this end, Edwards argues that:

> The aim is not to argue that job control *per se* has been more important in America than elsewhere, but to focus on the

intensity of control struggles as a key factor in the explanation of strike patterns. In other words, it is the particular pattern of the general struggle for control which is important. As noted above, strike patterns in several European countries have been influenced by the centralization and politicization of strike actions. This can be seen as one particular form of the institutionalization of the general struggle for control. In Britain and America, a different route has been taken. Here, the workplace has remained the center of attention. Not surprisingly, the strike patterns of the two countries have revealed important similarities, not simply in terms of the frequency and size of stoppages but also regarding the avoidance of 'political' strikes, the domination of strikes by individual trade unions, as distinct from national union federations, and several other points.[8]

For Edwards, the struggle for job control and the manner in which this struggle evolves affect the pattern of strike activity. This explanation is proposed in opposition to both the economic and political interpretations which he systematically criticizes. In looking at the Brazilian strike experience through the industrial relations-job control perspective, we find the approach inadequate, since it is difficult to ignore the fact that the dominant groups in Brazilian politics responded to the task of economic development by creating regimes that permitted them to manage, guide, and manipulate the transformation of economic and social structures at minimal costs to their power or ruling position.[9]

This is best illustrated by the corporatist system of industrial relations, in which the state holds the central position in the resolution of conflicts. The labor laws establish the restraints on both workers and employers, and also define the type, size, and geographical jurisdiction of the workers' organizations. Finally, the state reserves the right to intervene in the internal affairs of the unions if it becomes necessary. As a result, the authoritarian system of industrial relations stands in contrast to the pluralist nature of the system implicit in Edwards' argument.

Further, in the analysis of the transformation of strike patterns over the years, it is clear that the limitations on industrial conflict established by the labor laws have only had a strong impact on shaping strike activities during authoritarian governments, when the governing elites enforced the more repressive aspects of the system in order to bring labor under control. During these periods, strike dimensions corresponded to the provisions established by law. They were largely single category strikes restricted to the unions' jurisdiction and involving few establishments. But even in those years, strike frequency and duration declined, not because the bargaining process was a substitution for strike actions, but rather because of the intensity of the repression.

In liberal years, when the state refrained from using the repressive features of the labor laws, strike patterns corresponded less to the institutional constraints. In these periods, a lesser proportion of work stoppages was due to local, single category strikes. The larger mobilizations were mass strikes, which were responses not to the bargaining arrangements, but to the political conditions and the needs to take the workers' claims to the government. The mass strikes were not sanctioned under the industrial relations system, nor were their politically oriented demands. The loci of workers' collective actions were determined by the nature of the unions' demands. On the one hand, unions continued to utilize the labor relations institutions for the settlement of specific disputes over wages, working conditions, or benefits. On the other hand, working together in alternative organizations, outside the official union structure, labor leaders used mass strike actions to pressure government for broad reaching economic policies and political reforms.

Contrary to one of the basic assumptions of the industrial relations model, the Brazilian state definitely did not stimulate the development of independent and autonomous labor organizations at the local plant level, but promoted instead a bureaucratic union structure dependent on state auspices as an alternative to combative worker unions.[10] Consequently, industrial conflicts, when they erupt, have been from the outset confrontations with public authorities.

Edwards claims that "economic factors are common to all strikes, but political ones are likely to have an impact which is limited to a small range of strikes".[11] The analysis which he presents in the concluding portions of his study, however, point in another direction. For example, the author states that "a prominent characteristic of American strikes has been the uniformity of their shape,"[12] and explains that:

> ...it is obvious that strikes since the Second World War have differed in character from earlier disputes. Violence has largely, although not completely, disappeared; the language of management has come to stress accommodation with unions

> rather then outright hostility to them; the significance of disputes over union recognition has declined; and so on.[13]

After the allusion to the use of violence prior to the institutionalization of the bargaining structure, Edwards does not pursue either the question of violence in labor disputes, or the question of the state regulating industrial conflict. It is perplexing that he does not regard either as political factors in establishing parameters of industrial conflict.

This illustrates the difficulty that Edwards has in identifying political factors, a difficulty which is especially evident in his final analysis of the process of the institutionalization of the bargaining system:

> Finally, the [U.S.] government's attitude to intervention in strikes and to the isolation of economic and political matters has influenced the integration of trade unions into the existing political structure. As noted..., Shorter and Tilly see labor's political involvement in terms of a breakthrough by the working class to political recognition. But the government and employers have exerted a crucial influence on the terms of which 'recognition' is granted labor. Any breakthrough was on very limited terms, and did not challenge the basis of the system as a whole. Indeed, 'recognition' was granted largely because unions posed no serious challenge; it was not won by a working class determined to wrest political power from capitalists, but by a union movement which had already accepted the fundamentals of the system.[14]

Whether or not the American working class, prior to the institutionalization of collective bargaining, accepted the "fundamentals of the system" is an empirical question which Edwards does not analyze. The fact remains, however, that institutional constraints were imposed on workers and their collective actions on very "limited" terms by the country's powerholders. As a result, it is clear that the impact of the bargaining structures on strike activity by channeling strike actions to the plant level and focusing on restricted job control issues served the interests of those who defined the "terms of which recognition [was] granted to labor". The failure of Edwards to acknowledge the strong impact of political forces on the institutionalization of strikes was possibly the result of the difficulty of quantifying political factors.[15]

Edwards' analysis seems to indicate, however, that his definition of political factors is as vague as his notion of intensity of job control struggles.

Another reason why the author may have failed to detect the effects of political factors on strikes within the context of the United States is the country's decentralized system of political control, which makes quantification and statistical analysis problematic. In this respect, the study of the transformation of Brazilian strike activity was facilitated because of the centralization of power in the hands of the federal government and lack of autonomy of the subnational levels of government. This centralization, as was argued before, results in the more visible politicization of industrial strikes than in the more decentralized power structure of the United States.

The Political Organizational Approach

Economists and industrial relations scholars have not denied the existence of political factors, yet they have been unable to go beyond vague notions of a relationship between political forces and strike activity. In recent years, sociologists and political scientists have turned to examining the non-economic determinants of strike activity. From these efforts has arisen an analytical perspective which can be called the political organizational approach. This approach views strikes as forms of collective actions in power struggles between workers, employers, and authorities.

In general, studies which adopt this perspective have shown that strike activity has changed as labor acquires direct access to the national power structure and attempts to influence policies. In one of the few longitudinal studies of strikes, Shorter and Tilly summarized this approach as it applies to the French experience:

> This account of strike history over the last one hundred and fifty years suggests that there is a regular, intimate relationship between industrial structure, the organizational bases of working-class life, worker participation in politics and strike activity. Every new stratum of workers which economic modernization tosses to the surface will sooner or later demand participation in the nation's political life; and established groups

> will struggle against the eclipse of their present position of power by some upstart. Whether activation for this political struggle comes sooner or later depends on the challenger group's success in putting together an organizational launching pad.[16]

Along a similar line, Korpi and Shalev,[17] in their comparative study of eighteen industrialized countries, suggest some variants of the relationship between long-term changes in industrial conflict and the working class' access to the polity. The first is the case of Norway and Sweden, which have experienced a substantial decline in worker agitation since the Social Democratic Party rose to national power. A second case at the other extreme is that of the United States, Canada, and Ireland, where the working class has never played a significant role in national politics. These countries have shown no significant long run decline in industrial conflict, and remain the highest in strike intensity levels among the Western nations. Another variant is that in which working-class parties have considerable electoral support, but are excluded from the effective exercise of political power. In this situation, exemplified by France, Italy, and Japan, "conflict in the industrial arena becomes not only the inevitable alternative to a political conflict strategy: it also takes on the role of an extra-parliamentary vehicle of working-class political participation (as has been extensively argued for France by Shorter and Tilly)".[18] Lacking access to the state, the working class responds by using the strike as a vehicle of collective pressure.

Though the political organizational approach has produced a variety of treatments of industrial conflict, they all share a common premise: that industrial conflict results from wider struggles in which national power structures occupy a key position in shaping strikes and other forms of working-class protest. The basic assumptions of the approach applied to the Brazilian experience prove to be the most useful framework for understanding the changes in industrial strike activity. As has been argued throughout this study, the transformations which characterized Brazilian working-class collective action were outcomes of the interaction between the efforts of workers to attain a position of power in the polity and the resistance to this challenge by established elites. But the condition of late-industrialization has produced specific effects which make the Brazilian case somewhat different from the cases of Western Europe or North America.

As suggested before, there appears to be a strong relationship between the needs of late-industrialization and the rise of authoritarian regimes. Confronted with serious imbalances in the domestic economy, ruling elites have used the state as a means to force public and private capital accumulation necessary for accelerated industrial growth. In addition, the elites have also relied on the state to control the participation of the subordinate classes as these are incorporated into urban society by the industrialization process.

Unlike the prohibition of worker combinations characteristic of the first phases of industrialization in Europe and the United States, in modern authoritarian regimes working-class unions are institutionalized by the governing groups as part of the state apparatus. With the incorporation of working-class organizations into the state, control is accomplished through bureaucratic, as well as coercive means. Furthermore, the cooptation of labor leaders is facilitated by the close surveillance of union activities by the government. Finally, the close ties of the unions to the government have made them at times targets of manipulation and competition between contending political factions.

As principal mediator of industrial disputes, the state exercises direct power over both employers and workers. Because of this, economic elites take particular interest in the labor policies of the government, particularly since they are similarly dependent on the favors of the state. Unlike the advanced industrial societies, the late industrializing nation's economic elites rely more on the state for economic and political support.

In examining the organizational changes in strikes and the broader transformations in strike patterns, we find that these changes occurred not as a response to employers' strength or intransigence, as was the case elsewhere, but rather as a reaction to governmental repression and the need to alter power arrangements. At the same time, the fact that labor unions were subordinated to the state led to the creation of alternative forms of working-class organizations which paralleled the union structure. Unlike the case of the early industrializing nations, in which workers associations were proscribed and thus emerged in clandestine groups such as in pre-revolutionary Russia, in modern authoritarian regimes where an official union structure exists and where a certain amount of demand-making is tolerated, worker mobilization to contend for a place in the polity is done through parallel forms of associations with close ties to the official entities, as in the Brazilian case. These parallel organizations are not necessarily clandestine, but rather assume many of the political functions often prohibited to the official unions.

Furthermore, the need to find alternative forms of workers organizations has led as well to linking interpersonal social networks such as neighborhood associations, sports clubs, or church groups to worker mobilization. Since mobilizing the rank-and-file in the factories is closely regulated under the authoritarian regimes, these new forms of workers associations have proven to be effective under certain conditions. The support of the Catholic Church in the Brazilian case has been a key factor in the successful molding of neighborhood organizations to working-class political needs. Because of the recent emergence of this type of alternative, worker organizational response to government authoritarianism, further research is called for in order to better understand the consequences of these forms of workers organizations and to define the conditions which contribute to their emergence, permanence and linkages with union activism.

Alternative forms of popular organization in modern authoritarian regimes is only one topic of the broader area of labor studies which has received little attention in these societies. In general, the study of worker attitudes and participation is currently drawing more scholarly interest, due largely to the rise of working-class contention and outbursts in important countries in South America and in Eastern Europe where regimes are hard pressed by a resurgence of working-class opposition and demands for democratization of their societies.

In this study, we have raised as many questions about changes in strikes as we have answered. Most certainly, our intention to provide an overview of strike activity in Brazil has led to some broad generalizations which point toward questions for future research. Ultimately, the study has revealed that the mass politics notions inherent in the analysis of Latin American populism, and more recently in analysis of authoritarian regimes,[19] do not correspond to the complexity and extent of working-class political participation. For this reason, it is well to remember E. P. Thompson's concluding remarks in his classic study, *The Making of the English Working Class*:

> Yet the working people should not be seen only as the lost myriads of eternity. They had also nourished.... with incomparable fortitude, the Liberty Tree. We may thank them for these years of heroic culture.[20]

Notes

1. Roberto Franzosi, "One Hundred Years of Strike Statistics: Data, Methodology and Theoretical Issues in Quantitative Strike Research," *Industrial and Labor Relations Review*, v. 42, n. 3 (April 1989): 348-362.

2. P. K. Edwards, *Strikes in the United States 1881-1974* (Oxford: Basil Blackwell, 1981), p. 75.

3. Edward Shorter and Charles Tilly, *Strikes in France 1830-1968* (London: Cambridge University Press, 1974), p. 102.

4. Sylvia Ann Hewlett, *The Cruel Dilemmas of Development: Twentieth-Century Brazil* (New York: Basic Books, Inc.), pp. 110-112.

5. Douglas A. Hibbs, Jr., "On the Political Economy of Long Run Trends in Strike Activity," *British Journal of Political Science*, 8 (April 1978): 169.

6. P. K. Edwards, *Strikes in the United States*, pp. 233-242.

7. Ibid., pp. 232-233.

8. Ibid., p. 234.

9. Philippe Schmitter, "The Portugalization of Brazil?," in Alfred Stepan, (ed.), *Authoritarian Brazil* (New Haven: Yale University Press, 1973), p. 205.

10. Kenneth Scott Mericle, "Conflict Regulation in the Brazilian Industrial Relations System" (Ph.D. dissertation, University of Wisconsin, 1974), p. 316.

11. P. K. Edwards, *Strikes in the United States*, p. 80.

12. Ibid., p. 233.

13. Ibid., p. 213.

14. Ibid., p. 248.

15. Roberto Franzosi, among others, also has made the point that non-economic variables affecting strike activity may not lend themselves to purely quantitative analysis. See Roberto Franzosi, "One Hundred Years...," pp. 32-36.

16. Shorter and Tilly, *Strikes in France*, p. 347.

17. Walter Korpi and Michael Shalev, "Strikes, Industrial Relations and Class Conflict in Capitalist Societies," *British Journal of Sociology*, 30, 2 (June 1979).

18. Ibid, pp. 181-182.

19. Youssef Cohen, "The Benevolent Leviathan: Political Consciousness among Urban Workers under State Corporatism," *American Political Science Review*, 76 (1982): 47.

20. E. P. Thompson, *The Making of the English Working Class* (London: Victor Gollancz, Ltd., 1963), p. 832.

Appendix: Additional Secondary Data Tables

Table A.1 – Distribution of the Industrial Labor Force by Sectors and Branches of Industry with the Corresponding Rates of Growth between 1950 and 1980

Category & Branch of Industry	*1950 No. Employed*	*% of Total*	*1960 No. Employed*	*% of Total*	*1970 No. Employed*	*% of Total*
TRADITIONAL INDUSTRY	766,588	66.0	847,686	56.2	1,172,001	48.2
Textiles	313,845	26.7	306,122	20.3	335,711	13.8
Leathers	17,309	1.5	21,981	1.5	23,186	1.0
Food Inds.	211,948	18.0	217,621	14.4	311,288	12.8
Beverages	32,762	2.8	31,155	2.1	53,438	2.2
Printing	34,491	2.9	44,860	3.0	88,584	3.6
Wood Inds.	56,044	4.8	74,702	4.9	114,026	4.7
Furniture	31,672	2.7	52,974	3.5	82,544	3.4
Clothing	64,140	5.4	85,263	5.6	146,849	6.0
Tobacco	14,377	1.2	13,008	.9	16,375	.7
INTERMEDIATE IND.	175,419	14.9	229,627	15.1	346,885	14.2
Non-Metallic Materials	111,269	9.4	144,015	9.5	194,118	8.0
Rubber	9,137	.8	14,741	1.0	31,186	1.3
Mining	32,708	2.8	35,432	2.3	57,174	2.3
Paper	22,305	1.9	35,439	2.3	64,407	2.6
MODERN IND.	205,768	17.6	400,896	26.5	863,964	35.4
Metallurgy	90,203	7.7	151,001	10.1	246,144	10.1
Mechanics	21,798	1.9	49,000	3.2	167,393	6.9
Electrical Equip.	13,038	1.1	44,364	2.9	110,954	4.5
Automobile	15,121	1.3	63,229	4.2	149,954	6.1
Chemicals	65,608	5.6	92,502	6.1	189,519	7.8
OTHER INDUSTRIES *Not Classified*	19,869	1.5	31,504	2.1	56,134	2.3
Totals	1,177,644	100.0	1,509,713	100.0	2,438,984	100.0

continued

Table A.1 – Continuation

Category & Branch of Industry	*1980 No. Employed*	*% of Total*	*Annual Growth Rates* 1950-60	1960-70	1970-80
TRADITIONAL INDUSTRY	2,026,117	43.7	.88	3.24	3.52
Textiles	395,792	8.4	-.25	.92	1.64
Leathers	39,429	.8	2.39	.53	5.31
Food Inds.	566,833	12.0	.27	3.57	5.99
Beverages	53,647	1.1	-.50	5.39	.03
Printing	131,834	2.8	2.63	6.80	3.97
Wood Inds.	234,124	4.9	2.87	4.22	.71
Furniture	158,454	3.3	5.14	4.43	6.52
Clothing	427,192	9.0	2.84	5.43	10.67
Tobacco	18,812	.4	-.99	2.30	1.38
INTERMEDIATE INDUSTRY	619,654	13.4	2.69	4.12	5.79
Non-Metallic Materials	372,496	7.9	2.57	2.98	6.51
Rubber	55,546	1.2	4.78	7.49	5.77
Mining	83,739	1.8	.79	4.78	3.81
Paper	107,873	2.3	4.63	5.97	5.15
MODERN INDUSTRY	1,888,846	40.7	6.66	7.67	7.82
Metallurgy	526,672	11.1	5.20	9.24	7.60
Mechanics	515,237	10.9	8.10	12.28	11.24
Electrical Equip.	242,017	5.1	12.20	9.16	7.79
Automobile	264,853	5.6	14.30	8.63	5.68
Chemicals	340,067	7.2	3.43	7.17	5.84
OTHER INDUSTRIES *Not Classified*	103,759	2.2	4.61	5.77	6.14
Totals	4,638,376	100.0	2.48	4.79	6.63

Source: Industrial labor force data used in this analysis referred to in the table is based on those establishments employing five or more persons.

Instituto Brasileiro de Geografia e Estatística. Censo Industrial, 1950, 1960, 1970, 1980.

Table A.2
Brazilian Annual Growth Rates, 1921-1978

		Real Output Growth Rate (%)	
Year	*GDP*	*Agriculture*	*Industry*
1921-30	3.7	3.4	3.3
1931-30	4.6	4.3	5.2
1940-47	5.1	3.9	6.5
1948-56	6.4	3.9	8.8
1957-61	8.3	5.8	10.7
1962-67	3.5	3.9	3.5
1968-73	11.5	4.7	13.2
1974-78	7.5	md	md

md=missing data

Source: Fundação Getúlio Vargas, *Conjuntura Econômica*.
Table 2 in Sylvia Ann Hewlett, *The Cruel Dilemmas of Development: Twentieth-Century Brazil* (New York: Basic Books, Inc., 1980), p. 223.

Table A.3 – Indices of Real Wages for Various Occupational Groups (a)
1964-1974

	OCCUPATIONAL GROUPS WITH SALARY INCREASES DURING FIRST SEMESTER							OCCUPATIONAL GROUPS WITH SALARY INCREASES DURING SECOND SEMESTER						
Year	*Rubber Workers*	*Plastics (SP)*	*Metalworkers Interior (SP)*	*Chemical Workers Industrial Sec. (RJ)*	*Beverages (SP)*	*Bakers (SP)*	*Leather Workers (SP)*	*Metalworkers-JoãoMonlevade (MG)*	*Textile Workers (SP)*	*Metalworkers Capital (SP)*	*Newsprinting (SP)*	*Ceramic Workers (SP)*	*Chemical Workers Industrial Sec. (SP)*	*Metalworkers (RS)*
1964								100	100	100	100	100	100	100
1965	100	100	100	100	100	100	100	75	90	88	88	88	90	91
1966	90	91	87	88	95	72	92	62	75	75	73	71	73	73
1967	88	75	77	78	88	74	92	57	74	74	71	68	72	67
1968	89	74	78	80	89	74	96	59	74	89	73	69	75	68
1969	86	73	79	76	91	75	90	62	76	77	75	69	77	69
1970	92	75	82	82	93	80	96	65	82	82	79	73	82	72
1971	89	79	82	81	94	79	94	63	80	81	78	72	80	73
1972	92	77	83	83	93	77	99	64	79	79	78	71	78	73
1973	85	76	79	77	89	70	91	60	72	72	71	65	72	69
1974	79	71	71	70	80	73	83	62	74	74	73	65	73	---

(a) SP=São Paulo
RJ=Rio de Janeiro
MG=Minas Gerais
RS=Rio Grande do Sul

Source: Adapted from Tables IX and X cited in "Dez Anos de Política Salarial", *Estudos Socio Econômicos* 3 (August 1975), pp. 58-62.

Table A.4
Average Annual Work Time Necessary to Purchase the Minimum Ration of Essential Food Stuffs, 1965-1981

Year	*Worktime Necessary*	*Index*
1965	88 hours 16 minutes	*100.0*
1966	109 hours 15 minutes	*123.8*
1967	105 hours 16 minutes	*119.3*
1968	101 hours 35 minutes	*115.1*
1969	110 hours 23 minutes	*125.1*
1970	105 hours 13 minutes	*119.2*
1971	111 hours 47 minutes	*126.6*
1972	119 hours 08 minutes	*135.0*
1973	147 hours 04 minutes	*166.6*
1974	163 hours 32 minutes	*185.3*
1975	149 hours 40 minutes	*169.6*
1976	157 hours 29 minutes	*178.4*
1977	141 hours 49 minutes	*160.7*
1978	137 hours 37 minutes	*155.9*
1979	153 hours 04 minutes	*173.4*
1980	157 hours 32 minutes	*178.5*
1981	149 hours 40 minutes	*169.6*

Source: Departamento Intersindical de Estatística e Estudos Sócio-Econômicos, 1981, cited by Fernando Lopes de Almeida, *Política Salarial, Emprego e Sindicalismo 1964-1981* (Petropolis: Editora Vozes, 1982), p. 48.

Table A.5
Standards of Living for the Average Working-Class Family in São Paulo, 1958 and 1969

	1958	*1969*
Household members	4.5	4.9
Number employed	1.0	2.0
Monthly income (In current prices)	Cr$ 10.2	Cr$ 512.1
Real income (Prices of 1958)	Cr$ 10.2	Cr$ 9.2
Monthly earnings of head of household	Cr$ 8.5	Cr$ 316.0
Real income (Prices of 1958)	Cr$ 8.5	Cr$ 5.4

Source: Candido Procopio Ferreira de Camargo et al., São Paulo 1975: Crescimento e Pobreza (São Paulo: Edições Loyola, 1976), p. 67.

Table A.6 - Index of Worker Turnover: Number of Months Worked in the Year for Employees by Economic Sector and Minimum Wage Brackets in 1977

	Salary Level by Number of Minimum Wages Earned						
Economic Sector	< 1 M. W.	*1 to 3* M. W.	*4 to 7* M. W.	*8 to 10* M. W.	*10 to 15* M. W.	*> 15* M. W.	*Total*
Industry	5.76	7.68	9.48	10.20	10.32	10.32	7.80
Public Utilities	6.48	9.24	10.80	11.04	10.80	10.80	9.96
Construction	3.72	5.04	6.48	7.68	8.04	8.52	5.04
Agriculture	5.88	7.68	8.52	9.12	9.48	9.24	7.20
Services	5.52	7.20	9.00	9.72	9.84	9.96	7.44
Financial Sector	5.64	7.32	9.36	10.56	11.04	11.04	9.48
Commerce	6.00	7.44	8.64	9.24	9.48	9.48	7.32
Civil Service	9.84	10.80	11.28	11.40	11.16	11.16	10.92
Others	6.96	8.04	9.48	9.96	10.03	10.32	8.28
Total	5.76	7.68	9.48	10.20	10.32	10.32	7.80

Source: Andrea Calabi and Carlos A. Luque, "Observações Sobre o Padrão de Emprego e Remuneração nos Estabelecimentos Brasileiros" (São Paulo: Fundação Instituto de Pesquisas Econômicas, mimeograph, 1981), p. 22, based on data from "Relação Anual de Informações Sociais RAIS/1977, Ministerio do Trabalho, cited by Fernando Lopes de Almeida, *Política Salarial, Emprego e Sindicalismo 1964-1981* (Petropolis: Editora Vozes, 1982), p. 93.

Selected Bibliography

Books

Almeida, Fernando Lopes de. 1982. *Política Salarial, Emprego e Sindicalismo 1964/1981*. Petropolis: Editora Vozes.

Alves, Maria Helena Moreira. 1984. *Estado e Oposição no Brasil (1964-1984)*. Petropolis: Editora Vozes.

Andrade, Regis de Castro, ed. 1984. *Sindicatos em uma Epoca de Crise*. Petrópolis: Editora Vozes.

Antunes, Ricardo. 1988. *A Rebeldía do Trabalho: O Confronto Operário no ABC Paulista - As Greves de 1978/1980*. São Paulo: Editora Ensaio and Editora da UNICAMP.

_______. 1991. *O Novo Sindicalismo*. São Paulo: Editora Brasil Urgente.

Araujo, Braz José de. *Operários em Luta: Metalúrgicos da Baixada Santista (1933-1983)*. Rio de Janeiro: Editora Paz e Terra, 1985.

Baer, Werner. 1965. *Industrialization and Economic Development in Brazil*. Homewood, IL: Richard D. Irwin, Inc.

Banks, J. A. 1970. *Marxist Sociology in Action: A Sociological Critique of the Marxist Approach to Industrial Relations*. London: Faber and Faber.

Barsted, Dennis Linhares. 1982. *Medição de Forças - O Movimento Grevista de 1953 e a Epoca dos Operários Navais*. Rio de Janeiro: Editora Zahar.

Bendix, Reinhard. 1977. *Nation-Building and Citizenship*. Berkeley: University of California Press.

_______. 1956. *Work and Authority in Industry: Ideologies of Management in the Course of Industrialization*. New York: John Wiley and Sons.

Bernardo, Antonio Carlos. 1982. *Tutela e Autonomia Sindical: Brasil 1930-1945*. São Paulo: T.A. Queiroz.

Beynon, Huw. 1975. *Working for Ford*. London: EP Publishing Ltd., 1975.

Blaumer, Robert. 1964. *Alienation and Freedom: The Manual Worker in Industry*. Chicago: University of Chicago Press.

Boito Junior, Armando. 1991. *O Sindicalismo de Estado no Brasil: Uma Análise Crítica da Estrutura Sindical*. São Paulo: Editora da UNICAMP and Editora Huicitec.

______, ed. 1991. *O Sindicalismo Brasileiro nos Anos 80*. São Paulo: Editora Paz e Terra.

Braverman, Harry. 1974. *Labor and Monopoly Capital*. New York: Monthly Review Press.

Brito, José Carlos Aguiar. 1983. *A Tomada da Ford: O Nascimento de um Sindicato Livre*. Petropolis: Editora Vozes.

Bruneau, Thomas C. 1982. *The Church in Brazil: The Politics of Religion*. Austin: Latin American Mongraph no. 56, University of Texas Press.

Camargo, Candido Procopio Ferreira de, ed. 1981. *Crescimento e Pobreza 1975*. São Paulo: Edições Loyola.

Canedo, Leticia Bicalho. 1978. *O Sindicalismo Bancário em São Paulo*. São Paulo: Editora Símbolos.

Cardoso, Fernando Henrique. 1971. *Ideologia de la Burguesia Industrial en Sociedades Dependentes (Argentina y Brasil)*. México: Siglo Veintiuno Editores.

Castro, Pedro. 1986. *Greves, Fatos e Significados*. São Paulo: Editora Atica.

CEDAC-Centro de Ação Comunitária. 1980. *Perspectivas do Novo Sindicalismo*. São Paulo: Edições Loyola-CEDAC.

CEDI-Centro Eucumenico de Documentação e Informação. 1986. *Trabalhadores Urbanos no Brasil/82-84*. São Paulo: CEDI-Aconteceu Especial 16.

Cesarino Junior, A.F. 1968. *Estabilidade e Fundo de Garantia*. Rio de Janeiro: Editora Forense.

Chilcote, Ronald H. 1974. *The Brazilian Communist Party: Conflict and Integration 1922-1972*. New York: Oxford University Press.

Correa, Hercules. 1980. *O ABC de 1980*. São Paulo: Civilização Brasileira.

Costa, Sergio Amad. 1986. *Estado e Controle Sindical no Brasil*. São Paulo: T.A. Queiroz.

______. 1981. *O CGT e as Lutas Sindicais Brasileiras (1960-1964)*. São Paulo: Grêmio Politécnico.

Couto, Francisco Pedro de. 1966. *O Voto e o Povo*. Rio de Janeiro: Civilização Brasileira.

Crouch, Colin and Alessandro Pizzorno, eds. 1978. *The Resurgence of Class Conflict in Western Europe since 1968*. London: Macmillan Press Ltd.

Dean, Warren. 1971. *A Industrialização de São Paulo.* São Paulo: Difusão Europeia do Livro.

Debret, Guita Griu. 1979. *Ideologia e Populismo.* São Paulo: T.A. Queiroz.

Dickenson, John P. 1978. *Brazil.* Boulder: Westview Press.

Dulles, John W.F. 1970. *Unrest in Brazil.* Austin: University of Texas Press.

Edwards, P.K. 1981. *Strikes in the United States 1881-1974.* New York: St. Martins Press.

Erickson, Kenneth Paul. 1977. *The Brazilian Corporative State and Working Class Politics.* Berkeley: University of California Press.

Fajnylber, F. 1970. *Estrategia Industrial y Empresas Internacionales: Posición Relativa en America Latina y Brasil.* Santiago de Chile: United Nations-CEPAL.

Ferrante, Vera Lucia B. 1978. *FGST: Ideologia e Repressão.* São Paulo: Editora Atica.

Fiechter, Georges-André. 1975. *Brazil since 1964: Modernization under a Military Regime.* New York: John Wiley and Sons.

Flynn, Peter. 1978. *Brazil: A Political Analysis.* Boulder: Westview Press.

Frederico, Celso. 1978. *Consciência Operária no Brasil.* São Paulo: Editora Atica.

______. 1979. *A Vanguarda Operária.* São Paulo: Editora Símbolo.

Frei Betto. 1981. *O Que é Comunidade Eclesial de Base.* São Paulo: Editora Brasiliense.

Freire, Paulo-CEDAL/CEDETIM. 1979. *Multinacionais e Trabalhadores no Brasil.* São Paulo: Editora Brasiliense.

Freitas Junior, Antônio Rodrigues de. 1989. *Sindicato Domesticação e Ruptura.* São Paulo: Departamento Editorial, Ordem dos Advogados do Brasil, Secção São Paulo.

French, John D. 1992. *The Brazilian Workers' ABC: Class Conflict and Alliances in Modern São Paulo.* Chapel Hill: University of North Carolina Press.

Fuchtner, Jans. 1980. *Os Sindicatos Brasileiros: Organização e Função Política.* Rio de Janeiro: Editora Graal.

Grondin. Marcelo. 1985. *Perfil dos Dirigentes Sindicais na Grande São Paulo.* São Paulo: CECODE-Centro de Cooperação do Desenvolvimento.

Haimson, Leopold and Charles Tilly, eds. 1989. *Strikes, Wars and Revolutions in an International Perspective: Strike Waves in the Late Nineteenth and Early Twentieth Centuries.* Cambridge: Cambridge University Press-Editions de la Maison des Sciences de l'Homme.

Hewlett, Sylvia Ann. 1980. *The Cruel Dilemmas of Development: Twentieth-Century Brazil*. New York: Basic Books, Inc.

Hobsbawm, Eric J. 1964. *Essays in Labour History and Labouring Men*. New York: Basic Books, Inc.

______. 1974. *Labour's Turning Point 1880-1900*. Cranbury, New Jersey: Associated University Press, Inc.

Humphrey, John. 1982. *Controle Capitalista e Luta Operária na Industria Automobilistica Brasileira*. São Paulo: Editora Vozes/CEBRAP.

Hyman, Richard. 1975. *Marxism and the Sociology of Trade Unions*. London: Pluto Press, Ltd.

______. 1972. *Strikes*. London: Fontana-Collins.

Ianni, Octavio. 1980. *O ABC da Classe Operária*. São Paulo: Editora Huicitec.

______. 1974. *El Colapso del Populismo en Brasil*. México: Universidade Nacional Autonoma de México.

Jelin, Elizabeth. 1974. *El Protesto Obrero*. Buenos Aires: Ediciones Nueva Visión, no. 43.

Kahil, Raouf. 1973. *Inflation and Economic Development in Brazil 1946-1963*. Oxford: Clarendon Press.

Katznelson, Ira and Aristide R. Zolberg, eds. *Working-Class Formation: Nineteenth-Century Patterns in Western Europe and the United States*. Princeton: Princeton University Press, 1986.

Kornhauser, Arthur William, ed. 1954. *Industrial Conflict*. New York: McGraw-Hill.

Leite, Marcia de Paula. 1987. *O Movimento Grevista no Brasil*. São Paulo: Editora Brasiliense, Coleção Tudo é Historia no. 120.

Leite, Rosalina de Santa Cruz. 1982. *A Operária Metalúrgica: Estudo Sobre as Condições de Vida e Trabalho de Operárias Metalúrgicas na Cidade de São Paulo*. São Paulo: Editora Semente.

Lipset, Seymour Martin, Martin Trow and James Coleman. 1962. *Union Democracy*. New York: Doubleday Anchor Books.

Lopes, Juarez Brandão. 1967. *Crise de Brasil Arcaíco*. São Paulo: Difusão Europeia do Livro.

______. 1964. *Sociedade Industrial no Brasil*. São Paulo: Difusão Europeia do Livro.

Loyola, Maria Andrea Rios. 1980. *Os Sindicatos e o PTB*. São Paulo: Editora Vozes and CEBRAP.

Mainwaring, Scott. 1986. *The Catholic Church and Politics in Brazil 1916-1985*. Stanford: Stanford University Press.

Mallet, Serge. 1975. *The New Working Class*. Bristol: Spokesman Books.
Maranhão, Ricardo. 1979. *Sindicatos e Democratização (Brasil 1945-1950)*. São Paulo: Editora Brasiliense.
Marcondes, Freitas. 1964. *Radiografia da Liderança Sindical Paulista*. São Paulo: Instituto Cultural do Trabalho.
Maroni, Amneris. 1982. *A Estrategia da Recusa: Analise das Greves de Maio de 1978*. São Paulo: Brasiliense Editora.
Martins, Heloisa Teixeira de Souza. 1979. *O Estado e a Burocratização do Sindicato no Brasil*. São Paulo: Editora Huicitec.
McDonough, Peter. 1981. *Power and Ideology in Brazil*. Princeton: Princeton University Press.
Moisés, José Álvaro. 1978. *Greve de Massa e Crise Política (Estudo da Greve dos 300 Mil em São Paulo 1953-1954)*. São Paulo: Editora Polis, Ltda.
Moore, Jr., Barrington. 1987. *Injustice: The Social Bases of Obedience e Revolt*. White Plains, N.Y.: M E. Sharpe, Inc.
Morais, Reginaldo. 1986. *Pacto Social - Da Negociação ao Pacote*. Porto Alegre: L e PM Editor.
Morais Filho, Evaristo. 1966. *O Sindicato Único no Brasil*. Rio de Janeiro: Editora A Noite.
Neves, Lucilia de Almeida. 1981. *CGT no Brasil 1961-1964*. Belo Horizonte: Editora Vega.
Pazziannotto Pinto, Almir. 1980. *Central Unica: Porque?* São Paulo: Global Editora, Passado e Presente no. 7.
Pena, Maria Valeria Junho. 1981. *Mulheres e Trabalhadoras: Presença Feminina na Constituição do Sistema Fabril*. Rio de Janeiro: Editora Paz e Terra.
Pereira, Duarte. 1981. *Um Perfil da Classe Operária*. São Paulo: Editora Huicitec.
Perrot, Michelle. 1974. *Les Ouvriers en Greve: France 1871-1890*. Paris: Editions Mouton.
Rabello, Ophelia. 1965. *A Rede Sindical Paulista*. São Paulo: Instituto Cultural do Trabalho.
Rainha, Luis Flavio. 1980. *Os Peões do Grande ABC*. Petropolis: Editora Vozes.
Rainha, Luis Flavio and Osvaldo Martines Bargas. 1983. *São Bernardo: As Lutas Operárias e Sindicais dos Metalúrgicos, 1977-1979*. São Paulo: Editora FC, Sociedade Beneficiente e Cultural dos Metalúrgicos de São Bernardo e Diadema.

Rodrigues, Iram Jacome. 1990. *Comissão de Fábrica e Trabalhadores na Industria*. São Paulo: Editora Cortez e FASE.

Rodrigues, José Albertino. 1968. *Sindicato e Desenvolvimento no Brasil*. São Paulo: Difusão Europeia do Livro.

Rodrigues, Leôncio Martins. 1966. *Conflito Industrial e Sindicalismo no Brasil*. São Paulo: Difusão Européia do Livro.

______. 1990. *CUT: Os Militantes e a Ideologia*. Rio de Janeiro: Editora Paz e Terra.

______. 1970. *Industrialização e Atitudes Operárias*. São Paulo: Editora Brasiliense.

______. 1974. *Trabalhadores, Sindicatos e Industrialização*. São Paulo: Editora Brasiliense.

Roett, Riordan, ed. 1976. *Brazil in the Seventies*. Washington, DC: American Enterprise Institute for Public Policy Research.

Sader, Eder. 1988. *Quando Novos Personagens Entram em Cena: Experiências e Lutas dos Trabalhadores da Grande São Paulo 1970-1980*. Rio de Janeiro: Editora Paz e Terra.

Santos, Abdias José dos and Eracy Rocha Chaves. 1980. *Consciência Operária e Luta Sindical: Metalúrgicos de Niteroi no Movimento Sindical Brasileiro*. Petrópolis: Editora Vozes.

Schmitter, Philippe C. 1971. *Interest Conflict and Political Change in Brazil*. Stanford: Stanford University Press.

Schneider, Ronald M. 1971. *The Political System of Brazil: Emergence of the Modernizing Authoritarian Regime, 1964-1970*. New York: Columbia University Press.

Shorter, Edward and Charles Tilly. 1974. *Strikes in France 1830-1968*. London: Cambridge University Press.

Sitrangulo, Cid José. 1978. *Conteúdo dos Dissidios Coletivos de Trabalho*. São Paulo: Edições LTR.

Skidmore, Thomas E. 1967. *Politics in Brazil: 1930-1964, An Experiment in Democracy*. New York: Oxford University Press.

______. 1988. *The Politics of Military Rule in Brazil 1964-85*. New York: Oxford University Press.

Simão, Aziz. 1966. *Sindicato e Estado*. São Paulo: Dominus Editora.

Singer, Paul. 1973. *O Milagre Brasileiro: Causas e Consequências*. São Paulo: Editora Brasiliense.

Singer, Paul and Vinicius Caldeira Brant, eds. 1980. *São Paulo: O Povo em Movimento*. Petrópolis: Editora Vozes.

Spindel, Arnaldo. 1980. *O Partido Comunista na Gênese do Populismo, Análise da Conjuntura de Re-Democratização no Após-Guerra*. São Paulo: Editora Símbolo.

Stepan, Alfred, ed. 1973. *Authoritarian Brazil: Origins, Policies and Future*. New Haven: Yale University Press.

______. ed. 1988. *Democratizando Brasil*. Rio de Janeiro: Editora Paz e Terra.

______. 1971. *The Military in Brazil*. Princeton: Princeton University Press.

Teixeira, Nelson Gomes, ed. 1990. *O Futuro do Sindicalismo no Brasil: O Diálogo Social*. São Paulo: Livraria Pioneira Editora.

Telles, Jover. 1962. *O Movimento Sindical no Brasil*. Rio de Janeiro: Editora Vitora.

Thompson, E.P. 1963. *The Making of the English Working Class*. New York: Vintage Books, Random House.

Tilly, Charles. 1984. *Big Structures, Large Changes, Huge Comparisons*. New York: Russell Sage Foundation, 75th Anniversary Series.

______. 1978. *From Mobilization to Revolution*. Reading, Mass: Addison-Wesely Publishing Company.

Tilly, Charles, Louise Tilly and Richard Tilly. 1975. *The Rebellious Century 1830-1930*. London: J.M. Dent and Sons, Ltd.

Tilly, Louise A. and Charles Tilly, eds. 1981. *Class Conflict and Collective Action*. Beverly Hills: Sage Publications.

Touraine, Alain. 1966. *La Conscience Ouvriére*. Paris: Editions du Seuil.

______. 1981. *The Voice and the Eye: An Analysis of Social Movements*. London: Cambridge University Press-Editions de la Maison des Sciences de L'Homme.

Vianna, Luiz Werneck. 1976. *Liberalismo e Sindicalismo no Brasil*. Rio de Janeiro: Editora Paz e Terra.

Walsh, Kenneth. 1983. *Strikes in Europe and the United States: Measurement and Incidence*. New York: St. Martin's Press.

Weffort, Francisco Corrêa. 1974. *Clases Populares y Política (Contribución al Estudio del Populismo)*. San José de Costa Rica: Editorial Universitaria Centro-Americana.

______. 1978. *O Populismo na Política Brasileira*. Rio de Janeiro: Editora Paz e Terra.

Wesson, Robert and David V. Fleischer. 1983. *Brazil in Transition*. New York: Praeger Publishers.

Articles and Working Papers

Almeida, Angela Mendes de and Michael Lowy. "Union Structure and Labor Organization in the Recent History of Brazil." *Latin American Perspectives* (Winter 1976) 3: 98-119.

Almeida, Maria Herminia Tavares de. "O Sindicalismo Brasileiro entre a Conservação e a Mudança", in Bernardo Sorj and Maria Herminia Tavares de Almeida, eds., *Sociedade e Política no Brasil Pós-64*. São Paulo: Editora Brasiliense, 1983.

______. "O Sindicato no Brasil: Novos Problemas, Velhas Estruturas". *Debate e Crítica* (July 1975) 6: 49-74.

______. "Tendências Recentes da Negociação Coletiva no Brasil". *Dados-Revista de Ciências Sociais* (1981) 24, 2: 161-189.

"O Arrocho Treme nas Bases do ABC". *Ensaio* (April 1983) 4, 7.

Baer, Werner. "The Brazilian Growth and Development Experience: 1964-1975", in Riordan Roett, ed. *Brazil in the Seventies*. Washington, DC: American Enterprise Institute for Public Policy Research, 1976.

Cano, Wilson. "Industrialização e Absorção de Mão de Obra no Brasil". *Industria e Productividade* (June 1968) 1.

Cardoso, Fernando Henrique. "Condições Sociais da Industrialização: O Caso de São Paulo", in Fernando Henrique Cardoso, ed., *Mudanças Sociais na América Latina*. São Paulo: Difusão Europeia do Livro, 1969.

______. "Proletariado e Mudança Social em São Paulo". *Sociologia* (March 1960) 22, 1.

______. "Le Proletariat Brasilien - Situation et Comportament Social". *Sociologie du Travail* (1961) 4: 362-377.

Cline, William R. "Brazil's Emerging International Economic Role", in Riordan Roett, ed., *Brazil in the Seventies*. Washington, D.C.: American Enterprise Institute for Public Policy Research, 1976.

Cohen, Youssef. "The Benevolent Leviathan: Political Consciousness among Urban Workers under State Corporatism." *American Political Science Review* (1982) 76: 46-59.

Comissão Nacional de Planejamento do Segundo Congresso dos Metalúrgicos. "Os Metalúrgicos e a Industrialização". *Revista Brasiliense* (May-June 1960) 29: 79-93.

"Encargos Sociais e Fundo de Garantia". *Conjuntura Econômica* (January 1967) 21, 1: 57-64.

Erickson, Kenneth Paul and Patrick V. Peppe. "Dependent Capitalist Development, U.S. Foreign Policy and Repression of the Working Class in Chile and Brazil". *Latin American Perspectives* (Winter 1976) 3: 19-44.

Falletto, Enzo. "Industrialização e Classe Operária na América Latina", in Leôncio Martins Rodrigues, ed., *Sindicalismo e Sociedade.* São Paulo: Difusão Europeia do Livro, 1971.

Faria, Vilmar. "Desenvolvimento, Urbanização e Mudança na Estrutura do Emprego: A Experiência Brasileira dos Últimos Trinta Anos", in Bernardo Sorj and Maria Herminia Tavares de Almeida, eds. *Sociedade e Política no Brasil Pós-1964.* São Paulo: Editora Brasiliense, 1983.

Figueiredo, Argelina Cheibub. "Intervenções Sindicais e o Novo Sindicalismo," *Dados* (1978) 17: 135-155.

French, John D. and Mary Lynn Pedersen. "Women and Working-Class Mobilization in Postwar São Paulo." *Latin American Research Review* (1989) 24, 3: 99-125.

Gatica, Jaime. "Caracteristicas y Ajuste del Empleo Formal: Brasil 1985-1987". Brasilia: Texto de Discussão No.7, Ministério do Trabalho, Secretaria de Emprego e Salário, March 1988.

Gitahi, Leda, Helena Hirata, Elizabeth Lobo and Rosa Lucia Moisés. "Operárias: Sindicalização e Reinvindicações, 1970-1980". *Revista de Cultura e Política* (July 1982) 8: 90-116.

Gonçalves, J. Sergio R. C. "Perfil do Operariado numa Empresa da Industria Automobilistica de São Paulo". *Contexto* (July 1977) 3: 33-49.

"Greves... e Há mais do que isso". *Cadernos do CEAS* (September-October 1979) 63: 49-58.

Hadler, Maria Silvia Duarte. "A Política de Controle da Classe Operária no Governo Vargas,." *Cara a Cara* (July-December 1978) 1, 2: 107-114.

Harding, Timothy Fox. "Implications of Brazil's Third Labor Congress". *Hispanic American Report* (October 1960) 13: 567-572.

______. "Labor Challenge to Dictatorship". *Brazilian Information Bulletin* (Spring 1974) 13: 2-5.

______. "Laboring under the Dictatorship". *Brazilian Information Bulletin* (June 1973) 10: 8-10.

Hibbs, Douglas A. "Industrial Conflict in Advanced Industrial Societies". *American Political Science Review* (1976) 70: 1033-1058.

______. "On the Political Economy of Long-Run Trends in Strike Activity". *British Journal of Political Science* (1978) 8: 153-175.

Hobsbawm, Eric J. "The British Standard of Living, 1790-1850", in *Labouring Men: Studies in the History of Labour*. New York: Basic Books, Inc., 1964.

______. "La Conciencia de Clase en la Historia", in Istvan Meszaros, ed. *Aspectos de la Historia y la Conciencia de Clase*. México: Universidade Nacional Autonoma de México, 1973.

______. "Considerations sur le 'Nouveau Syndicalisme' 1889-1926". *Les Mouvements Socials* (October-December 1968) 65: 71-80.

______. "The Labour Aristocracy in Nineteenth-Century Britain", in *Labouring Men: Studies in the History of Labour*. New York: Basic Books, Inc., 1964.

______. "Movimento Operário e Política". *Contexto* (March 1977) 2: 1-14.

______. "Trends in the British Labour Movement since 1850", in *Labouring Men: Studies in the History of Labour*. New York: Basic Books, Inc., 1964.

Humphrey, John. "Labour Use and Labour Control in the Brazilian Automobile Industry". *Capital and Class* (Winter 1980-81) 12: 43-57.

Ianni, Octavio. "Populismo e Classes Subalternas". *Debate e Crítica* (July-December 1973) 3: 7-17.

______. "Transformações no Comportamento Político Operário", in *Industrialização e Desenvolvimento Social no Brasil*. Rio de Janeiro: Editora Civilização Brasileira, 1963.

Jelin, Elizabeth. "Espontaneidad y Organización en el Movimento Obrero". *Revista Latinoamericana de Sociologia* (1974) 2.

Keck, Margaret E. "O Novo Sindicalismo na Transição Brasileira", in Alfred Stepan, ed. *Democratizando Brasil*. Rio de Janeiro: Editora Paz e Terra, 1988.

Korpi, Walter. "Conflict, Power and Relative Deprivation". *American Political Science Review* (1974) 68, 4: 1569-1578.

Korpi, Walter and Michael Shalev. "Strikes, Industrial Relations and Class Conflict in Capitalist Societies". *British Journal of Sociology* (1979) 30, 2: 164-187.

Leite, Marcia de Paulo. "Tres Anos de Greves em São Paulo 1983-1985". *Revista São Paulo em Perspectiva* (July-September 1987) 1, 2: 50-64.

Leite, Marcia de Paula and Sudney Solis. "O Ultimo Vendaval: A Greve dos 700 Mil". *Cara a Cara* (July-December 1978) 1, 2: 115-151.

Lessa, Carlos. "Fifteen Years of Economic Policy in Brazil". *Economic Bulletin for Latin America* (November 1964) 9: 153-214.

"A Lição das Greves - Chega de Pelegos". *Cadernos Políticos* (1980) 1.

Linz, Juan. "An Authoritarian Regime: Spain", in Stein Rokkan, ed. *Mass Politics*. New York: Basic Books, Inc., 1970.

______. "The Future of an Authoritarian Situation or the Institutionalization of an Authoritarian Regime: The Case of Brazil", in Alfred Stepan, ed. *Authoritarian Brazil*. Pp. 233-254. New Haven: Yale University Press, 1973.

Lowey, Michel and S. Chucid. "Opiniões e Atitudes de Lideres Sindicais Metalurgicos". *Revista Brasileira de Estudos Políticos* (January 1962) 13: 132-169.

Loyola, Maria Andrea Rios. "Racionalização do Trabalho e Atitudes Operárias". *Revista de Administração de Empresas* (November-December 1975) 15, 6: 71-92.

______. "Trabalho e Modernização na Industria Textile". *Revista de Administração de Empresas* (September-October 1974) 14, 5: 19-31.

"A Luta por um Sindicato de Base: Histórico da Oposição Sindical". *Cadernos CEAS* (September-October 1979) 63: 8-11.

Macedo, Roberto B.M. "Algumas Dificulades na Interpretação dos Dados de Salário e Salário Medio da Industria". *Planejamento e Conjuntura* (August 1974) 79: 63-67.

Maia, Rosane. "As Greves em 1989: Os Trabalhadores na Corda-Bamba na Hiperinflação". Brasilia: Texto de Dicussão no. 22, Ministério do Trabalho, Secretaria de Emprego e Salários, February 1990.

______. "Relatório de Pesquisa No. 2 - Sistema de Greves no MTb-SIGREV". Brasilia: Ministério do Trabalho, Assessoria Econômica, November 1989.

Maia, Rosane and Rosangela Saldanha. "Abrindo a Caixa Preta... (Estudo sobre a Evolução do Emprego na Administração Pública Estadual e Municipal)". Brasilia: Texto de Dicussão no. 12, Ministério do Trabalho, Secretaria de Emprego e Salários, February 1988.

McDonough, Peter. "Mapping an Authoritarian Power Structure: Brazilian Elites during the Medici Regime". *Latin American Research Review* (1981) 16, 1: 79-106.

Mericle, Kenneth S. "Corporatist Control of the Working Class: Authoritarian Brazil Since 1964", in James M. Malloy, ed. *Authoritarianism and Corporatism in Latin America*. Pp. 303-338. Pittsburgh: University of Pittsburgh Press, 1977.

"Os Metalurgicos e a Industrialização". *Revista Brasiliense* (May-June 1960) 29: 79-93.

Moisés, José Álvaro. "Experiência de Mobilização Popular em São Paulo". *Contraponto* (September 1978) 3, 3: 69-86.

______. "What is the Strategy of the 'New Syndicalism'?". *Latin American Perspectives* (Fall 1982): 55-73.

Morais Filho, Evaristo. "O Erro Sindical". *Jornal da Tarde* (14 October 1978): 6.

______. "A Regulamentação das Relações de Trabalho no Brasil". *Revista Brasileira de Ciências Sociais* (July 1963).

"Movimento Operário: Novas e Velhas Lutas". *Escrita/Ensaio* (1980) 3, 6.

Munhoz, Fabio. "Sindicalismo e Democracia Populista: A Greve de 1957". *Cadernos CEDEC* (1978) 2.

Oliveira, Lucia Lippi. "O Movimento Operário em São Paulo 1970-1985", in Emir Sader, ed. *Movimentos Sociais na Transição Democrática*. São Paulo: Editora Cortez, 1987.

"Quarenta e Um Dias de Resistência e Luta: Uma Análise da Greve Feita por Quem dela Participou", in *Cadernos do Trabalhador 1*. São Paulo: Editora do ABCD Sociedade Cultural/URPLAN da Pontifícia Universidade Católica de São Paulo, 1980.

Ramos, Carlos Alberto. "O Desempenho do Mercado de Trabalho em 1988". Brasilia: Texto de Dicussão no. 16, Ministério do Trabalho, Assessoria Econômica, July 1989.

"Relações Trabalhistas," in NEPP-Nucleo de Estudos de Políticas Públicas. *Brasil 1986 - Relatório sobre a Situação Social do Pais*. Campinas: Universidade Estadual de Campinas, 1988.

"Relações Trabalhistas," NEPP-Nucleo de Estudos de Políticas Públicas. *Brasil 1987 - Relatório sobre a Situação Social do Pais*. Campinas: Universidade Estadual de Campinas, 1989.

Rodrigues, José Albertino. "Movimento Sindical e Situação da Classe Operária". *Debate e Crítica* (January-June 1974) 2: 98-111.

______. "Padrão de Vida da População Brasileira". *Revista de Estudos Sócio-Econômicos* (November 1961) 1, 3.

______. "Situação Econômica-Social da Classe Trabalhadora no Brasil". *Revista de Estudos Sócio-Econômicos* (September 1961) 1, 1.

Rodrigues, Leôncio Martins. "Bibliografia Sobre Trabalhadores e Sindicatos no Brasil". *Estudos CEBRAP* (January-March 1974) 7: 151-171.

______. "Classe Operária Prefere Lutar Hoje por Sindicalismo Autonomo". *Jornal do Brasil* (13 August 1978): 29.

______. "O Poder Sindical na Nova Constituição". *RH - Informação Profissional - Edição Especial: Os Direitos Sociais e Trabalhistas na Constituição de 1988*. São Paulo: Associação Brasileira de Recursos Humanos, October 1988.

______. "Professor Condena Imobilismo Sindical". *O Estado de São Paulo* (15 January 1978): 46.

______. "O Sindicalismo Corporativo no Brasil", in Leôncio Martins Rodrigues, ed. *Partidos e Sindicatos: Escritos de Sociologia Política*. São Paulo: Editora Atica, 1990.

______. "O Sindicalismo nos Anos 80: Um Balanço". *Revista São Paulo em Perspectiva* (January-March 1990) 4, 1: 11-19.

______. "Tendências Futuras do Sindicalismo". *Revista de Administração de Empresas*, 19, 4 (October-December 1979) 19, 4: 45-54.

Rowland, Robert. "Classe Operária e Estado de Compromisso (Origens Estruturais da Legislação Trabalhista e Sindical)". *Estudos CEBRAP* (April-June 1974) 8: 5-40.

Sader, Eder and Paulo Sandroni. "Lutas Operárias e Tacticas Burguesas: 1978-1980". *Cadernos PUC/SP* (1981) 7.

Sandoval, Salvador A. M. "General Strikes in Brazil, 1980-1989". *Latin American Labor News* (1990) 2 & 3: 11-13.

______. "Greves e Flutuações Econômicas no Brasil, 1945-1968". *Estudos Econômicos* (September-December 1990) 20, 3: 479-498.

Sandoval, Salvador A. M. and Sonia M. de Avelar. "Conciencia Obrera y Negociación Colective en Brasil". *Revista Mexicana de Sociologia* (1983) 3: 1027-1047.

Schmitter, Philippe C. "The Portugalization of Brazil?", in Alfred Stepan, ed. *Authoritarian Brazil*. Pp. 179-232. New Haven: Yale University Press, 1973.

Singer, Paul. "Desenvolvimento e Repartição da Renda no Brasil". *Debate e Crítica* (July-December 1973) 1: 67-94.

______. "Força de Trabalho e Emprego no Brasil: 1920-1969". *Cadernos CEBRAP* (1971) 3.

______. "Movimentos de Bairro", in Paul Singer and Vinicius Caldeira Brant, eds. *São Paulo: O Povo em Movimento*. São Paulo: Editora Vozes/CEBRAP, 1980.

Soares, Glaucio Ary Dillon. "The New Industrialization and the Brazilian Political System", in James Petras and Maurice Zeitlin, eds. *Latin America: Reform or Revolution*. New York: Fawcett Books, 1966.

Souza, Amaury de e Bolivar Lamounier. "Governo e Sindicato no Brasil: A Perspectiva dos Anos 80". *Dados* (1981) 24, 2: 139-159.

Thompson, E.P. "Eighteenth-Century English Society: Class Struggle without Class?". *Social History* (May 1978) 3, 2: 133-165.

______. "Time, Work-Discipline, and Industrial Capitalism". *Past and Present* (December 1967) 38: 56-97.

Tilly, Charles. "Britain Creates the Social Movement". Ann Arbor, Michigan: CRSO Working Paper No. 232, Center for Research on Social Organization, The University of Michigan, 1981.

______. "Capital Implodes and Workers Explode in Flanders, 1789-1914". Ann Arbor, Michigan: CRSO Working Paper No. 296, Center for Research on Social Organization, The University of Michigan, 1983.

______. "Does Modernization Breed Revolution". *Comparative Politics* (April 1973): 425-447.

______. "How (And to Some Extent, Why) to Study British Contention". Ann Arbor, Michigan: CRSO Working Paper No. 212, Center for Research on Social Organization, The University of Michigan, 1980.

______. "Social Movements and National Politics". Ann Arbor, Michigan: CRSO Working Paper No.197, Center for Research on Social Organization, The University of Michigan, 1979.

______. "Strikes, Demonstrations and Social Movements in Twentieth-Century France". Ann Arbor, Michigan: CRSO Working Paper No. 311, Center for Research on Social Organization, The University of Michigan, 1984.

Touraine, Alain. "Industrialization et Conscience Ouvriére a São Paulo". *Sociologie du Travail* (1961) 3, 4: 77-95.

Touraine, Alain and Bernard Mottez. "Clase Obrera y Sociedad Global", in Georges Friedmann and Pierre Naville, eds. *Tratado de Sociologia del Trabajo*. México: Fondo de Cultura Economica, 1963.

Touraine, Alain and Daniel Pecaut. "Working Class Consciousness and Economic Development in Latin America", in Irving Louis Horowitz, ed. *Masses in Latin America*. New York: Oxford University Press, 1970.

Valentine, Cynthia E. "Internal Union Democarcy - Does It Help or Hinder the Movement for Industrial Democracy". *The Insurgent Sociologist* (Fall 1978) 8, 2/3: 40-51.

Vianna, Luiz Jorge Werneck. "Sistema Liberal e Direito do Trabalho". *Estudos CEBRAP* (January-March 1974) 7: 115-149.

Walker, Neuma Aguiar. "The Organization and Ideology of Brazilian Labor", in Irving Louis Horowitz, ed. *Revolution in Brazil.* New York: Dutton, 1964.

Wallerstein, Michael. "The Collapse of Democarcy in Brazil: Its Economic Determinants". *Latin American Research Review* (1980) 15, 3: 3-43.

Weffort, Francisco Corrêa. "Origens do Sindicalismo Populista no Brasil (A Conjuntura da Após-Guerra)". *Estudos CEBRAP* (April-June 1973) 4: 65-106.

______. "Democracia e Movimento Operário: Algumas Questões para a História do Período 1945-1964, I". *Revista de Cultura Contemporânea* (July 1978) 1,1: 7-13.

______. "Democracia e Movimento Operário: Algumas Questões para a História do Período 1945-1964, II". *Revista de Cultura Contemporânea* (January 1979) 1, 2: 3-11.

______. "Democracia e Movimento Operário: Algumas Questões para a História do Período 1945-1964, III". *Revista de Cultura Contemporânea* (August 1979) 1, 1: 11-18.

______. "Participação e Conflito Industrial: Contagem e Osasco, 1968". *Cadernos de CEBRAP,* (1972) no. 5.

______. "Raizes Sociais do Populismo em São Paulo". *Revista Civilização Brasileira* (May 1965).

______. "State and Mass in Brazil". Studies in *Comparative International Development* (1966) 2, 12.

Wells, John. "Industrial Accumulation and Living Standards in the Long Run: The São Paulo Industrial Working Class, 1930-75 (Part I)". *The Journal of Development Studies* (1983) 19, 2: 145-169.

______. "Industrial Accumulation and Living Standards in the Long Run: The São Paulo Industrial Working Class, 1930-75 (Part II)". *The Journal of Development Studies* (1983) 19, 3: 297-328.

Unpublished Works

Alem, Silvio Frank. 1981. Os Trabalhadores e a 'Redemocratização' (Estudo sobre o Estado, os Partidos e a Participação dos Trabalhadores Assalariados Urbanos na Conjuntura da Guerra e do Pós-Guerra Imediata) 1942-1948. Master Thesis, Universidade Estadual de Campinas.

Almeida, Maria Herminia Tavares de. 1978. Estado e Classes Trabalhadoras no Brasil (1930-1945). Ph.D. Disseration, Universidade de São Paulo.

Avelar, Lucia Mercês de. 1983. O Voto Operário. Master Thesis, Pontíficia Universidade Católica de São Paulo.

Avelar, Sônia Maria de. 1985. The Social Bases of Workers' Solidarity: A Case Study of Textile Workers in São José dos Campos, Brazil. Ph.D. Dissertation, The University of Michigan.

Cohen, Youssef. 1979. Popular Support for Authoritarian Governments: Brazil under Medici. Ph.D. Dissertation, The University of Michigan.

Faria, Hamilton José Barreto. 1986. A Experiência Operária dos Anos de Resistência: A Oposição Sindical Metalurgica de São Paulo e a Dinâmica do Movimento Operário: 1964-1978. Master Thesis, Pontíficia Universidade Católica de São Paulo.

French, John. 1985. Industrial Workers and the Origin of Populist Politics in the ABC Region of Greater São Paulo, Brazil 1900-1950. Ph.D. Dissertation, Yale University.

Harding, Timothy Fox. 1973. The Political History of Organized Labor in Brazil." Ph.D. Dissertation, Stanford University.

Humphrey, John. 1975. A Classe Operária no Brasil na Epoca Atual (Materiais de Pesquisa sobre Operários na Industrial Automobilistica). Manuscript in CEBRAP. São Paulo.

Leite, Marcia de Paula. 1983. Sindicatos e Trabalhadores na Crise do Populismo. Master Thesis, Universidade Estadual de Campinas.

Macedo, Roberto B.M. 1977. Uma Revisão Crítica da Relação entre a Política Salarial Pós-1964 e o Aumento da Concentração da Renda na Década de 1960. Manuscript, Faculdade de Econômia e Administração, Universidade de São Paulo.

Mericle, Kenneth Scott. 1974. Conflict Regulation in the Brazilian Industrial Relations System. Ph.D. Dissertation, University of Wisconsin.

Piozzi, Patricia. 1982. O Ato Livre: Considerações a Respeito da Política Operária. Master's Thesis, Faculdade de Filosofia, Letras e Ciências Sociais, Universidade de São Paulo.

Sandoval, Salvador Antonio Mireles. 1984. Strikes in Brazil, 1945-1980. Ph.D. Dissertation, The University of Michigan.

Souza, Amaury Guimaraes de. 1978. The Nature of Corporatist Representation: Leaders and Members of Organized Labor in Brazil. Ph.D. Dissertation, Massachusetts Institute of Technology.

Verardo, Luiz Humberto. 1992. Educação Política no Sindicato: Estudo de uma Experiência Recente. Master's Thesis, Faculdade de Educação, Universidade Estadual de Campinas.

Weffort, Francisco Corrêa. 1972. Sindicato e Política. Thesis of "Livre Docência", Universidade de São Paulo.

Documents

Brazil, Instituto Brasileiro de Geografia e Estatística. *Anuário Estatístico do Brasil 1952-1982*. Rio de Janeiro, Fundação Instituto Brasileiro de Geografia e Estatística, 1953-1984.

______. *Censo Industrial*. Rio de Janeiro: Fundação Instituto Brasileiro de Geografia e Estatística, 1940, 1950, 1960, 1970, 1980.

______. *Industria de Transformação*. Rio de Janeiro: Fundação Instituto Brasileiro de Geografia e Estatística, 1966, 1967, 1968.

______. *Produção Industrial*. Rio de Janeiro: Fundação Instituto Brasileiro de Geografia e Estatística, 1966, 1969, 1970, 1971.

______. *Produção Industrial Brasileira*. Rio de Janeiro: Fundação Instituto Brasileiro de Geografia e Estatística, 1952, 1953, 1954.

______. *Produção Industrial do Brasil*. Rio de Janeiro: Fundação Instituto Brasileiro de Geografia e Estatística, 1958.

______. Departamento de Emprego e Rendimento. *Pesquisa Nacional por Amostra de Domicilio, 1986. Suplemento No. 1, Associativismo*. Rio de Janeiro: Fundação Instituto Brasileiro de Geografia e Estatística, 1988.

______. Departamento de Estatísticas e Indicadores Sociais. *Participação Político-Social, 1988: Brasil e Grandes Regiões*. Rio de Janeiro: Fundação Instituto Brasileiro de Geografia e Estatística, 1990.

______. Departamento de Estatísticas e Indicadores Sociais. *Sindicatos: Indicadores Sociais, 1987*. Rio de Janeiro: Fundação Instituto Brasileiro de Geografia e Estatística, 1989.

______. *Pesquisa Industrial*. Rio de Janeiro: Fundação Instituto Brasileiro de Geografia e Estatística, 1977, 1978, 1979, 1980, 1981, 1982.

______. *Sinopse Preliminar do Censo Industrial - 1980*. Vol. 3, Book 1. Rio de Janeiro: Fundação Instituto Brasileiro de Geografia e Estatística, 1982.

Brazil, Ministério da Industria e do Comércio-CCE. *Registro Industrial*. Rio de Janeiro: Ministério da Industria e do Comércio-MIC, 1962.

Conferência Nacional dos Bispos do Brasil-CNBB. *Comunidades Eclesiais de Base no Brasil: Experiências e Perspectivas*. São Paulo: Estudos da CNBB no. 23, Edições Paulinas, 1979.

______. *Comunidades Igreja na Base Perspectivas*. São Paulo: Estudos da CNBB no. 3, Edições Paulinas, 1977.

______. *Diretrizes Gerais da Ação Pastoral da Igreja no Brasil 1979/1982*. São Paulo: Documentos da CNBB no. 5, Edições Paulinas, 1977.

______. *Exigências Cristãs de uma Ordem Política*. São Paulo: Documentos da CNBB no. 10, Edições Paulinas, 1978.

______. *Pistas para uma Pastoral Urbana*. São Paulo: Estudos da CNBB no. 22, Edições Paulinas, 1979.

______. *Subsidios para uma Política Social*. São Paulo: Estudos da CNBB no. 24, Edições Paulinas, 1979.

DIEESE-Departamento Inter-Sindical de Estatística e Estudos Sócio-Econômicos. *Boletim DIEESE*. São Paulo, 1983 to 1990.

______. "Cinquenta Anos de Salário Minimo". São Paulo: Position Paper no. 16, July 1990.

______. "Dez Anos de Política Salarial". *Estudos Sócio-Econômicos*, 3 (August 1975).

______. "Salário Minimo". *Divulgação*, 2 (1977).

______. "Produtividade e Campanha Salarial". *Estudos Sócio-Econômicos*, 4 (December 1979).

______. *Salário Minimo desde 1940*. São Paulo: DIEESE, 1986.

______. *Pesquisa DIEESE: Emprego e Desemprego na Grande São Paulo, Conceitos, Metodologia e Principais Resultados 1981-1983*. São Paulo: DIEESE, July 1984.

United States, Department of Commerce, Industry and Trade Administration. *A Survey of U.S. Export Opportunities: Brazil*. Washington, D.C.: U.S. Government Printing Office, 1979.

United States, Department of Labor, Bureau of Labor Statistics. *Analysis of Work Stoppages - 1955*. Bulletin No. 1196. Washington, D.C.: U.S. Government Printing Office, June 1956.

______. *Labor in Brazil*. BLS Report No. 191. Washington, D.C.: U.S. Government Printing Office, January 1962.

______. *Labor Law and Practice in Brazil*. BLS Report No. 309. Washington, DC: U.S. Government Printing Office, 1966.

"Tese de Oposição Sindical Metalurgica-Texto Aprovado no Primeiro Congresso da Oposição Metalurgica de São Paulo, Abril 1979". *Cadernos do CEAS*, 63 (September-October 1979): 12-18.

Newspapers and Magazines

O Estado de São Paulo, 1947, 1949, 1955, 1963, 1970, 1978, 1979, 1980.
Folha da Manhã. 1945-1959.
Folha de São Paulo. 1960-1980.
O Jornal do Brasil. 1978-1980.
Isto É.
Veja.

Index